USING HUMOR TO
MAXIMIZE LIVING

USING HUMOR TO MAXIMIZE LIVING

CONNECTING WITH HUMOR

Second Edition

Mary Kay Morrison

Bruce Quast, cartoonist

ROWMAN & LITTLEFIELD EDUCATION

A division of
ROWMAN & LITTLEFIELD PUBLISHERS, INC.
Lanham • New York • Toronto • Plymouth, UK

Cartoons by Bruce Quast. Used with permission.

Published by Rowman & Littlefield Education
A division of Rowman & Littlefield Publishers, Inc.
A wholly owned subsidiary of The Rowman & Littlefield Publishing Group, Inc.
4501 Forbes Boulevard, Suite 200, Lanham, Maryland 20706
www.rowman.com

10 Thornbury Road, Plymouth PL6 7PP, United Kingdom

British Library Cataloguing in Publication Information Available

Library of Congress Cataloging-in-Publication Data

Morrison, Mary Kay, 1946-
  Using humor to maximize living : connecting with humor /
Mary Kay Morrison. — 2nd ed.
    p.   cm.
    Summary: "Using Humor to Maximize Living affirms, sustains, and encourages people in the practice of humor, not only as a personal tool to optimize a healthy life style, but also to maximize the benefits of humor in everyday life. Check out the research that includes a review on the use of humor to nurture creativity, to increase the capacity for memory retention, to support an optimal work environment, and to build safe communities that reflect the relational trust necessary for maximizing living."— Provided by publisher.
    ISBN 978-1-61048-487-9 (hardback)—ISBN 978-1-61048-488-6 (paper)—
  ISBN 978-1-61048-489-3 (electronic)
  1. Educational psychology.   2. Wit and humor in education.   3. School environment.
  I. Title.
  LB1051.M67   2012
  370.15—dc23
                                                                    2012001386

∞™ The paper used in this publication meets the minimum requirements of American National Standard for Information Sciences—Permanence of Paper for Printed Library Materials, ANSI/NISO Z39.48-1992.

Printed in the United States of America.

In loving memory of my father, Bill Wiltz, whose laughter affected the lives of all he touched, especially his sweet cookie: my mother, Ruth Wiltz.

To my loving husband, Don Morrison, who has inspired, encouraged, supported, and loved me. To our children, their spouses, and our precious grandchildren, who enrich our lives with their love: William, Jennifer, Ben, Tyler, Emma, Andy, Julie, Andrew, Mimi, Stephen, Rachael, Jason, Katie, Cloe, Peter, Val, Samuel, Christine, Isaiah, Jennifer, and Beth.

CONTENTS

FIGURES AND TABLES

PREFACE

My first book was written because I strongly believe that humor belongs in schools and is an integral part of learning. I have realized in the subsequent four years that people from all walks of life really do need the affirmation that humor, fun, and laughter provide. Laughter and humor definitely belong not only in our schools but in factories, hospitals, offices, funeral homes, and homeless shelters.

As I continue to provide workshops on humor and stress, I have found a universal desire for joy and happiness. Humor is needed in all occupations and by all professions. I have been invited to present to numerous groups and organizations and have had the privilege of sharing information to many around the world. There have been numerous individuals and groups who have requested that I write this sequel. I am eager to share my vision on how humor practice can be an integral part of optimal living.

The past few years, I have been blessed and privileged to teach an international graduate course for the Association of Applied and Therapeutic Humor (AATH). This organization is a community of professionals who study, practice, and promote healthy humor and laughter. It has also been my honor to serve on the AATH board of directors for the past several years and to work alongside the most amazing leaders in the field of humor and laughter in the world.

Several years ago, at the urging of the board and with the support of countless folks, I developed the AATH Humor Academy. There are currently nine advisors and nine instructors who volunteer their time and talents for the Humor Academy program. We are all committed to sharing the information and research about humor with other like-minded individuals. At the end of the first year of the program, I was elated that we had twenty-four graduates who wrote about their insights and participated in study groups throughout the year. I have learned so much from all of these individuals. This book could not have been written without them. You will find their contributions throughout this book.

Through AATH, I have found that there are countless folks who are passionate about applying and practicing humor in all walks of life, from funeral directors to caring clowns, from military personnel to physicians. These members have expressed the hope that their ideas and humor work can be shared. I have had the privilege to work within this community of like-minded humorists who affirm and support my humor practice.

This book is written with love and with gratitude to all of my fellow humor practioners who allowed me to put their voices and passion into print so the benefits of humor can be shared with others. Many people have written contributions about how they apply and practice humor in their respective fields. You will find their names in the appendix. I am thrilled to share their stories, experiences, and strategies with you.

I want to emphasize that the research on humor is in preliminary stages of development. It is a difficult topic to explore as it is such a multifaceted topic. The exploding rate of research in numerous fields makes it difficult for even the most committed practitioner to stay abreast of the growing knowledge base. Cellular and genetic research, imaging technology, and new ways to look at psychology (including positive psychology) are providing us with valuable information. Almost all of the research strongly supports the benefits of using humor to maximize living. I have done my best to provide current information and up-to-date research in this book. I will continue to share insights and resources on my website, through social networks, and of course through AATH and the Humor Academy. I am grateful to you for joining me on my humor journey.

ACKNOWLEDGMENTS

A huge thank you to my family, especially to my husband, Don, who constantly supports my humor practice and without whom I could not have completed this book. Special gratitude goes to my mom, Ruth Wiltz. Our kids and grandkids are mentioned frequently in this book, as they make sure that I find humor in everyday living. They bring incredible joy into my life: William, Jennifer, Ben, Tyler, Emma, Andy, Julie, Andrew, Mimi, Steve, Rachael, Jason, Katie, Cloe, Peter, Val, Samuel, Christine, Isaiah, Jennifer, and Beth. My friends, aunts, uncles, and cousins have stimulated my laugher and encouraged my efforts over the years. You are treasured! There are quotes and comments from my family scattered throughout this book.

A special thanks to the Association of Applied and Therapeutic Humor (AATH) members and Humor Academy advisors who have supported and encouraged me as we have collaborated on ways to share information about humor and laughter. Heartfelt thanks to Barbara Miller, Karyn Buxman, and Chip Lutz for their initial support and advice in starting the AATH Humor Academy. To the amazing advisors and instructors in AATH, including Don Baird, Lee Berk, Cheri Campbell, Dwayna Covey, Lenny Dave, Deb Gauldin, Roberta Gold, Deb Hart, Earl Henslin, Jill Knox, Linda MacNeal, Paul McGhee, Joyce Saltman, Enid Schwartz, Joel Schwartz, Steve Sultanoff, Steve Wilson, and Patty Wooten. Thank you also to the first graduating class of the Humor Academy! I greatly appreciate your enthusiastic support.

To my incredible colleagues who generously contributed their personal insights, their research, and their information about humor in their fields, I am grateful beyond words. Thanks to Chris Balmer, Lee Berk, Ron Berk, Hamish Boyd, Karyn Buxman, Judy Carter, Kay Caskey, Pat Conklin, Mark Clarke, Pat Conklin, Dwayna Covey, Adrienne Edmondson, Kelly Epperson, Fif Fernandes, Deb Gauldin, David Granirer, Deb Hart, Kris Harty, Earl Henslin, Nick Hoesl,

David Jacobson, Leigh Anne Jasheway, Kathy Keaton, Allen Klein, Jackie Kwan, Kathy Laurenhue, Chip Lutz, Lois McElravy, Paul McGhee, Don and Alleen Nilsen, Cheryl Oberg, Sharon Olds, Hob Osterlund, Kathy Passanisi, Katherine Puckett, Amy Robbins, Bronwyn Roberts, Joyce Saltman, Susan Sparks, Ron Sudenick, Enid Schwartz, Joel Schwartz, Ed Singer, Tony Trunfio, Heather Wandell, Steve Wilson, Leslie Yerkes, and Laurie Young.

Thanks also to Bob Sylwester, who encouraged my fledgling efforts from the very beginning and who continues to provide resources and moral support. My deep appreciation also goes to Bev Letcher, who helped proof the initial copy. Thanks to Thomas F. Koerner, editorial director at Rowman & Littlefield Education, for his support, Mary McMenamin, Laura Grzybowski, and all those at Rowman & Littlefield for their assistance.

A special thanks to Bruce Quast from Rockford, Illinois, for his amazing cartoons in this publication.

I am grateful to those who have participated in my workshops and who have enriched me with their insights and feedback. Thanks to those who had faith in the power of humor and contacted me to facilitate a staff development workshop for their organization. Your trust led to this book.

INTRODUCTION

What is humor, exactly? How do you get a sense of humor? Once you find yours, how do you use it to maximize living? If it is so important, why is it rarely mentioned in college courses without some clues for finding and using it?

The purpose of this book is to affirm, sustain, and encourage people in the practice of humor not only as a personal tool to optimize a healthy lifestyle but to maximize the benefits of humor in everyday life. These benefits include current research-based data on the use of humor to nurture creativity, to increase the capacity for memory retention, to support an optimal work environment, and to build safe communities that reflect the relational trust necessary for maximizing living.

People value humor. References to the importance of having a sense of humor are liberally sprinkled throughout the popular media. It is usually mentioned as a factor to look for when hiring as well as one of the qualities of effective employees. It is without a doubt the one quality that most of us agree is needed in life. However, it is rare to find much on the study of humor practice and the benefits gained by practicing humor.

Where does humor exist in the brain? This book is the result of a twenty-year journey delving into the connections between brain science and humor. As frequently noted, humor research is in the pioneering stages. The purposeful inclusion of stories, jokes, and quotes is designed to bring some levity to an otherwise serious look at this topic.

The benefits of humor are identified and celebrated throughout in the hopes that you will be encouraged to think about your own humor style and humor practice. Form a study group or employ this book as part of a basic technique to learn more about humor. There are several interactive components at the end of each chapter for you to utilize in a variety of ways and in a variety of group settings.

This is an invitation to you to try the tools in the "jest for fun" boxes, the café conversations, the anecdotes, the appendices, and the powerful leadership strategies. All suggest strategies on how you can have some fun and bring "humergy" into your personal and professional life.

> *I have always been a huge admirer of my own work. I'm one of the funniest and most entertaining writers I know.*
>
> —Mel Brooks

Here is a brief overview of the chapters.

CHAPTER 1: HUMOR—THE TONIC FOR TIRED BLOOD

Step right up and get your humor here! The benefits of humor are extraordinary. When there is a fusion of enthusiasm, energy, joy, and hope, a peak experience emerges that most of us identify as a sense of humor. The relatively new field of positive psychology strives to understand and promote human potential that enables individuals and communities to thrive. Humor is one of the cognitive strengths connecting our basic temperament and our lifetime experiences.

This chapter provides foundational information for improving humor practice. Definitions, a historical perspective, and the benefits of humor are explored. The phenomenon of humergy, the energy that comes from humor, is investigated. Get ready for a spoonful of fun, provoking a belly laugh or at least a chuckle or two.

CHAPTER 2: DEVELOPING YOUR HUMOR BEING: A NUT IS BORN

Each infant's brain contains a unique blueprint for humor maturation. Universal patterns of humor development are the foundation for cultivating individual growth and determining what type of humor is possible for each age or stage of development. The "growing up funny" list is an investigation of distinct phases of humor development.

1. Peek-a-boo
2. Knock-knock
3. Riddle-de-dee
4. Pun fun
5. Joy-flow

Play is an integral part of humor development at all of these stages. Most children are finding a reduction of *free* play as structured activities and studying consume more and more of their time. Employees are searching for ways to keep their employees happy and productive. Play is becoming more popular as an option in creating an optimal working environment.

Did you grow up funny? What is your humor foundation and current humor practice? This exploration of humor development will encourage you to begin to examine your own unique humor growth and practice.

CHAPTER 3: EXAMINING BRAIN RESEARCH AND HUMOR: MOUSE DROPPINGS

What have we learned from brain research about humor? Two kinds of mice are providing us with information about laughter, fun, and positive emotionality.

1. Mice are frequently used in research, providing a foundation for what we know about the emotions and the field of humor studies.
2. Another type of *mouse manipulation*, using computerized imaging techniques, is advancing research at an incredible speed and actually allows us to see brain activity levels.

A staggering amount of data is emerging from the biological research and imaging technology to provide compelling evidence on the significance of humor in our lives. While it is clear that fear and stress inhibit productivity and do have a correlation with depression, the research on humor and joy is a more complex process. An increasing number of studies confirm the relationship between the positive emotions and optimal living. This chapter includes a synopsis of the humor research with evidence that humor skills have a direct relation to reducing stress and increasing happiness. Information is included on what we are learning from brain imaging.

CHAPTER 4: HURTFUL HUMOR IS NO LAUGHING MATTER

There are moments in history when nations wonder if the ability to use humor has been lost to an extraordinary tragedy, such as 9/11. There are also moments in our own lives when humor seems to be lost. The current emphasis on accountability and increased productivity has raised stress levels of many people.

Negative humor often emerges from excess stress and fear. An examination of how fear triggers an unhealthy emotional climate and how humorphobia (the fear of humor) inhibits learning is examined in this chapter. The nature of inappropriate humor, including that of bullies and victims, will be investigated. Recognizing humordoomer behavior is the key to understanding possible strategies for building better relationships with these individuals. Strategies for coping with humordoomers will be explored.

CHAPTER 5: THE HUMOR WORKOUT: PUMPING UP WITH PRACTICE

What is your humor style? The humor styles inventory will assist you in understanding why we all find humor in different things. Although both nature and nurture contribute to our sense of humor, humergy is a skill that can be enhanced with practice. While we are not exactly born with a sense of humor, temperament is a significant factor in humor development. Life experiences, age, gender, cultural background, work situation, relationships, and personality all have an impact on our humor approach. Join the humor marathon. With effort anyone can increase and enjoy a humor power workout that will improve their humor core.

Your humor workout provides benefits that:

- Maximize creativity and comprehension
- Increase ability to take risks and try new things
- Expand ability to generate ideas
- Capture attention
- Increase memory storage and retrieval
- Respond to change and crisis with positive energy
- Facilitate communication with individuals and in groups
- Enable observation of internal emotional state
- Reflect the inner spirit of self and others
- Increase ability to "read" the emotions of others
- Reduce tension, fear, and anger
- Nurture trust
- Increase group energy and positive group dynamics

CHAPTER 6: HUMOR AT WORK: STORIES OF COURAGE

This is it! Humor is a powerful tool for energizing peak performance and increasing productivity. This chapter highlights the stories of over thirty individuals who purposefully use humor as a tool in their work. You will be amazed at the impact they are having on so many others in various walks of life.

The goal of this chapter is to provide poignant stories from humor practioners on how they integrate and incorporate humor into their workplace culture. Humor can make a difference in every career path and job situation. Included are stories of using humor at funeral services and as a coping strategy for caregivers. Some descriptions include the use of humor in the grieving process and as a way to decrease the pain of those going through chemotherapy. But it is the multifaceted experiences of musicians, doctors, social workers, educators, and grief counselors that provide insights into how our lives can be enhanced with humor and laughter. These stories are riveting and will provide the opportunity for you to imagine how a focus on humor practice can energize your workplace.

CHAPTER 7: LEADERSHIP IS A FUNNY THING

If you walk into your organization or place of work, do you find happy employees and administrators? Is the emotional climate one of trust and positive energy? Three distinct leadership styles are observed in relation to humor:

1. Authoritarian
2. Laissez faire
3. Participatory

The belief systems of leaders impact their emotional contribution to the level of happiness found in a work environment. The philosophy of servant leadership as a belief system will be explored, including the following principles:

- *Transformation* as a vehicle for personal and institutional growth
- *Personal growth* as a route to better serving others
- *Enabling environments* that empower and encourage service
- *Service* as a fundamental goal
- *Trusting relationships* as a basic platform for collaboration and service
- *Creating commitment* as a way to collaborative activity
- *Community building* as a way to create environments in which people can trust each other and work together
- *Nurturing the spirit* as a way to provide joy and fulfillment in meaningful work. The level of humor, laughter, and fun will be evident in workplaces that have high levels of trust.

The study of humor provides new perceptions into critical issues facing leaders. It allows the freedom to not only think "out of the box" but to have fun while doing so.

Significant areas of impact include the ability of humor to:

- Define the ability of a leader to build a culture of trust
- Maximize the capacity of individuals for effective communication
- Create an optimal working environment
- Plant information into the long-term memory
- Reduce stress

A framework for leaders is introduced that examines the content, process, and context of building leadership skills.

> *I handed in a script last year and the studio didn't change one word. The word they didn't change was on page 87.*
>
> —Steve Martin

1

HUMOR: THE TONIC FOR TIRED BLOOD

I was put on this earth to accomplish a certain number of things . . . right now I am so far behind I will never die!

—Anonymous

Have you been exhausted, worried, or just plain weary lately? Has the current focus on bad news, accountability, and crazy politics made you irritable? This is your lucky day! Step right up for a sure-fire remedy guaranteed to bring vitality and energy to your everyday life. You will be amazed by the advantages of the humor tonic.

But be warned: humor is more than the snake-oil skill of telling jokes. Also be warned that the research contained here focuses on many preliminary findings and could be biased toward the positive benefits of humor. The focus in this book has been to search for the advantages for all who want to increase humor in their lives. Humor is just the tonic needed by those of us stressed by the challenges of everyday life, so the reviewed studies and insights are presented through a rosy and optimistic lens.

If you want to add a little fun to your life, this book is for you! Humor is the real thing. It cures the blues. It knocks the socks off of boredom. It tickles, splits guts, and generates bellyaches while curing whatever ails you. It might even be funny. The six benefits of humor are explored in depth later in this book. But for now, just take a peek at what a healthy dose of humor might do for you. Just a spoonful!

1. CONTRIBUTES TO MIND/BODY BALANCE

Health nuts are going to feel stupid someday, lying in a hospital dying of nothing.

—Redd Foxx

A sense of humor can create a remarkable feeling of control. Learning to use humor as the binoculars for life's challenges can amplify confidence in your own internal power to cope. The optimistic energy that comes from humor will enable you to embrace difficulties with resilience. Some people purposefully use laughter to ease pain and promote physical healing. There is some experimental research indicating that laughter and humor might actually cure illness and provide effective therapies for a number of disorders. Some claim that laughter relieves pain, reduces stress, and improves the immune system response (Harvey, 1998). Although many studies are preliminary, numerous indicators are confirming the benefits and applications of positive humor.

Got stress? The purposeful use of humor can help you feel more optimistic about your life, knowing that you can choose how to respond to stress. Humor elevates mood and has been known to be a deterrent to depression. Stress reduction is considered one of the most important benefits of humor. A little humor will go a long way in helping us balance the challenges of high-speed living. Research on stress and depression will be explored more fully in Chapter 3.

2. MAXIMIZES BRAIN POWER

If you haven't got a sense of humor, you haven't any sense at all.

—Mary McDonald

Humor has the ability to capture the attention of the brain. "Emotion drives attention and attention drives learning" (Sylwester, 1995). A brain cannot learn if it is not attending. The surprise elements of humor alert the attentional center of the brain and increase the likelihood of memory storage and long-term retrieval. Humor has the potential to hook easily bored and inattentive participants in a workshop. It can help the stressed or shy employee to relax. As brain food, humor can't be beat. Brain scans reveal that humor "lights up" huge areas of the brain.

Word play, puns, stories, jokes, and riddles all involve the creative use of language. Maximizing the capacity to use language through the skillful use of humor will increase the number and speed of the neural connections in the brain. Humor is often used as one of the ways to identify gifted students in schools.

Just how effective can humor be? The marketing industry gives us an indication. Many of us watch the Super Bowl just to see the commercials. The money spent for air time is mind-boggling. Advertisers have less than two minutes to get your attention and put their product into your long-term memory, and they spend zillions of dollars to capture the attention of this large viewing audience.

Not only do people watch these commercials, but also, the next day, animated discussion about favorite Super Bowl commercials takes place around office water coolers. There is a good reason for humor in advertising. An analysis of the retention rate for commercials found that the highest rate of recall was when humor was used (Stewart & Furse, 1986).

The research is clear that strong emotional connections enhance learning. Which emotion is your trigger of choice for memory? Fear and anger can permeate lives and bombard the senses with negative information on a daily basis. Choose joy! Remember that humor will help put information into long-term memory.

3. ENHANCES CREATIVITY

The latest survey reports that 3 out of 4 people make up 75 percent of the population.

—Unknown

Creativity is the ability of the brain to bring together diverse ideas that will generate the thinking necessary for complex problem solving. Humor and creativity are great companions, each a perfect complement for the other in nourishing thinking. Risk taking is the nucleus of creativity and of humor; the freedom to express wild ideas activates spirited conversation and sparks the imagination. The creative process flourishes when accompanied by a sense of humor.

McGhee (1999) talks about creativity in his book *Health, Healing and the Amuse System.* He says that creative thinking in the workplace is becoming more significant because of the rapid pace of change that has been occurring. Businesses are realizing that the old solutions don't work any more.

It takes creativity and practice to be able to change negative thinking. Exploring the benefits of creative thinking has reaped big benefits for companies like Google, which has unorthodox "rules" for employee behavior. Their website states that employees can create their office environment by showcasing team interests and personality. Bikes are often used for efficient travel between meetings. It is not unusual to see dogs, lava lamps, and massage chairs in office spaces. There are volleyball courts, pianos, ping-pong tables, and pool tables. Healthy lunches are served in the café, with snacks and drinks in the break rooms. This is not your typical workplace, but doesn't it sound like a fun place to work? One reason Google has been so successful is because of their emphasis on creativity.

Humor increases the potential for divergent thinking and the capacity for solving complex problems. By linking diverse areas of the brain, humor forges new neural connections involving previously existing concepts. Voila—creativity flourishes. This means that it is essential to encourage the employees in your organization to "think outside the box." An ever-more-competitive international marketplace requires increased levels of creativity (McGhee, 1999).

Paul McGhee writes that there are three ways to boost the level of creativity within your organization: "1) create a work environment conducive to more creative thinking, 2) hire more creative employees, and 3) find ways to build up the creative abilities of the employees you have." For maximum results, you can try all three guidelines at the same time and maximize the creativity in your organization (McGhee, 1999).

4. FACILITATES COMMUNICATION

> *If you're going to tell people the truth, you'd better make them laugh. Otherwise, they'll kill you.*
>
> —George Bernard Shaw

Using humor to build and maintain relationships is an invaluable skill. Emotional intelligence (EI), the ability to perceive, assess, and influence one's own and other people's emotions, is essential for knowing when and how to use humor effectively (Goleman, 1998). The ability to use humor as a part of interpersonal dialogue requires confidence in one's own humor strengths; a fun-loving, playful spirit; and the willingness to risk the extraordinary.

As long as distinctions are made between management and nonmanagement employees, there will always be barriers to good communication. Some managers have a style that discourages open communication. When a manager uses humor (especially occasional self-directed humor), however, it says to everyone on the team that he or she is a "regular" person—he or she is one of us. To function as a team, you need openness and comfort in bringing up difficult issues, and shared positive humor is a powerful means of achieving that. "Any organization that wants or needs the full commitment of its employees to work as a team needs to establish a relaxed and open work atmosphere. A manager who shows that s/he has a good sense of humor goes a long way in establishing this atmosphere" (McGhee, 1999).

Humor generates trust among colleagues and can facilitate a reduction in tension, fear, and anger. Leaders who have the ability to assist others in seeing the humor in difficult situations can nurture communication and ease tense situations. Exaggeration, puns, and self-deprecating humor are tools of the trade. Humorists are able to use reframing (for example, highlighting the ridiculous or exaggerating) as a device to facilitate a shift in context. This shift encourages both individuals and groups to think creatively through shared humor. Laughter can quickly dispel tension and increase the capacity for dialogue.

The use of humor as a tool in communication is rarely taught. However, it is the first thing that parents nurture in their children. Parents across cultures strive to entice their baby to smile and laugh. The use of humor is a skill requiring multifaceted levels of knowledge and ability. Purposeful humor integration provides a distinct advantage in conversation. Politicians, managers, and coaches seeking to ease tension and promote dialogue have embraced the use of humor.

> *After eating an entire bull, a mountain lion felt so good he started roaring. He kept it up until a hunter came along and shot him. The moral: When you're full of bull, keep your mouth shut.*
>
> —Will Rogers

5. SUPPORTS THE CHANGE PROCESS

Nothing new should be done for the very first time.

There are volumes written about organizational change. It is a hot topic in all fields of work. When encountering everyday small disruptions or a major crisis situation, the response pattern for change varies greatly among individuals and within organizations.

Humor can be an indicator of the change response. It is similar to taking the temperature of an individual or an organization. Belief systems, coping skills, physical being, temperament, experiences, culture, and gender all blend within the individual neurological system and result in generating an individual response pattern for change. The humor response of any group is a reflection of organizational thinking and can reflect the ability of that culture to adapt.

Brains crave familiar patterns. Think about the structure, procedure, and familiar schedule in your everyday life. Unexpected change, suffering, and loss disrupt normal routines. When an individual experiences humor as a response to life challenges, it is easier to heal and move forward. Painful experiences, if met with hope and optimism, can produce remarkable growth opportunities. In fact, humor frequently emerges from the downside of life. Laughter and tears are closely related, which is why many comedians began their careers by laughing through the tragedy in their lives. This ability for humorous optimism in the face of difficulty is truly a miracle tonic.

Change is good—you go first.

6. CREATES AN OPTIMAL ENVIRONMENT AND WORKPLACE CULTURE

Logic is a systematic method of coming to the wrong conclusions with confidence.

An expert is one who knows more and more about less and less until he knows absolutely everything about nothing.

A meeting is an event at which the minutes are kept and the hours are lost.

—Murphy's laws

Look for laughter, joy, spirit, and enthusiasm in the workplace and you'll find an environment in which learning and productivity thrive. Humor contributes to that optimal work environment. It is brain-compatible in creating an enriched context both for working and for assisting individuals in becoming engaged in their jobs. When you find fun, laughter, and leaders with a sense of humor, people thrive.

Leadership is correlated with building relationships based on trust. Trust is considered the basis for creating successful learning communities because it facilitates teamwork and is the foundation for cultivating relationships. A strong bond of trust among members of an organization is essential for growth.

But what does trust look like? It's simple to observe if you know the indicators. Look for laughter, fun, and joy. When you walk into a work environment and you can actually feel the joy, you'll recognize the existence of a high level of trust. Humor thrives in an environment of trust and is a major factor that contributes to building trust. When multiple choices are available to an individual within a relationship or within an organization, there are increased opportunities for a sense of humor to thrive. Fun is an indicator of trust (Yerkes, 2001).

"Mirthium" is a review of sixty-plus studies conducted over the past forty years, and it gives the reader a clear synopsis of exactly what benefits humor will provide as well as clarifying some of the existing misperceptions.

"Oscar makes me take **Mirthium II**® *every day before I go to work."*
—Felix Unger (*The Odd Couple*)

MIRTHIUM II®

(*Generic:* Laughtilyouplotz)

If you have been diagnosed with chronic humor impairment, jocularitis, jesticulosis, or just plain "seriousness," talk to your humor professional about Mirthium II®. This is the more potent, turbo-charged version of Mirthium®.

Reported benefits are based on randomized, quadruple-blind (even the researcher doesn't have a clue what's happening), placebo, controlled clinical trials worldwide on 9 semi-human HMO CEOs, conducted by several disreputable, highly stressed university researchers. Those results were replicated in studies with 3 blind mice, 5 Chinese hamsters, and a partridge in a pear tree, plus a convenience sample of sheep from New Zealand.

BENEFITS

Based on nearly 100 scientific studies of the psychophysiological effects of humor and laughter conducted over the past half century, the major benefits follow:

Humor

1. Reduces negative emotional consequences of stress, anxiety, and tension
2. Decreases depression, loneliness, and anger
3. Improves mood
4. Increases self-esteem
5. Promotes a sense of empowerment

Laughter

6. Increases pain tolerance and threshold
7. Improves respiration and breathing (exercises lungs and raises blood oxygen levels)
8. Improves mental functioning (alertness, creativity, and memory)
9. Exercises facial, abdominal, and thoracic muscles
10. Relaxes muscles/decreases muscle tension

WARNINGS

There are certain claims or common beliefs about the effects of Mirthium II® which are false. Research has been conducted on all of the following topics. However, the scarcity of studies, weaknesses in design and execution, or conflicting results render their conclusions as questionable. Seriously, despite the encouraging direction of the findings, there is insufficient research evidence to support the following claims:

Humor

1. Decreases symptoms of illness and medical problems
2. Enhances interpersonal relationships, intimacy, and marriage satisfaction
3. Increases longevity

Laughter

4. Stimulates the production of endorphins which decrease pain

Figure 1.1   Mirthium

Reprinted with permission of Ronald A. Berk (2011), academic physician and scientist.

5. Prevents or alleviates pain
6. Lowers heart rate
7. Lowers blood pressure
8. Decreases heart disease
9. Decreases stress hormones (serum cortisol, dopac, and epinephrine)
10. Boosts immune system functions to fight viral and bacterial infections and disease
    - increases immunoglobulin A(IgA), M(IgM), and G(IgG)
    - increases natural killer cell activity (NKA)
    - increases number of activated T-lymphocytes (T4 and CD4 cells)
    - increases T-cell helper/suppressor ratio
    - increases levels of Complement 3
    - increases number of B-cells
    - increases gamma-interferon levels

DOSAGE

Place 1 delayed-release, red transdermal patch on the tip of your nose every 24 hours

- Recommended by the American Association of Polymorphous Prescriptions

- #1 choice of professors, physicians, nurses, administrators, accountants, engineers, IT specialists, lawyers, insurance brokers, IRS auditors, FBI agents, and TSA personnel

- *FAST RESULTS*: Laugh within 30 min. after 1st dose, as patch dissolves in your nose

CONTRAINDICATIONS

Mirthium II® is contraindicated in humans and assorted livestock who have a known hypersensitivity to anything or with nail fungus, a hernia, humongous prostate, cataracts, or irritable howl syndrome. Tell your humor professional about any over-, under-, or around-the-counter medications. Mirthium II® interacts with every medication.

SIDE EFFECTS

No severe allergic reactions other than convulsive hysteria and shrieking like a banshee. If laughter continues for more than 48 hours, you should be so lucky. Side effects include: trichinosis, halitosis, gingivitis, hallucinations, drooling, erectile dysfunction (of course), sleep apnea, athlete's foot, urge to smoke, memory loss, gangrene, incontinence, and necrophilia.

QUESTIONS

Ask your humor professional about Mirthium II® today. Call 1-555-YO-FUNNY for your free information guide on Mirthium II® or visit http://www.mirthium.com.

BERK PHARMACEUTICALS
(A name you used to be able to trust!)

Figure 1.1 (continued)

DOSES OF HUMOR ARE VITAL

Noting all the benefits of humor, one would assume that humor studies would be a core component of research on leadership, organizational development, and workplace studies. However, humor as a fundamental skill is rarely the focus of research studies, and it's certainly generally neglected as a topic for serious consideration.

Even so, it's frequently mentioned as a quality that is invaluable. For instance, would you want to hire someone without a sense of humor? Of course not! Although humor is mentioned frequently in the literature as exceedingly important (even being considered an essential quality in the hiring process), it's usually neglected as a topic of significant study. As a result of this benign neglect, the exploration and study of humor is a pioneering effort. This is an invitation to take this miracle tonic of humor seriously.

This is not a joke book. Although you may laugh when reading this book and find that parts of it are pretty funny, the primary intent is not to tell jokes. Though you will smile and even chuckle as you read, the primary purpose is to share information about humor and laughter. This is rather a practical look at a topic that is often ignored.

The purpose of this book is to affirm, sustain, and encourage everyone in the practice of humor not only as a personal tool to optimize a healthy lifestyle but also to maximize the benefits of humor in everyday living. These benefits include current research-based data on the use of humor to nurture creativity, to increase the capacity for memory retention, to support an optimal work environment, and to build safe communities that reflect the relational trust necessary for collaborative learning and living. (See "Benefits of Humor," Figure 1.2.)

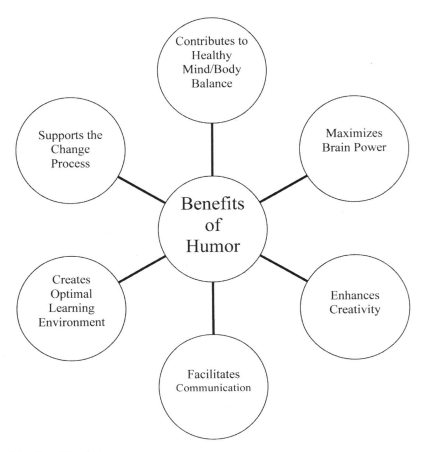

Figure 1.2   Benefits of Humor

THE ENERGY OF HUMOR: HUMERGY DEFINED

> *Analyzing humor is like dissecting a frog. Few people are interested and the frog dies of it.*
>
> —E. B. White

At the risk of squashing your interest, clarifying the wriggly aspects of humor is fundamental to the ability to improve humor practice. Laughter and humor are related but are not exactly the same (Provine, 2000). Since laughter has such a strong link to humor, a common misperception is that humor is the ability to make people laugh by telling jokes. While the ability to tell jokes is a valued skill, it does not begin to reflect the complexity of humor.

Spontaneous group laughter is often impossible to describe. The ability to laugh with others at the discrepancies of life certainly contributes to the humor experience. Although jokes and funny stories generate laughter, it is generally found that laughter occurs during normal everyday interactions. When someone walks up to a group of folks who are laughing hysterically and wants to know what is so funny, it is impossible to explain. You finally sputter through your tears: "You just had to be there!" Phrases that make people laugh are often not very funny when the actual words are examined (Provine, 2000).

Comedy, mirth, stories, wit, and joking are all part of the external experience of laughing with other people. However, humor experienced with others is different from an individual's unique sense of humor. It is essential to distinguish between the two.

The word *humor* by itself, without any sense as in "sense of humor," is defined in the dictionary as the "quality that makes something amusing or laughable." Humor, then, is that which would be considered funny. When you bring a "sense" to humor a metamorphosis occurs. A *sense of humor* is the capacity of a human being to respond to life challenges with optimistic enjoyment (Morrison, 2005).

Just because laughter is a universal human trait does not guarantee that there exists a universal understanding of humor. Cognitive, emotional, behavioral, psychophysiological, and social components are all factors of humor (Martin, 2001). The multifaceted nature of humor can pose numerous challenges for valid research. At the risk of oversimplifying the complexity of humor, the abovementioned definition will be used in this book. Additional definitions are found in Appendix 1, "Humor Terminology."

An individual sense of humor is inseparable from the whole being. It is intrinsically woven into the emotional and social psyche and reflects an individual's ethics and belief systems. The ability to adapt to change with enjoyment or at least a positive acceptance defines the essence of having a sense of humor.

Joy-Flow Experiences

Age doesn't always bring wisdom, sometimes age comes alone.

Enthusiasm, energy, joy, and hope merge to create the peak experiences most of us identify with a sense of humor. The relatively new field of positive psychology strives to understand and promote the human potential that enables individuals and communities to thrive. Humor is one of the complex cognitive strengths that connect basic temperament and lifetime experiences. The energy of humor, or "humergy," is an indicator of reaching the "self-actualization" level on Maslow's hierarchy of needs scale (Maslow, 1968).

Maslow generalized that self-actualizing people tend to respond to life challenges with a spontaneous and creative personality. He defined profound moments of joyful understanding as peak experiences with heightened sensory experiences integrating hope, optimism, and peace. It's difficult to find specific terminology that expresses Maslow's peak experience. The vitality of humor energy that emerges from a hopeful, joyful spirit of humor needs defining. I have identified this peak experience of a vigorous, optimistic energy as *humergy*.

Humergy is the energy that emerges from the joy and optimism of the inner spirit, reflecting a unique personality and nourishing a healthy mind–body balance. It's possible to clarify the characteristics that inhibit humergy and those that promote its development, as shown in Table 1.1. Stress, fear, and pessimism hinder the ability of an individual to enjoy the fullness of a humergy lifestyle. Healthy relationships, optimism, and an environment of trust nurture the growth of humergy.

Table 1.1   Humergy Characteristics

Humor Inhibitors	*Humor Developers*
Stressful relationships	Healthy relationships
Low self-confidence	Self-confidence
Authoritarian environment	Trust: risk taking environment
Anxiety, fear of fun and play	Joyfulness, playfulness
Helplessness	Hopefulness
Pessimism	Optimism

Source: Developed by Mary Kay Morrison

This energy is being explored in several fields, including that of positive psychology, which addresses the study of positive emotions. Richard Davidson's research on "approach-related positive emotion" characterizes certain individuals as having enthusiasm, alertness, energy, and persistence in goal orientation (Davidson, 2000). The purpose of positive psychology is to understand and promote the human strengths that enable individuals and communities to thrive.

The Positive Emotions and Psychophysiology (PEP) Lab at the University of North Carolina Chapel Hill is conducting one of the most fascinating projects in studying positive emotions. The research is based on the belief that positive emotions extend the capacity for attention, cognition, and action. The goal of the PEP Lab is to focus on how positive emotions enable human beings to "flourish." When positive emotions are absent, people lose their freedom of choice, stagnate, and are predictable. When there is ample supply of positive emotionality, people are creative, resilient, and unpredictable (Fredrickson, 2003).

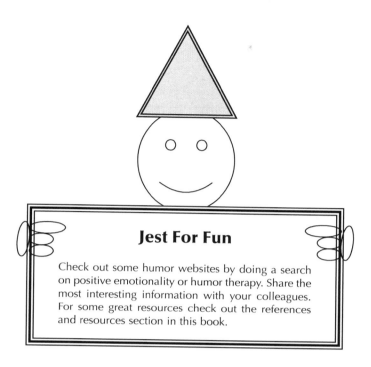

Jest For Fun

Check out some humor websites by doing a search on positive emotionality or humor therapy. Share the most interesting information with your colleagues. For some great resources check out the references and resources section in this book.

Pioneering efforts are being made by counselors and psychologists to incorporate humor into therapy treatments for patients. The use of humor in the medical field was highlighted in the movie *Patch Adams*, the story of Hunter Adams, who promoted the use of humor as a medical practice. His goal was to fulfill his patients' fantasies, ease their fears, and increase their endorphin levels. Several not-for-profit organizations promote humor therapy and humor research. Numerous references to these organizations are interspersed throughout this book.

A SHORT HISTORY OF FUNNY PEOPLE

The kind of humor I like is the thing that makes me laugh for five seconds and think for ten minutes.

—William Davis

In addition to Maslow, an odd assortment of characters from history provide insights into the current understanding of humor. It is claimed that humor was invented in the 1400s by Duke Knock of the Knock, who was trying to ascertain why doth ye chicken traverse ye thoroughfare. Others assert that humor was invented by Al Gore to alleviate boredom with politics.

The role of early medicine was to keep the humors in balance. Hippocrates clarified the Greek idea of four humors, which were related to temperament and disposition. In the 1600s it was determined by physicians that four liquids called humors determined a healthy balance of mind and body. These were blood, black bile, yellow bile, and phlegm. An imbalance of humors signaled abnormal behavior or mental illness.

During the Renaissance period, *humorous* actually referred to anyone who was considered demented. In fact, it was not until the 1700s that humor was considered normal behavior. Puritans actually forbade the use of most comedy, play, and fun. Some think that this negativity toward humor persists in several forms today.

Shakespeare contributed to an understanding of the terminology of comedy and tragedy through his literary works. Comedy was not really "humorous" but depicted ordinary characters who triumphed, while tragedy involved great characters who made mistakes or suffered painful experiences, often resulting in death. Shakespeare interspersed comedy and tragedy with an emotional impact that has survived over the years and still remains as an important work.

Charlie Chaplin, known as the "tramp philosopher," began his film career with the release of a silent picture, *The Tramp* (1915). He energized audiences with his tragicomic portrayal of a little guy against the world. He focused his work on the premise that people can and should laugh at life's tragedies.

Mark Twain, born Samuel Clemens in 1835, is known as one of the greatest American humorists. Twain wrote *The Adventures of Tom Sawyer* and *The Adventures of Huckleberry Finn*, both examples of finding humor in everyday life. His literature has long been a familiar staple on the reading lists for students.

> *Suppose you were an idiot and a member of Congress. But I repeat myself.*
>
> —Mark Twain

Will Rogers, born in 1879, had top billing with a vaudeville act in the renowned Ziegfield Follies. As a syndicated column writer, he intertwined humor, current events, and human idiosyncrasies. His ability to poke fun at politicians endeared him to the American public. His career included work in the movies, and he became a well-known figure. His quotes are still applicable today.

> *There's no trick to being a humorist when you have the whole government working for you.*
>
> *Be thankful we're not getting all the government we're paying for.*

Everything is changing. People are taking their comedians seriously and the politicians as a joke.

I don't make jokes; I just watch the government and report the facts.

—Will Rogers

Abraham Lincoln was known for his animated storytelling. His clever wit was often used to disparage political opponents. His most engaging quality was the ability to laugh at his own physical imperfections, a trait that endeared him to the American public.

If I were two faced, would I be wearing this one?

Common looking people are the best in the world; that is the reason the Lord made so many of them.

—Abraham Lincoln

Norman Cousins is the person credited with the initial research on the relationship between laughter and wellness. He wrote about his experiences in his best-selling book, *Anatomy of an Illness as Perceived by the Patient: Reflections on Healing and Regeneration*, published in 1979. His personal story of a life-threatening illness and his belief that laughing would help him to heal have become legendary. He checked himself out of a hospital and into a motel to watch funny movies as part of his therapeutic process. He recovered fully and decided that humor was a major part of his healing process.

Lucille Ball captured the hearts of the world with her portrayal of an everyday housewife who turned ordinary events into an extremely funny sitcom. She had an enormous impact on the transition of the media from movies to television and was one of the first women to become a nationally known television star.

The secret of staying young is to live honestly, eat slowly, and lie about your age.

You see much more of your children once they leave home.

—Lucille Ball

Bob Hope performed in radio, movies, and television and became famous for his one-liners. He is cited by the Guinness Book of Records as the most honored entertainer in the world. He performed for the American military troops stationed overseas and won the hearts of the soldiers during those performances with his ability to help them laugh at their own difficult situation.

> *If you haven't any charity in your heart, you have the worst kind of heart trouble.*
>
> *A bank is a place that will lend you money if you can prove that you don't need it.*
>
> *I love to go to Washington, if only to be near my money.*
>
> —Bob Hope

Bill Cosby has touched people's lives by providing humorous insights into everyday situations of parenting and family life with his television sitcom. As an author and speaker, he continues to share his wit and insights. Recently he has used his comic visibility to espouse his opinions about controversial racial issues. These are not laughing matters to Cosby, who strongly advocates views that are not typically verbalized. He uses humor to communicate the following:

> *A word to the wise ain't necessary—it's the stupid ones who need the advice.*
>
> *Always end the name of your child with a vowel, so when you yell the name will carry.*
>
> *Let us now set forth one of the fundamental truths about marriage: the wife is in charge.*
>
> —Bill Cosby

Erma Bombeck was a journalist who wrote a weekly humor column focusing on life as a parent. Her books became best-sellers and often focus on helping parents laugh at the challenges of having children. When she became a cancer survivor, she helped many learn to laugh through this illness. Her courage and ability to laugh during her cancer battles continue to inspire those suffering from terminal illness.

> *Humor is a spontaneous, wonderful bit of an outburst that just comes. It's unbridled, it's unplanned, and it's full of surprises.*
>
> *If you can't make it better, you can laugh at it.*
>
> —Erma Bombeck

Jest For Fun

Pick a humorist who makes you laugh. Search the web for their bibliography and famous quotes. Post your findings your staff bulletin board. (See Appendix 4, "Comedian List.")

Johnny Carson, David Letterman, Jon Stewart, and Jay Leno have helped many Americans end their day with laughter. Late-night television is a way of life for many Americans. Often the humor revolves around current political situations. The format allows us to laugh at the unusual things national figures say and do. Letterman's top ten list has become a part of American culture and is included in this book as a strategy to teach various aspects of humor.

The list of comedians who have influenced the understanding of humor is immeasurable. An expanded list of comedians is in Appendix 4. This comedian list can be used for several of the activities described in this book. You can identify your own favorite comedian when exploring your humor style.

A humorist is a person who feels bad but who feels good about it.

—Don Herold

THE TONIC OF HUMOR IS CONTAGIOUS—CATCH IT!

Can you believe that the tonic of humor is available free of charge with great side effects of laughter and fun? The joy-flow experience of humergy is observed when enthusiasm, excitement, and energy are bubbling from individuals who are passionate about their work. This synergy is experienced in an environment that is humming with the spirit of joyful learning and living.

Humergy is reflected in the excitement of employees as they exude a zest for life and a quest for knowledge. Many organizations are devoted to the research and sharing of humor resources. Catch their humor energy and take advantage of their resources.

- The Association of Applied and Therapeutic Humor (AATH) is an organization that is mentioned frequently in this book. It has served me as a community of colleagues that have supported my efforts to explore the research and write this book. I currently serve on the board of directors and am actively serving as director of the Humor Academy for AATH. This organization is open to all who are interested in promoting the positive benefits of humor. AATH defines humor as "any intervention that promotes health and wellness by stimulating a playful discovery, expression or appreciation of the absurdity or incongruity of life's situations. This intervention may enhance health or be used as a complementary treatment of illness to facilitate healing or coping, whether physical, emotional, cognitive, social, or spiritual" (http://www.aath.org/).
- The International Society for Humor Studies (ISHS) is a scholarly and professional organization dedicated to the advancement of humor research. Many of the society's members are university and college professors in the arts and humanities, biological and social sciences, and education. The society also includes professionals in the fields of counseling, management, nursing, journalism, and theater. All of the members are interested in humor's many facets, including its role in business, entertainment, and health care as well as how humor varies according to culture, age, gender, purpose, and context (http://www.hnu.edu/ishs). I had the privilege of presenting "Teaching with Humor" at ISHS at the Long Beach Campus of the University of California in 2008.
- The Laughter Arts and Science Foundation is a comprehensive program founded by Steve Wilson that promotes education, training, and research in laughter, humor, and mirth. There are several projects within this wonderful organization. I am honored to serve as an advisor to the Funny Lit project that Steve initiated several years ago. The purpose is to promote literacy through the use of humor and laughter (http://www.laughter foundation.org/index-new.asp).
- The purpose of the American Humor Studies Association is to foster and promote study, criticism, and research in American humor in all its varied aspects (http://www.slu.edu/academic/ahsa/journalhome.htm).
- Comedy Cures is an organization founded to bring joy, laughter, and therapeutic humor programs to kids and grown-ups living with illness, depression, trauma, and disabilities (http://www.comedycures.org/).

Additional organizations are listed in the resource guide.

> *A humorist facilitates the capacity of self and others to adapt to every-day events or global change, with laughter and optimistic humor.*

—Mary Kay Morrison

SUMMARY

Humor is an oft-overlooked skill that has many benefits, including providing stress relief, maximizing brain capacity for learning, increasing creativity, improving communication skills, and creating an environment of trust. Humor is inseparable from the whole human being. It is intrinsically woven into the emotional and social psyche, reflecting ethics and belief systems.

The numerous definitions of humor include "what makes you laugh" or "what is amusing." However, a sense of humor is the capacity of a human being to respond to life challenges with optimistic amusement. There is a synergy evident in people who have such an optimistic sense of humor. Humergy is the energy that radiates the joyful optimism of the inner spirit, reflecting a unique personality and nourishing a healthy mind–body balance (Morrison, 2005).

When there is a fusion of enthusiasm, energy, joy, and hope, a peak experience emerges that most of us identify as a sense of humor. The relatively new field of positive psychology strives to understand and promote the human potential that enables individuals and communities to thrive. Humor is one of the complex cognitive strengths that emerge connecting basic temperament and lifetime experiences.

Many people and organizations have contributed to the field of humor. Humorists purposefully and deliberately use humor to focus on truth. Effective leaders understand that the energy of humor is a sign of a healthy organization built on trust.

POWERFUL PRACTICE—STRATEGIES FOR LEADERS

- Staff meeting activity: post humor definitions from a variety of sources on the walls. Participants choose the definition that most closely aligns with their beliefs, then physically go and stand by their choice. The gathered group will discuss why they chose that quote. They can report their discussion highlights to the rest of the staff. This is a good activity for an initial discussion on differing humor beliefs. (See Appendix 1 for definitions.)

- Expand the humor selection in your staff library or resource center. Encourage discussion and sharing of joyful practice.
- Encourage flexibility in workplace norms. When you provide the freedom for individuals to accomplish their work within their own time frame, you are letting them know you trust them as professionals. The rigid imposition of rules (such as "you must stay in the building until 4:00 p.m.") decreases the ability for fun and laughter and increases the likelihood of low morale. Allow access to the building over the weekend and other times so work can be accomplished within the individual's time frame.
- Provide the opportunity for staff to discuss this book as outlined in the first section of the study group format. Invite participation and encourage attendance with prizes, food, and fun.
- Invite employees to share the funniest thing that has happened to them either in their personal lives or in their work life. Compile these into an internal booklet or through social networks and blogs. Numerous folks are finding creative ways to share the humor in their respective fields. For example, stories in the field of nursing are shared in the *Journal of Nursing Jocularity*. This is a free publication for medical folks edited by my friend and colleague Karyn Buxman (http://www.journalofnursing jocularity.com/).
- Use your humor initiatives as a marketing tool. Contact the media with a story of how your organization is using humor to create an optimal work environment.
- Conduct a staff survey to explore beliefs about humor in the workplace. Compile the results and discuss. You can adapt or use the Humor Reflections (Appendix 5) or the Humor Belief Inventory (Appendix 6).

STUDY GROUP FOCUS

- Have a staff meeting devoted to exploring the benefits of humor. Brainstorm ways that humor can be integrated in the workplace or within the organization.
- Publish the benefits of humor in your office or organizational newsletter. Highlight examples of individuals exemplifying these benefits with connections to the benefits for living.
- Identify and celebrate the areas of humor strength that currently exist both on an individual and a collegial basis. Share the ways your staff currently have fun.
- Brainstorm ways to increase the fun and trust opportunities that will optimize living and learning. Develop an action plan for your organization.

CAFÉ CONVERSATIONS

- Discuss your favorite historical contribution to the field of humor. How could this information contribute to the improvement of your life today? For instance, how did Norman Cousins's work impact the field of health?
- Share your favorite television commercial during lunch breaks. Numerous websites post award-winning commercials. How can you apply this type of creativity to your organization or field of work?
- How does the field of positive psychology correspond to your line of work? What is happiness, and what is the relationship between happiness and humor?

Never miss a good chance to shut up.

Always drink upstream from the herd.

Good judgment comes from experience, and a lot of that comes from bad judgment.

—Will Rogers

2

DEVELOPING YOUR
HUMOR BEING:
A NUT IS BORN

Today's mighty oak is just yesterday's nut that held its ground.

In a nutshell, humor is a fundamental and integral core of cognitive and emotional growth. The fertile ground of trust and the elements of nurturing relationships are required for humor to take root. How can parents and teachers nourish the little nuts that are searching for the ground in which their humor can flourish?

Each nut has the capacity for humor development, and studies of early humor development reveal universal patterns of growth. Each child is born with a unique disposition. Although essential questions revolve around the relationship between the environment and the humor developmental process, there are significant factors that support optimal humor maturation.

While it is understood that children are born with an inherent predisposition for temperament, the environment significantly impacts "nuttiness." Let's look at both the nature and nurture of humor maturation.

NATURE OF THE NUT

Are you born with your sense of humor? A glimpse into the research on temperament provides convincing evidence that some humor characteristics emerge from one's biologically based temperament. Innate individual differences usually remain somewhat stable throughout life and impact the response to one's environment.

If you are the parent of more than one child, you will have noticed individual differences among siblings from birth. There are nine temperament characteristics detailed in *The Temperament Perspective* (Kristal, 2005). Each infant has a different degree of each of the identified characteristics. A few of these are worth noting because they can impact humor style and humor growth.

Intensity is the reactive energy of a response, whether happy, sad, or angry—that is, how expressive a child is. The emotional response varies greatly among young children. For instance, some children will smile a little at peek-a-boo games while others laugh loudly.

Adaptability describes how easily a child adjusts to changes and transitions. A sense of humor is closely related to the capacity for flexibility during change. The ability to laugh in new situations is apparent even with very young children. Some are at ease right away while others may hide behind a parent when in a new situation.

Mood is the basic quality of disposition. It may be more positive (a happy or cheerful child) or more negative (a cranky or serious child). Some researchers think that mood is a parallel characteristic or that it overlays one's basic temperament.

Approach/withdrawal is the child's initial response to novelty: new places, people, situations, or things (Kristal, 2005). It takes a certain degree of risk taking to experiment with humor. "Class clowns," for instance, are pretty comfortable with new places and situations. They approach situations with enthusiasm, zest, and unbridled risk taking.

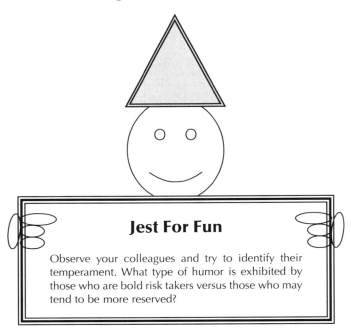

Jest For Fun

Observe your colleagues and try to identify their temperament. What type of humor is exhibited by those who are bold risk takers versus those who may tend to be more reserved?

Moment-to-moment experiences contribute to feelings and are based on the presence or absence of certain chemicals in the brain. As feelings fluctuate, emotions are somewhat restricted to the range and scope of innate temperamental structure.

What influences an individual's humor style? While temperament forms the basis for the energy of a humor style, one can increase one's humor capacity with intentional efforts. Understanding temperament contributes to the ability to maximize the development of a unique humor style and humor strength. Details on humor strength and style are included in Chapter 5 of this book. Think about how your basic temperament has shaped your "nuttiness."

NURTURING *YOUR* NUT

The opposite of play is depression (Brown, 2009). Experiential play is a critical component for learning. Play encourages the discovery skills that generate neural connections while promoting creativity, critical thinking, risk taking, and social bonding. Free play in the classroom is considered to be child directed rather than adult directed. Choice, risk taking, and exploration are the foundation for humor development and form the basis for learning through play. This type of play is also significantly important for adults as well. Brown notes that nothing lights up the brain like play. While many people assume that play is for children, human brains are really designed to play throughout life. The basis of trust is actually given through play signals (Panksepp, Dong, Wayman, & Guerra, 2009).

Today, according to the National Institutes of Mental Health, at any given time there are around 15 million clinically depressed people in the United States. Most are being treated with an ever-increasing array of antidepressants. There is an increasing awareness that depression is more than an insufficiency of chemicals like serotonin. There are also malfunctions in brain circuitry, which are the pathways by which neurons communicate in the brain. Jake Panksepp and his team are investigating this circuitry, along with the genetic and epigenetic factors that regulate these pathways as well as possible circuitry disorders. Panksepp is doing research to see if play experiences early in life can protect against depression later (WSU News, 2009).

Exercise can be as effective as medication for reducing depression. Exercise has also been shown to increase the retention rates of high school students who exercised daily before school (Ratey, 2008). The current research on play, laughter, fun, and exercise is exciting as it indicates promising new ways to treat depression and provide a healthy lifestyle.

There is a dedicated "play" circuitry in the brain equivalent to the circuits of fear and love (Panksepp, 2003). In studies of juvenile rats, it was found that play

Jest For Fun

There was a 102-year-old woman who was asked the top ten reasons that she lived so long. She replied that she "jumped" every day—and then she proceeded to do so to the delight of those around her. So do jump for joy everyday! (Roberts, 2011)

strengthens the social connections among the young rodents by producing sig-nals that Panksepp believes are similar to human laughter. Playing contributes to young mammals by building a memory base in the brain. In mammals, vo-calization sounds emerge from tickling and roughhousing activity.

In humans this vocalization is called laughter. Laughter is a human response to a social connection (Provine, 2000). Neural systems are designed to mirror emotions expressed either verbally or through facial expressions and body language. Play strengthens these social connections.

Physical strength, mental agility, and social skills improve with play. Children laugh often during early childhood. There are references to the number of times that adults laugh as opposed to the frequency of childhood laughter, but claims that children laugh more frequently then adults have not been substantiated (Martin, 2007).

Two studies show supporting evidence for the link between human play and learning. In a fascinating look at the role of play and its effects on primate learn-ing, Lee Alan Dugatkin (2002) suggests that research is pointing to play in child-hood as a means of learning to handle unexpected events in adulthood. It is possible to better prepare an individual for everything from disappointment to physical error, from submission to dominance, from reading social cues to know-ing social limits. In humans, measures of rough-and-tumble play in childhood correlate with scores on social problem-solving tests. In addition, the neural cir-cuitry of play suggests a possible link between play and learning. Although this theory has been explored and supported many times before, recent research has been on the study of the frontal lobes.

There are indications that play increases the versatility of choices, either in decisions, emotional reaction, or physical movement. Play may create a reper-toire of sensorimotor experiences that can be used as measuring sticks for effec-tive response choice in the future.

By renaming play as exploratory time, Steven Wolk (2001) emphasizes the importance of self-discovery and of having the student in control of his or her own learning. Wolk asserts that during exploratory time children build the cogni-tive skills needed to accelerate learning.

I want to live forever. So far, so good.

PLAY AND PREJUDICE

The belief that play has no place in the serious business of work has been wo-ven into the fabric of many organizational systems. This belief has been rein-forced by the intense focus on productivity, accountability, and mandates. The

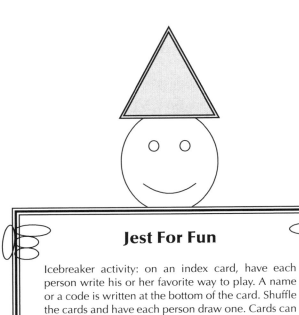

Jest For Fun

Icebreaker activity: on an index card, have each person write his or her favorite way to play. A name or a code is written at the bottom of the card. Shuffle the cards and have each person draw one. Cards can be read out loud with guessing as to who wrote the card, or folks can find a partner and have time to share twice, once as the player and the second time as the play teacher. Actual play is encouraged. (See Figure 2.1.)

very word *play* is repulsive to some people who think of it as the antithesis of "hard work."

Educators compel young children to "do worksheets" rather than allow cognitive growth through the natural exploration that play provides. Ask a young child their favorite subject, and "recess" becomes the increasingly frequent answer as children progress through school. Learning is perceived as "work." Recess is often the only time that children have free choice. Play is a critical component for humor development, yet the opportunities for play in educational systems are near extinction for both children and adults. (See Figure 2.1.)

Play is usually considered to be suitable only for very young children. Using the word *play* in connection with adult meetings often triggers an intense negative reaction. There are those who express a disdain for the use of any activities perceived as "okay" for elementary and early childhood educators but certainly not appropriate in the "higher" cognitive processes necessary after fifth or sixth grade. Conventional wisdom dictates a general belief that learners need to buckle down, work harder, play less, and quit clowning around as they grow.

As children advance through school, auditory methodology increases so that by high school many classes are in a lecture format with few games and ac-

Many believe that play should be banned in the workplace!

Figure 2.1 "No Play"

tivities. Therefore high school and middle school teachers have immense obstacles to overcome in providing opportunities for play. These obstacles need to be addressed by increasing the awareness that humor facilitates learning, play encourages memory retention, and laughter relieves the stress that inhibits cognitive processing. Research on these factors will be explored further in Chapter 3.

Henry Ford had the philosophy that work and play did not mix. Employees were seen as insubordinate and even could be fired if they were humming, whistling, or smiling. Ford thought that work and play was a toxic combination. Today, there are an increasing number of organizations that espouse play as contributing to productivity and peak performance. Several companies are hiring consultants from Serious Play, which is a technique that uses Lego blocks to train executives (Pink, 2006). Think tanks, meditation rooms, team building activities, and actual opportunities to use toys have found their way into boardrooms and businesses. Companies have found increased productivity with increased opportunities for fun (Yerkes, 2001). See Appendix 8, "Take It and Make It Funny."

> *You can discover more about a person in an hour of play than in a year of conversation.*
>
> —Plato

Play is an important component in adult learning. Many organizations have incorporated play into their staff development and work culture. Play encourages creativity, productivity, and enthusiasm. Stress can vanish with the opportunity to play, laugh, and have fun. A sense of play nurtures a sense of humor.

Bring purposeful play into your staff meetings. Do you hate meetings? If so, you are like the majority of people in the world. Meetings can be productive and fun. Check out the Education Learning Network in the resources section for website access to my webinar titled *Staff Meetings with Pizzazz!*

SO PLAY AROUND!

The motivation to play and laugh is innate to the human species (McGhee, 2002b). Young children play and laugh even without efforts to nurture these behaviors. Widespread differences in the development of humor skills can be seen as children grow older. Increased opportunities for humor development will foster key intellectual, social, and emotional life skills.

Integrating play into your practice is a purposeful, challenging, and splendid responsibility. It also brings great satisfaction. Don't be afraid of being silly or looking ridiculous. Have courage! Live on the wild side with the purposeful inclusion of humor and fun in your personal and professional life.

As a child develops, the chemical composition of the brain combines with positive environmental factors to cultivate a sense of trust. A feeling of con-

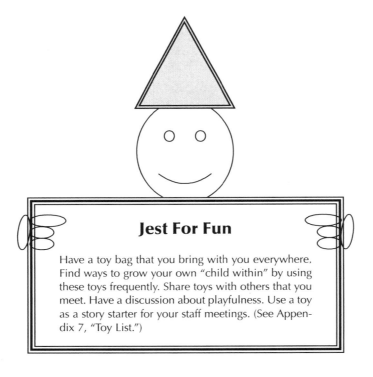

Jest For Fun

Have a toy bag that you bring with you everywhere. Find ways to grow your own "child within" by using these toys frequently. Share toys with others that you meet. Have a discussion about playfulness. Use a toy as a story starter for your staff meetings. (See Appendix 7, "Toy List.")

trol over one's environment (by providing choices) gives hope to individuals in their inherent determination to reach developmental goals. Trust and hope provide a basic foundation for developing a sense of humor. Note there is a pattern of development that can be recognized, nurtured, and cultivated. Researchers D. H. Fuhr, Paul McGhee, E. A. Schwartz, and Avner Ziv have explored the idea of developmental stages of humor. As with any maturational sequence, characteristics of these stages are flexible, and there will be variances as to when the growth of the emerging nut occurs. (See Figure 2.2.)

> *The new word for the day is the term neoteny, which means the retention of immature characteristics into adulthood.*

GROWING UP FUNNY: AGES AND STAGES OF HUMOR DEVELOPMENT

These stages of emotional progression are observed most often through play and are the essential foundation for the development of a sense of humor. Hope, trust, positive emotionality, and optimism are integral to the maturation process. Each of these stages is identified by a prevalent game or activity that is reflective of the particular stage.

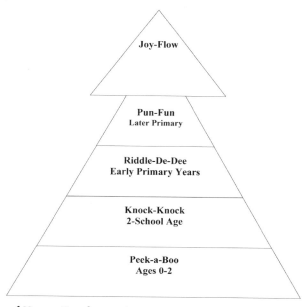

Figure 2.2 Stages of Humor Development

Peek-a-Boo (Birth to Two Years)

Parents work very hard to elicit that first smile from their newborn. When Rachael and her husband, Jason, had their first daughter, Katie, they were typical of parents around the world. From the moment she was born they cooed, smiled, and talked to her. When she smiled, they responded with great enthusiasm. They were ecstatic about capturing her first outburst of laughter on video as a response to Jason acting silly with a toy elephant. Rachael and Jason have made sure that Katie's humor journey is beginning.

Babies carefully observe their caregivers and intently respond to smiles with mirroring smiles and mimicking laughter. The process of reading the faces of others initiates social development and provides a basis for bonding between caregivers and the child. Around five or six months, babies recognize parents and caregivers and will frown or cry when strangers approach.

There is fascinating research on the impact of mirror neurons on the ability to socialize and learn. At all stages the brain mirrors the expressions and actions of various relationship interactions. The universal practice of parents actively eliciting smiles and laughter is a great example of mirror neurons at work (or at play!).

When Isaiah was born, his siblings and cousins smothered him with kisses, hugs, and laughter. At four weeks he was smiling and responding to their repeated attempts to get him to smile. If you use these same smiling techniques in your everyday life, smiling at strangers and laughing with your family, you will discover these mirror neurons at work. Of course the opposite is true. Negativity and frowns also stimulate the mirror neurons. Purposeful use of smiling and laughter can stimulate the positive energy that is possible through mirror neuron activation.

The game of peek-a-boo assures the child that what disappears will reappear. This game helps children understand that their caregiver will return. The initial fear of loss is replaced with surprised relief, which eventually results in laughter. Adults delight in this laughter, and the game is frequently repeated. At age ten months, Cloe found great delight in pulling the diaper off of her mother's face in a reverse game of peek-a-boo.

Adults engage infants in numerous games that provide the basic skills for the "reading" of emotions. Silly noises, hiding objects, repetition of nonsense sounds, and roughhousing all elicit laughter while forming the trusted relationships necessary for humor development. These playful games also contribute to the foundation of a strong attachment between parent and child.

Around the age of one year, incongruent behavior on the part of a caregiver (such as pretending to eat the child's cracker) will evoke laughter (Ziv, 1984). Repetition of silly behaviors will amuse children of this age, while rhythm and rhyme engage their sensory abilities.

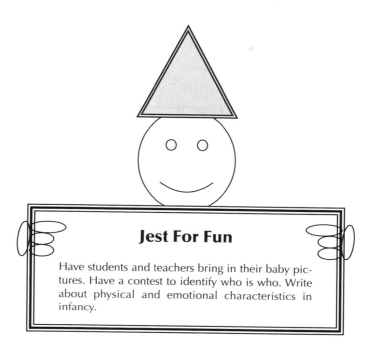

Jest For Fun

Have students and teachers bring in their baby pictures. Have a contest to identify who is who. Write about physical and emotional characteristics in infancy.

When the twins Benjamin and Tyler were twenty-two months old, one of their favorite songs was "Twinkle, Twinkle, Little Star." While singing with them in the car, their grandmother changed the word *star* to their names and then a variety of other names. They kept saying, "No Grandma, star!" When she finally sang it the right way, Ben said "No Grandma—Tyler!" followed by laughter. He obviously was able to understand and replicate the surprise change pattern or "joke."

Chasing games and physical contact play are important aspects of this stage. At eighteen months, cousins Andrew and Samuel were laughing and coming back for more when their caregiver would say: "I'm going to get you!" followed by a chase around the dining room table.

The peek-a-boo stage builds the relational foundation of trust and hope necessary for emotional intelligence and for building infant attachment to a primary caregiver. It also supports the ability of the toddler to understand disruption in normal patterns of human behavior so he or she can transition to the knock-knock phase.

Knock-Knock (Two Years to School Age)

At age two-and-a-half Samuel declared that his father was sure silly when he sang and exaggerated the movements to several songs. Pretend behaviors, exaggeration of reality, and imagination emerge in this stage of humor development. Two-year-old Cloe loves to run up the stairs with a "tiger" big sister roaring after her. In this stage emerges the capacity of children to appreciate fantasy creatures and to employ their own imagination to create silly stories and drawings. Dramatic play begins with children imitating adult behavior. They use their imagination to pretend, often laughing at their own ingenuity.

After making cookies, twenty-three-month-old Andrew was helping to wipe up the crumbs on the floor. He wiped the top of his mother's feet and looked up with a smile. When his silly behavior was acknowledged by his mother's laughing, he also laughed heartily, obviously happy that she "got his joke." He repeated this silly pattern several times, always looking to be sure that she appreciated his humor.

Bathroom humor emerges at this stage and reflects the concerns that children have with their own bodily functions. Taboo words and laughter about body parts are common in early childhood. Jokes about elimination and sexual ideas are often accompanied with giggles. Numerous creative books have been written on these topics.

When a busy mom was at the sink helping Mimi brush her teeth, her three-year-old brother Steve was in the tub playing with the tub toys. He asked his mom if she had "heard that." He wanted to be sure to let her know that he had created loud "bubbles" in the tub. He thought his production of gas in the water was hilarious.

Know why Miss Tomato turned red? Because she saw Mr. Green Pea!

It is intriguing to note the use of humor in children's literature. Word play and repetition are important in the knock-knock stage of humor development. Three- to five-year-olds begin to find humor in things that appear incongruent, such as an elephant washing a car. Dr. Seuss has become a timeless example of the combination of rhythm, rhyme, ridiculous characters, and imaginative storylines that appeal to children of all ages. Media exposure has made Big Bird and Cookie Monster, as well as Barney and Elmo, common household names. Many movies today have a parallel humor track appealing to the different cognition levels of both children and adults. *Finding Nemo, Shrek,* and *Antz* delight audiences of all ages.

Emerging social relationships start to mirror group laughter and humor. Group glee is a wave of laughter that emerges from a group of playing children. Christine, Mimi, and Katie are five-year-old cousins. One day they jumped on the bed together laughing and singing, "No more monkeys jumping on the bed! One fell off and cracked her head! Grandma called the doctor and the doctor said, 'No more monkeys jumping on the bed!'" Their laughing became uproarious, and they fell down hugging each other in uncontrollable giggles. This type of bonding led one of them to proclaim that they are not cousins but triplets.

One reason early childhood educators enjoy teaching young children is that they find humor in most situations, and they easily share the laughter. Children take pleasure in trying to fool adults with "knock-knock jokes" and silly riddles. Parents who take the time to nurture this stage are encouraging the capacity for the future divergent thinking required for innovative problem solving and creativity. Encouraging the use of nonsense words, word plays, and rhyme supports the acquisition of the foundational tools necessary for humor skills.

Knock-knock jokes are actually a fairly advanced skill since there are five steps in the process:

1. The originator says: "Knock-knock."
2. The recipient says: "Who's there?"
3. The originator responds, usually with a first name.
4. The recipient asks for clarification by saying the name plus "Who?"
5. The punch line is a deliberate addition to the word set up in the third response. This is usually in the format of a last name and linked to the first name so that the first name has a different meaning.

Knock-knock.
Who's there?
Dewey.
Dewey who?
Dewey like knock-knock jokes?

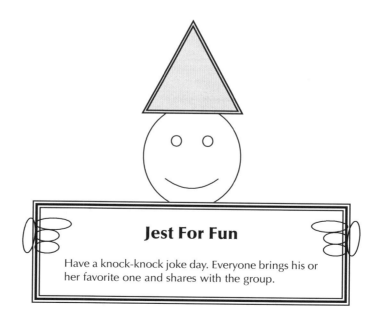

Jest For Fun

Have a knock-knock joke day. Everyone brings his or her favorite one and shares with the group.

This format is a good basis for children beginning to understand that words can have two meanings. Unfortunately for parents and teachers of children at this stage, these jokes can get pretty tedious. When Emma was learning this format, her parents encouraged her sense of humor by laughing at some of her knock-knock "jokes" that really did not make sense. She had heard her older brothers get huge laughs from their knock-knock jokes, and she wanted to learn how to make others laugh using this format.

Riddle-De-Dee (Early Primary Years)

Parents and educators have a significant role in modeling humor and providing strategies to build relationships. "Children with the ability to use humor skills in social interactions were found to be chosen for social activities more often than children with less developed skills" (McGhee, 2002b).

The comprehension of verbal irony seems to emerge between five and six years of age. Jokes, riddles, and clowns begin to be appreciated by children. Practicing jokes and repeating riddles are valuable components in this stage of humor development. Teachers can generate excitement for reading through joke and riddle books, especially for those students who might not be too enthusiastic about other kinds of literature. Since children are drawn to these books, many educators use them to promote vocabulary development, encourage creativity, and improve reading skills.

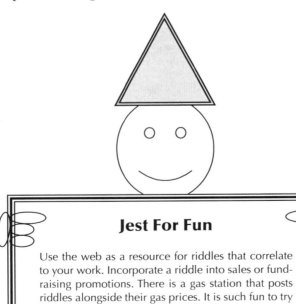

Jest For Fun

Use the web as a resource for riddles that correlate to your work. Incorporate a riddle into sales or fundraising promotions. There is a gas station that posts riddles alongside their gas prices. It is such fun to try to guess these riddles as one travels. Of course gas prices are even a riddle these days!

Andrew, at eight years of age, asked what ducks like to eat. Of course he was enthusiastic to tell me the answer: "Quackers." Comic books, funny stories, and cartoons embedded in the curriculum contribute to the fun of learning. A great resource for children on how to create riddles is *Stumble Bees and Pelephones* (McGhee, 2002a). McGhee says that humor is really a form of intellectual play. Playing with ideas forms the foundation of creative thinking.

My dog can lick anyone.

Pun Fun (Later Primary Years, Grades 4–8)

Children at this stage are moving toward increased understanding of the subtle differences in language, and their more fully developed language skills accelerate their humor appreciation. Word play, language variations, and the magic of language become a magnet that will captivate children during grades 4 through 8. This is the period where the students will be able to detect and enjoy a language twist at the end of a story. They will also be able to understand a subtle variance in word selection and therefore "get the joke." Puns and satire are beginning to be understood by students, and there are initial attempts to invent their own pun fun.

The ability to discern the variances in language is essential for humor development. Ziv, in his book *Personality and a Sense of Humor* (1984), wrote that in order to enjoy humor a person must understand the nuances of language. Understanding the nature of humor development can be invaluable for both teachers of special education and for teachers of talented students. Special education teachers find that using jokes and riddles can assist in the language and reading skill development of their students. And since a sense of humor is an indicator of language comprehension, it is often one of the characteristics for identifying linguistically talented students.

The pun-fun stage also requires the capacity to perceive differences between feelings of joy, surprise, silliness, happiness, and sarcasm, all necessary elements for humor development. The emotional growth of the child is an important factor in appreciating and learning to use humor at this stage. This can have negative as well as positive results. Since slapstick humor and laughing at the mistakes of others are commonly experienced within the social structure of these grades, teachers need to be prepared to share positive humor techniques with their students. It's important for students to have positive role models for humor practice.

The middle school years initiate the emergence of puberty with jokes about sex and aggressive behavior. Adolescents experience anxiety about the changes they are experiencing physically, and this sexual humor can provide relief from the stress of puberty. As with the bathroom humor of earlier ages, physical changes evoke challenges for preteens, who resort to laughing with others as a coping device. Note that some folks never outgrow the bathroom and sexual humor stages.

Puns emerge from the clever massaging of language, usually evoking groans from listeners. These groans act as fertilizer for the pun nuts, as it definitely encourages them to expand their punning. Groups of punsters can be dangerous. They build on each other and delight in how far they can string out a punny. Many students love using puns related to the lesson. Ask them to think of puns on the topic of the day. A lesson on the importance of calcium and the consumption of milk can lead to puns on the good mood that milk provides and how it is udderly delicious. Whether it is creating puns, practicing the rhymes of Dr. Seuss, or doing a comparative analysis of Shakespeare's tragedies and comedies, there is a tremendous opportunity to nurture humor at this stage.

> *Time flies like an arrow. Fruit flies like bananas.*
> *A dog gave birth to puppies near the road and was cited for littering.*
> *I wondered why the baseball was getting bigger. Then it hit me.*
> *There was a person who sent ten puns to friends, with the hope that at least one of the puns would make them laugh. No pun in ten did.*

A word about class clowns—these are the entertainers trying to get the entire class or office to laugh. There is no doubt about the havoc that class clowns can bring to a classroom and to the workplace. Even though the ability to create group

Jest For Fun

Sponsor a "Pun Day Fun Day." Encourage various pun formats throughout the day. For example, you can incorporate puns into office memos. Notice the impact on the energy levels in your workplace.

laughter is a valued life skill, these attempts are usually negated and even punished by the initial attempts of these risk-taking youngsters in schools. These folks can shine if encouraged to use their humor to strengthen social bonds. Numerous comedians admit to starting their careers in school as class clowns. Fortunately they had teachers who provided the solid ground necessary for these nuts to succeed in the world of comedy. Channeling the energy and creativity of those who seek attention through laughter can be a challenge for administrators.

A good time to keep your mouth shut is when you are in deep water.

Joy-Flow (Maturation of Humor Style, High School to Adult)

We have mentioned the ultimate or peak experience as identified by Maslow and described by Mihaly Csikszentmihalyi as a flow or a spiritual experience (Csikszentmihalyi, 1997). *Humergy is extraordinary optimism and a passionate energy for life combined with a gentle understanding of others. It describes the energy that radiates the optimistic joy of the inner spirit, reflecting a unique personality, and nourishing a healthy mind–body balance* (Morrison, 2008). Joy-flow is the degree to which humans have accomplished optimal growth and self-discovery. This peak experience exemplifies the capacity to view challenges with optimistic amusement. A heightened state of positive emotionality defines the fun-finder's peak experience. For many, joy-flow is a spiritual journey.

Becoming aware of one's sense of humor provides an opportunity to expand humor energy through humor practice. This experience of flow and energy will create a natural euphoric high. Do take this opportunity to review the humor strength reflections (Appendix 5). Take the time to reflect on what types of humor produce a joy-flow in you.

Once there is an understanding of the emotional self, it transcends to an understanding of others. Humergy encourages listening and honoring feelings, both of self and of others. It is an understanding that anger often mirrors feelings of fear. The experience of humergy in groups encourages trusting relationships, providing mutual support for facing life challenges.

Joy-flow also is evident within groups. Visualize a classroom of laughing students filled with excitement, where each school day offers opportunities for brain-compatible learning facilitated by passionately optimistic teachers. Picture an office with laughing employees energized by the prospect of providing a fun-filled sales promotion or by bringing laughter to their clients.

Humergy is the energy that radiates the humorous optimism of the inner spirit. It is the positive emotionality that creates a healthy mind–body balance. It is observed in all who are passionate about living in joy, in those who are ecstatic about life opportunities that support positive emotionality, and where

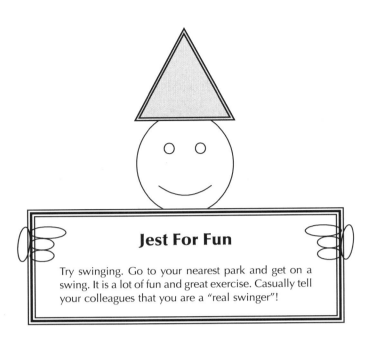

Jest For Fun

Try swinging. Go to your nearest park and get on a swing. It is a lot of fun and great exercise. Casually tell your colleagues that you are a "real swinger"!

fun is an integral part of living. This joy-flow state and the possible connections to human growth provide significant opportunities for further study.

HUMOR ACROSS CULTURES

"Spam!" was my first reaction when I received the email inviting me to speak at a Humor Conference in Izmir, Turkey. It is a miracle that I did not delete that email. It was indeed an invitation to present at a Humor in Education conference in Izmir, Turkey, from Handan Oktar, who is an amazing educator and principal of a pre-K–12 school. This conference was for over 250 educators from all over Turkey and was held at Isikkent Egitim Kampusu in March 2010. Handan and I Skyped and collaborated on the aspects of culture that might be a challenge for my presentation.

In preparing, I learned about Turkish folklore and traditions. My preparation included consulting with various colleagues who had visited Turkey and reading numerous articles about humor in Turkey. I have to admit that I was a bit anxious about the language translation and likely cultural differences. My PowerPoint slides were translated into Turkish, and there were two interpreters who did a live translation during the presentation. My worries were initially confirmed when the first story told did not get much of a reaction.

Relief followed in thirty seconds when the audience began to laugh and I realized that the translation process created a delayed laughter response.

Handan taught me so much about humor through her desire to incorporate fun and laughter into the educational process in Turkey. Her leadership led to the incorporation of humor into the lives of over 5,000 students in Turkey. Handan recently sent me a joke that made me laugh out loud.

Dear Santa:

My wish this year is for a big fat bank account and a thin body.
Please, do not mix the two like you did last year!

Humor is universal. Regional differences make for quite a few jokes in the United States. I currently teach an AATH Humor Academy graduate-level class that has had students from Australia, Venezuela, Canada, Brazil, and the United States. There are more similarities than differences. If you are working with people from other countries, you might chat about historical and cultural humor. A colleague from China shared that humor is not encouraged in parts of his country; in fact it is discouraged. This information is helpful in encouraging humorous interactions in an increasingly interconnected world.

Even regional differences make for quite a few jokes in the United States:

- A Tennessee State trooper pulled over a pickup on I-65. The trooper asked, "Got any ID?" The driver replied, "Bout whut?"
- The young man from Mississippi came running into the store and said to his buddy, "Bubba, somebody just stole your pickup truck from the parking lot!" Bubba replied, "Did you see who it was?" The young man answered, "I couldn't tell, but I got the license number."
- You can say what you want about the South, but you never hear of anyone retiring and moving North.

UNIVERSAL HUMOR ELEMENTS

Woven through these developmental stages are several elements that have a profound impact on the development of humor beings. These cut across the temperament and developmental aspects of humor and are the emotional components of trust, hope, optimism, and loving relationships. In efforts to learn about humor it is helpful to review in depth the emerging research about the significant impact emotions have on learning presented in Chapter 3. However there is a need to mention a few of the emotional indicators that are lifelong partners of humor development and practice.

- *Trust:* Fun and laughter are indicators of a high level of trust within a healthy organization.
- *Hope:* Humor is the sign of optimism within individuals and organizations. Humor expresses the hope that humans can survive tragedy, difficulty, and change and not only survive but thrive.
- *Optimism:* Depression and pessimism are often linked. The energy of humor is a reflection of an optimistic spirit.
- *Love:* When looking for a mate, the number one characteristic mentioned as necessary is a sense of humor. Humor is the universal bond for building relationships and reflects one's affection for others.

Finding and nourishing the nut within you is a lifelong adventure. The energy that comes from humor supports the ability to be optimistic, to have trust and hope, and to experience loving relationships.

Even Rednecks have a sense of humor!

A redneck was stopped by a game warden in Central Mississippi recently with two ice chests full of fish. He was leaving a cove well known for its fishing. The game warden asked the man, "Do you have a license to catch those fish?" "Naw, sir," replied the redneck. "I ain't got none of them there licenses. You must understand, these here are my pet fish."

"Pet fish?"

"Yeah. Every night, I take these here fish down to the lake and let 'em swim 'round for awhile. Then, when I whistle, they jump right back into these here ice chests and I take 'em home."

"That's a bunch of hooey! Fish can't do that."

The redneck looked at the warden for a moment and then said, "It's the truth, Mr. Government Man. I'll show ya. It really works."

"O.K.," said the warden. "I've got to see this!"

The redneck poured the fish into the lake and stood and waited. After several minutes, the warden says, "Well?"

"Well, what?" says the redneck.

The warden says, "When are you going to call them back?"

"Call who back?"

"The *fish*!" replied the warden.

"What fish?" replied the redneck.

Moral of the story: we may not be as smart as some city slickers, but we ain't as dumb as some government employees.

SUMMARY

This chapter examines the impact of temperament on development and the power of play in brain growth. Humans are born with a temperament that impacts humor development and an environment nurtures the growth of a sense of humor. There are five defined stages of humor development:

1. Peek-a-boo, ages zero to two
2. Knock-knock, ages two to school age
3. Riddle-de-dee, early primary years
4. Pun fun, later primary years
5. Joy-flow, maturation of humor style, high school to adult

Each stage has opportunities for enhancing learning, and it is important for educators to have an awareness of the developmental characteristics of each stage. Each infant's brain contains a unique blueprint for humor maturation. Recognition of universal patterns of humor development provides the foundation for cultivating individual growth through specific jokes and humorous techniques for that particular phase.

Play is an integral part of brain growth and of humor development. Play provides powerful practice opportunities for cognitive development. There is some research to indicate that play in childhood inhibits depression as an adult. Unfortunately, in this age of accountability, play is seen as a nonproductive activity. Playfulness is deemed acceptable only in controlled situations and with certain rituals that permit the expression of silliness, fun, and wild laughter. Play necessitates a level of risk taking rarely tolerated as acceptable behavior in most groups. Yet many organizations are recognizing the importance of play in generating creativity, productivity, and employee well-being. A sign of a healthy work environment is that it is filled with fun and laughter. Playfulness produces signals of trust.

Humor is an indicator of a high level of trust within a culture. Diversity will lead to unique historical and cultural perspectives on humor. Humor is reflected in the universal positive elements of trust, hope, optimism, and love.

POWERFUL PRACTICE—STRATEGIES FOR LEADERS

- Use humor as an intentional attentional tool.
- Generate discussion of these definitions among the staff. Divide staff into several or all of these groups. Have them design activities based on their topic:

- Practicing Play: How Do You Play?
- The Art of Fun: Define Possible Staff Activities
- Mindful Mischief: Minimize Misbehaviors with Mirth
- Class Clowns: What Happens to Class Clowns?
- Funny Papers: Writing with Humor and Use of Cartooning

- Start staff meetings honoring the person who has created the most laughter in the workplace that week. Have a traveling "Oscar" trophy.
- Have a "lettuce entertains you" salad luncheon for a staff development day. Take pictures of staff with "make-overs" as clowns. Let different groups create games, activities, and opportunities for fun.
- Sponsor a "Letterman top ten list" for some of the problems or situations in the workplace. (For example: "The top ten reasons why board meetings are fun to attend" or "The top ten reasons for being the first person in the building in the morning").
- Start a comedy club. Invite all interested to join in sharing jokes, stories, and cartoons. Meet weekly, beginning with a half-hour time slot. This could be over the lunch hour, before, or after work. Use a deck of cards to begin the session. The person who draws the "joker" first gets to begin the session.
- Do a climate survey of staff before implementation of a focused effort to increase creativity and play. After a year of implementation do a follow-up survey. Note any change in climate, stress, employee job satisfaction, and so forth.

STUDY GROUP FOCUS

- Share your observations about the humor practice of the people in your workplace.
- Brainstorm with your group some ways to optimize play both in your professional and personal lives.
- Create a plan to increase the humor resources in the resources available to employees.
- Discuss how creativity and humor are related. How can humor be used to increase creativity?
- How was your sense of humor formed? Think of the impact of both nature and nurture.

CAFÉ CONVERSATIONS

- Discuss the play research found in this chapter. Expand the discussion to include the views and climate in different departments within the organization. Is there a difference in the way play is considered as a part of the work environment?

- What is creative thinking? After coming to a shared agreement, explore the various ways that your workplace encourages creativity. Explore additional options.
- What are the benefits and challenges of spontaneous play in your workplace? List ways that organizations can take advantage of the people who initiate fun. Read about the Fish Philosophy or check it out at http://www.charthouse.com/content.aspx?name=home2

Even a blind squirrel finds a nut once in awhile.

3

EXAMINING BRAIN RESEARCH AND HUMOR: MOUSE DROPPINGS

It has recently been discovered that research causes cancer in rats.

Pioneering research continues to unravel ways in which humor and learning are linked. Two kinds of mice are providing increasingly detailed information about the role of the emotions in the learning process. These "mouse droppings" provide powerful incentives to take a fresh look at humor as a significant factor in the learning process.

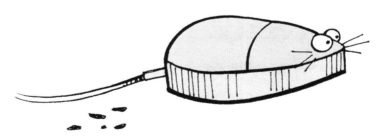

Mouse Droppings

- *Laboratory mice.* Those little critters and their researchers persist in providing data about the links among the emotions, learning, and humor.
- *Computer mouse.* Another type of mouse manipulation is found in the use of computerized imaging. The ability to observe brain activity has accelerated the understanding of cognitive research. Cognitive neuroscience continues to address how brain biology addresses the emotions and learning.

The future of humor research and related fields involves complex processes for looking at the brain and reviewing the results from a variety of devices including magnetic resonance imaging (MRI), functional MRI (fMRI), positron emission tomography (PET), and transcranial magnetic stimulation (TMS) (Fry, 2002). Humor appreciation is a complex information-processing task incorporating mechanisms of pattern recognition, categorization, meaningful search, and emotionality (Fry, 2002). Humor is difficult to study. This chapter will include a review of studies that do not specifically mention humor but examine related research like positive emotions, well-being, and happiness. I believe that the potpourri of ideas will give some indication of the complexity of the task and some foundational knowledge about the impact of humor on living.

Technology does provide some mesmerizing data on what positivity (including humor) looks like in the brain. Machines are able to measure variations in chemical composition, blood flow, and electromagnetic fields. This technology has dramatically advanced the ability of brain scientists to provide clinical applications. The research on humor shows that the chemical reactions that occur during laughter are complex, which affirms that what is known about humor and cognition is primitive at best. The quest for knowledge linking the positive emotions and learning can be compared to a mouse in a maze looking for the cheesy humor. It will be a long journey! Please note that the research on laughter and humor is still in the preliminary stages and there is much debate about the implications of the research that is mentioned in this chapter.

Funny, isn't it? Humor has not even been on the radar screen of most researchers until recently. Following the trail of mouse droppings has been a pioneering adventure. However, there are several pellets that make the case for developing a sense of humor to maximize living. This chapter will examine the research on the role of emotions in fear, stress, and depression including a look at what can be inferred from current research on how humor can:

- Maximize learning
- Build relationships
- Create an environment of trust
- Relieve stress
- Manage pain.

BRAIN IMAGES: THE EMOTIONS AND HUMOR

I have long been fascinated with neuroscience and how humans learn. Several key points are emphasized in this section. Brain research is in its infancy. Only recently has technology been in existence to let scientists "see" the brain. As the pioneers in neuroscience and information explore both the biological sciences and brain imaging technology, it is evident that humor is a significant factor in the way people approach living! Humor does maximize living, and brain science is underscoring this in research study after research study.

What do you remember from second grade (Figure 3.1)? Think about your most vivid memory. Chances are that it is tied to a pretty strong emotion. I remember being put in the coat closet (yes, that is what we had back then) for talking too much. I was really angry, as it was not my fault and I was scared to tell my parents. I remember it being smelly and dark in there. My strong feelings put this memory into my long-term memory. I do not remember much else from second grade. I would bet that your memories of grade school are linked to equally strong emotions.

> *A little girl had just finished her first week of school. "I'm just wasting my time," she said to her mother. "I can't read, I can't write and they won't let me talk!"*

An overview of the research confirms that humor is a complex process involving the emotional being. This research on emotions provides the essential foundation necessary for humor studies. Emotion is an unconscious arousal system that helps to alert the brain to potential dangers as well as opportunities. The emotions identify the dynamics of challenge and activate the problem-solving systems to respond. Almost everything humans do begins with the complex processing system of emotion (Sylwester, 2005).

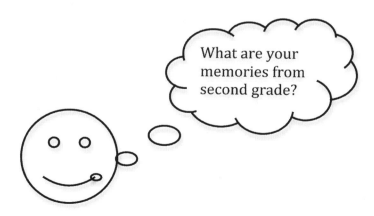

Figure 3.1   Second Grade Memories

Learning must go through the brain's emotional filter, so memories are composed of experiences that are linked to strong emotions. Thus, emotional memory is a critical component for the learning process. These emotions are either positively or negatively linked.

Emotional well-being is dependent on the ability to be mindful of emotional state. Part of humor practice, which is detailed in Chapter 5, is making a conscious effort to be aware of feelings. Positive psychology sometimes refers to this practice as *being mindful*. Some people keep a daily gratitude journal so they can focus on their positive emotions and strengthen those neural pathways.

Our friend the imaging mouse drops the information that much of the activity of humor occurs in the frontal lobes of the brain. The frontal lobes are the problem-solving, decision-making, action-initiating, paired lobes in the front part of the cerebral cortex (Sylwester, 2005). The frontal lobes recognize incongruities or discrepancies between the predicted developments and what actually occurs.

All of the senses are designed to go on high alert when observing unusual patterns in the field of vision because the human stress-driven reflective response system is designed to detect anything that might inflict harm. If what occurs is what is expected, the brain does not take notice. However, without effective internal coping strategies, if what occurs is unexpected and negative (danger), a distrustful state of fear, pessimism, anger, and so forth emerges.

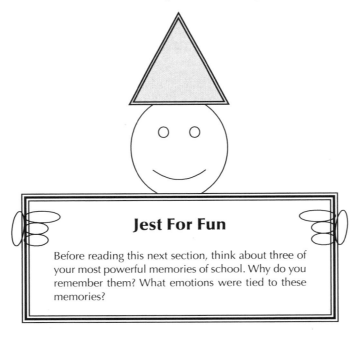

Jest For Fun

Before reading this next section, think about three of your most powerful memories of school. Why do you remember them? What emotions were tied to these memories?

Conversely, if what occurs is unexpected and positive (opportunity) and resources are available to respond effectively, humans move into a state of joy—becoming happy, optimistic, and so forth. Memory is strongly linked to positive or negative emotions.

The emotions are a critical force in the learning process. According to Antonio R. Damasio, "emotion is a very adaptive form of physiological response, and it regulates our lives." He states that emotion is part of the reasoning and decision-making process and is critical to learning and memory. Our very survival depends upon the emotions as part of our regulatory system (Damasio, 1999). Sylwester (1995) says, "Emotions drive attention, attention drives learning."

Candice Pert (1997), a pioneer in cellular research, hypothesizes that emotions exist in every cell of the body. She actually started investigating neuropeptides when she read Norman Cousins's work *Anatomy of an Illness* (1979). Her research explores the brain chemicals of mood and behavior and how they communicate with the immune system, and she was interested in Cousins's theory that endorphins are the key to the healing power of laughter. Her theory is that because emotions exist in every cell in the body and not just in the brain, when a strong emotion emerges, it is felt in the entire body. Although there is some controversy about this theory, there is no doubt that emotions play a vital role in attention, memory, and learning. They also impact day-to-day emotional well-being.

If there were a mouse in the corner of your workplace or at your family gatherings, what emotions would be observed among your family and colleagues? Would there be joy with positive interactions? Is there anger, fear, or resentment? Does the energy and mood change frequently?

Since fear can and does immediately activate the reflective response system of the brain, it has long been used to manipulate behavior within organizations. This controlling tactic is evident in many systems, including the workplace. The fear of evaluations or confrontations with the boss, the fear of being assigned additional or difficult responsibilities, and the fear of not getting a raise are widespread fear-based factors in the workplace. Both employers and employees must frequently navigate the emotional minefield of fear-based emotions in business. Do take a close look at the emotion of fear in order to better understand humor.

Fear is the most powerful emotion. It has the primary purpose of protecting us from harm. Humans are programmed to pay attention to fear because this emotion alerts the brain if safety is threatened. Fear has been the focus of considerable cognitive research. Imaging technology makes it relatively easy to locate fear in the amygdala and hippocampus regions of the brain. Fear signals danger and immediately alerts the brain to pay attention.

While this fear is critical to survival, it is tempting to use this emotional reaction to control the actions of others. Humans live within societies driven by fear. Excess fear causes chronic stress. This stress is killing us (Sapolsky, 1999)!

If you want to read an eye-opening account of what this stress can look like in the brain, check out my friend and colleague Dr. Earl Henslin's book *This Is Your Brain on Joy* (2008). Henslin works at Amen Clinics in California, which has the mission of helping people with distressed brains to find balance. These clinics use sophisticated imaging technology to discover how to improve brain functions (Figure 3.2). I am grateful to Dr. Henslin for permission to use these images to share the contrast between a peaceful brain and an anxious or stressed brain.

In his book, Henslin explores the impact that lifestyle has on brain health and proceeds to share numerous brain scans and information. Please note the figure and compare a "joyful, peaceful" brain with one that is in emotional pain. As you can see, the patterns that emerge depict quite a contrast. The areas where fear and sadness are located pop out in the second image, the one on the right side. Thanks to imaging technology, you can actually see a visual of the activity in our brains (Henslin, 2008). Again, a word of caution—scientists are in the infancy of learning what these brain scans mean, but the information that is

Brain Scans are giving us more information.

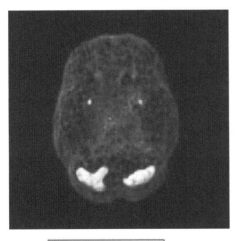

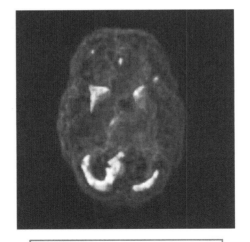

Peaceful Brain

Anxious, Worried, Depressed Brain

Figure 3.2   **Henslin Brain Scans.** Printed with permission of Dr. Earl Henslin.

gathered is showing great promise for those who work with patients who are stressed, addicted, or depressed.

Joy is a terrible thing to waste.

—Dr. Earl Henslin

Another person who has identified humor in the brain through imaging fMRI scans is Rita Carter (2009). When showing cartoons to subjects, images of the areas activated by the first frame of a cartoon include activity in the temporal lobe, the parietal lobe, and the cerebellum. When an expectation is subverted (surprise factor), the amygdala becomes active. Studies on the humor that arise from unconnected ideas between coworkers suggest to Carter that keeping workers laughing may "jump-start" their creative juices. She suggests that humor forces people to attend to distractions, making them more receptive to new information. Humor elevates the brain's "reward" circuit. This elevates circulating levels of dopamine, which is linked to motivation and the anticipation of pleasure (Carter, 2009).

STRESS AND WELL-BEING

Our brain is wired to notice unusual movement and abnormal activity. This information is filtered by the reflexive response system of the brain and alerts it to possible danger. This same system also feels relief if the danger is nonexistent. This feeling of relief is often what triggers humor, so humor is a tool that can be used by the reflexive response center of the brain that monitors the environment for fear. When the brain discovers there is no danger, the surprise brings relief that often generates laughter and humor. Thus humor can provide the tools needed to cope with fear and stress.

Posts on the positive psychology listserv include those by Martin Seligman, who has written a new book, *Flourish: A Visionary New Understanding of Happiness and Well-Being*. He describes well-being with the acronym PERMA, with five measurable elements:

- Positive emotion
- Engagement
- Relationships
- Meaning and purpose
- Accomplishment

Seligman says that no one of these elements by itself depicts well-being, but all contribute to it and are needed. These are all based on perceived strengths. According to Christopher Peterson and Martin Seligman in *Character Strengths and Virtues* (2004), humor does include playful recognition and enjoyment of incongruity, which includes a cheerful view of the light side of adversity and the ability to make others smile and laugh. The values in action (VIA) inventory of strengths includes *humor and playfulness* as one of twenty-four character strengths. In the description of correlates and consequences, best established are the conclusions that humor is linked to good disposition and that it buffers the effects on mood of life pressures and hassles (Peterson & Seligman, 2004).

A request on the positive psychology listserv for further information on humor and positive psychology was met with a referral to Willibald Ruch. He has done extensive research on humor and exhilaration along with numerous other related works. One Ruch study involved writing a humor diary modeled on the gratitude diary, in which a person writes what they are grateful for each day. People were encouraged to write the funniest three things that happened to them that day. This intervention was shown to increase life satisfaction and decrease depression and still had an effect three months later (Ruch, Proyer & Weber, 2010).

Excess fear causes stress. There is mounting scientific evidence that suggests that excess stress has an adverse impact on learning. Yet, according to many teachers, children are exposed to stress at escalating rates. There has been increased high-stakes testing in schools, and many districts have implemented paper-and-pencil testing for students as young as four and five years old. Numerous schools are testing kindergarten children three times a year on a computer. There has been an increasing pressure to focus on what has mandated assessment (reading and math) at the expense of the arts, physical education, and play. Grades are considered extremely important and actually have been found to drive most students' learning instead of the desire to learn.

On the first day of school, a first-grader handed his teacher a note from his mother. The note read, "The opinions expressed by this child are not necessarily those of his parents."

A look at some of the research heightens awareness of the possible dangers that excess stress creates for both students and teachers. Although there are no firm conclusions, some of the recent theories on the relationship between stress, depression, memory, and learning are intriguing.

An impoverished and stressful childhood may diminish learning by having a negative impact on the medial temporal memory of a child. Prenatal stress and the stress that comes from living in poverty have been found to have a negative impact on neurological development and subsequent ability to learn (Farah, Noble, & Hurt, 2005).

Human beings all encounter certain amounts of stress, and while stress has a bad reputation, some stress is good for us. It keeps the brain alert to danger and creates the energy needed to face challenges. The source of most stress is in the brain itself (Mellin, 2010). Mellin identifies three things that people who are stressed often do. When stressed, people often seek pleasure responses that are not healthy. She identifies these "not so healthy" responses as things you "acquire, ingest or inject."

Pleasure really comes from "the desire to be of service, to do good." A brain that is stuck in stress produces an excess of stress hormones including cortisol. This stress becomes cumulative, and in time what was designed to protect you from stress can actually become a magnet for symptoms. The goal, according to Mellin, is to reverse the allostatic load by using simple tools that give you the capacity to achieve a state of joy. Instead of tolerating stressed-out feelings, you identify your level of stress and choose a tool to switch your brain to a state of well-being. Mellin describes the goal as being to actually rewire the brain to increase the joy circuits. She discusses joy as a brain state that is similar to humergy.

National Geographic has produced a revealing DVD called *Stress: Portrait of a Killer* (2008). It features numerous researchers, including Robert Sapolsky, who extensively studied stress in apes in Africa. By living with these primates and taking their blood samples, he determined that stress can lead to actual negative physiological consequences. Sapolsky found that the impact of stress is found deep within us, shrinking our brains, adding fat to our bellies, and even unraveling our chromosomes. Stress is measurable and can be downright dangerous (National Geographic, 2008).

Excess fear might lead to actual memory loss. Sapolsky conducted a mesmerizing study examining the brains of World War II veterans who had survived intense trauma during the war. He found that the hippocampus of these men was usually smaller than that of nonveterans in the same age category. He noted an actual loss of part of the hippocampus in these veterans as well as a resulting memory loss (Sapolsky, 1999). Current studies corroborate this relationship between excess stress, damage to the hippocampus, and subsequent memory loss, but no firm conclusions can be made yet.

Overuse or misuse of the reflexive response system can escalate simple anger and assertiveness into reflexive physical aggression. Some people constantly live in an insecure, fearful environment, producing a learned helplessness response (Sylwester, 2005). Often people just give up when they feel they have no control over their environment. "A reflexive stress response occurs unconsciously, and so reduces our ability to create factual memories" (Sylwester, 2005).

Lee Berk and Stanley Tan both gave presentations at the 2011 AATH conference based on their research. They reported that laugher stimulates the immune system and counteracts stress by lowering serum cortisol levels, increasing the amount of activated T-lymphocytes, and increasing the number and activity of natural killer cells (Berk & Tan, 1997). Both have been involved in numerous studies on the impact of laughter on stress. Berk has published a memorable poster that summarizes the research studies that have been conducted on joyful or mirthful laughter. This type of laughter is considered a positive stress (eustress) with a complex physiology that involves brain, hormone, and immune system interconnections that lead to potential benefits on health and wellness. As Berk shares through his presentations, the science of psychoneuroimmunology provides strong scientific evidence of the interconnectedness that everyday lifestyle behaviors and emotions have on modulating the physiological mechanisms.

> *I have been to a lot of places, but I've never been in Cahoots. Apparently you can't go alone. You have to be in Cahoots with someone. I've also never been in Cognito, either. I hear no one recognizes you there. I have, however, been in Sane. They don't have an airport; you have to be driven there. I have made several trips—thanks to friends and family. I would like to go to Conclusions, but you have to jump. . . . I'm not much on physical activity.*
>
> —Anonymous Facebook post

DEPRESSION

There is hope for depression. A team of researchers at Washington State University has been researching the underlying causes of depression. Over the last decade, there has been an increasing awareness that depression stems from more than just a shortage in brain chemicals like serotonin. Scientists have recently discovered that the disorder is also linked to malfunctions in brain "circuitry"—the intricate pathways by which neurons communicate in the brain. Panksepp believes that depression is tied to three main brain circuit disorders. "You can make the case for opioids as well as the dynorphin or glutamate systems," Panksepp said (Panksepp, Dong, Wayman, & Guerra, 2009).

Pharmaceuticals are not the only option for reversing brain degeneration associated with depression. Studies show that exercise, for example, can in some cases be as effective for reducing depression as medication.

When you enrich a rat's environment with play, interaction and toys, the neurons in the hippocampus bloom and generate more synapses. The rats become smarter and learn more quickly. BDNF levels increase too. (Panksepp, Dong, Wayman, & Guerra, 2009)

Wayman and Panksepp are using play as a model to determine if play experiences early in life can protect against depression later in adulthood (Panksepp, Dong, Wayman, & Guerra, 2009).

Dong looks at dynorphin, which is a naturally occurring brain opiate related to the endorphins and enkephalins that are responsible for producing "runner's high." But instead of promoting euphoria, dynorphin makes people feel dysphoric—grumpy and unhappy. Dynorphin receptors are deeply concentrated in a circuit called the "brain reward pathway (BRP)," which is activated after pleasurable events, "like a good meal." From his research on heroin and cocaine addiction, Dong hypothesizes that dynorphin "hijacks" the BRP, causing an individual to feel despondent (Panksepp, Dong, Wayman, & Guerra, 2009).

Wayman has researched brain circuitry to identify genes that directly regulate those pathways and contribute to the development of depression. One pathway he is investigating involves brain-derived neurotrophic factor (BDNF)—an important substance for ordinary brain development. "During major depressive disorder, BDNF levels crash in several areas of the brain—such as the hippocampus, which is important for learning, memory and emotional processing" (Panksepp, Dong, Wayman, & Guerra, 2009).

Wayman goes on to explain that when BDNF levels diminish, the hippocampus shrinks and nerves alter structurally. The dendritic processes at the end of nerves lose their spines and wither. This damage impairs the capacity of nerves to communicate and dispatch impulses through the synapses. So the power of play might be an alternative "medication" for depression. As mentioned in Chapter 2, play has a powerful beneficial impact on the brain and on the development of positive emotions. Play usually induces laughter, revitalizing the body with the humergy of renewed energy and joy.

People who are prone to depression may secrete more cortisol during a stressful time. There may also be decreased prefrontal cortex activity, causing moody and negative behavior. Depressed people have trouble concentrating. Symptoms of depression also include deteriorating efficiency, sloppy work, numerous sick days, verbal outbursts, and social rejection (Sylwester, 2005).

Depression should not be overlooked when it comes to its impact on productivity. "It is not possible to explain either the disease or its treatment based solely on levels of neurotransmitters," says neurobiologist Ronald Duman (Duman, Malberg, & Thome, 1999).

There is evidence that indicates that recurrent depression is in fact a neuro-degenerative disorder, disrupting the structure and function of brain cells—destroying nerve cell connections, even killing certain brain cells, and precipitating cognitive decline. At the very least, depression sets up neural roadblocks to the processing of information and keeps us from adaptively responding to whatever challenges life throws our way (Estroff, 1999).

David Granirer is the founder of Stand Up for Mental Health, a project teaching stand-up comedy to people with mental illness. He has taught individuals with depression, cancer, and addictions. His success is inspiring. He believes negative emotions can be the key to happiness. If a person takes his or her negative emotions and creates comedy about it, it can lead to healing. Humor is a powerful tool to accept and learn from dysfunctions. You can read a bit more about David's novel program in Chapter 6. Humor and laughter can be the first drugs of choice for depression. More and more therapists are being trained to use laughter therapy in treating people with depression.

Do not disturb! I am disturbed enough already!

—Anonymous Facebook post

MAXIMIZING LEARNING WITH HUMOR

How does humor enhance learning? The humor elements of learning are grouped here into the metaphor of "hook, line, and sinker." These are described as tools that can fill the "learner's tackle box" (see Figure 3.3):

1. The hook: capture and retain attention
2. The line: expand comprehension
3. The sinker: increase the opportunity for memory retention

How do you activate the hook, line, and sinker tools in your tackle box? Hook it with humor. Cast in the line of practice and repetition, and sink information into long-term memory with feedback and reflection.

The process described in this metaphor involves a purposeful and determined use of humor for the purpose of memory retention. Humor has the power to capture attention (hook), manipulate this information in the working memory (line), and become a part of the automatic response system (sinker).

Your Tackle Box
Hook, Line, and Sinker

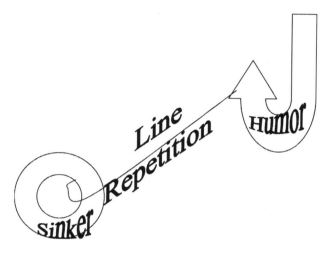

Figure 3.3   Hook, Line, and Sinker

The Hook

The brain is hardwired to familiar patterns. Driving and solving a math problem become routine with practice. Over time, repetitious daily activity follows established habits of behavior. As previously mentioned, fear protects from danger. In order to do this, the brain is alerted to a pattern disruption or any surprise element. Fear serves as a protective device when something out of the ordinary is observed. This surprise component is what provides the opportunity to effectively use humor in the teaching and learning process because humor usually contains an element of surprise.

Surprise defies the brain's predictions and expectations. When someone acts out of the ordinary or when something unusual happens, the brain pays attention. It is often recommended in implementing differentiation strategies that teachers change state every ten to fifteen minutes to "wake up" the attentional center of the brain. This change of state assists the learners who may have difficulty paying attention. A humor hook is perfect bait for the learner's tackle box. If you want to learn something, do try to find the humor in it!

The Line

The hook is followed with a line, a direct connection that links past experiences with the new information. The emotional memory is strong. Humor can be used to activate the brain by linking to the emotional context of humor, thus finding the information that needs to be remembered. This humor context can be attained through repetition and practice. These are the critical components in creating strong lines or neural pathways to the long-term memory. Neurons that fire together wire together. Practice and repetition condition the brain to form pathways that will become hardwired. These neural connections streamline the learning process. Learning is quicker, more automatic, and more efficient when pathways in the brain are frequently traveled.

The more humor that is interjected into the learning process (instead of boring rote stuff), the more likely learners will want to repeat the information and strengthen the neural pathway. A strong line is dependent on frequent usage. If it's fun, it will be practiced.

The Sinker

Several authors of the neuroscience literature detail strategies for using feedback and reflection as tools for sinking the information into long-term memory and ensuring recall (Jones, 2003). Humor can be used to assist when knowledge is accessed. Again, the more humor links (emotional memory) provided for the brain, the better chance there will be for recalling information. Reflection is another opportunity to use humor, and it can be a powerful tool for subsequent memory recall. Other powerful sinker techniques are summary, assessment, and authentic assessment (performing a real life task).

So humor has the power to capture attention (hook). If you manipulate this information through practice and repetition in the working memory (line), it becomes a part of the automatic response system (sinker) with feedback and reflection. The frequency of humor implemented at any of these points improves the probability that the emotional memory will be found and the learner will remember the information.

Many teachers informally use humor as an integral part of teaching for memory retention and recall. However, what is suggested here is a purposeful use of humor applied to what is already known from cognitive research.

Enid Schwartz has spent years developing courses for medical personnel on humor. She now teaches her course "Humor in Health Care" online. Her groundbreaking work includes cartoons in the text of her book along with jokes, quips, and quotes throughout the text (Schwartz, 2010). She shares how she uses humor online. She purposefully injects humor into every aspect of the curriculum. Many appreciate her willingness to try laughter online!

Learning is not just for school. Healthy adults are usually lifelong learners. A focus on productive, active learning is associated with extended healthy living. It is important as aging occurs to continue to find ways to challenge the adult brain towards new and different ways of learning. Check out my original book for details on more research on humor and learning (Morrison, 2008).

I'm having amnesia and déjà vu at the same time. I'm sure I've forgotten this before.

—Steven Wright

HUMOR BUILDS RELATIONSHIPS WITH FRIENDS AND COLLEAGUES

Developing positive relationships with colleagues is one of the greatest benefits of humor. Laughter is a visible sign of humor in action and reflects the social side of humor. Why do humans laugh? When do you laugh? What connection does laughter have to humor? Robert Provine, in his book *Laughter, a Scientific Investigation* (2000), makes it clear that it is difficult to research humor because of the variety of definitions and vague terminology. However, laughter is observable, and "because laughter is unplanned and uncensored, it is a powerful probe into social relationships" (Provine, 2000).

While laughter is generally thought to be an expression of humor or comedy, it is observed most often during social interactions with others and does not necessarily result from jokes or funny stories. Provine uses the term *sidewalk science*, which he says is a low-tech approach to brain and behavior research based on everyday experience. His observations of human laughter and an analysis of subsequent recorded conversations are the basis for his interpretation that laughter can be considered a distinct vocalization that usually occurs during positive social interactions (Provine, 2000).

Philosopher John Morreall (1997) speculates that human laughter may have its biological origins as a shared expression of relief at the ending of danger. The relaxation felt after laughing may help inhibit the fight-or-flight response, making laughter a behavioral sign of trust in one's companions.

Laughter is a part of human behavior regulated by the brain. It helps humans clarify their intentions in social interaction and provides an emotional context for conversations. Laughter is used as a signal for being part of a group—it signals acceptance and positive interactions. Laughter is sometimes contagious; the laughter of one person can provoke laughter from others. This may account for the popularity of laugh tracks in situation comedy television shows. Imaging studies reveal that the limbic system is involved in laughter. The limbic system is a primitive part of the brain that is involved in emotions and helps us with basic functions necessary for survival. Two structures in the limbic system are involved in producing laughter: the amygdala and the hippocampus (Morreall, 1997).

The Rotman Research Institute at the University of Toronto released the first study to show that the frontal lobe plays a prominent role in the ability to appreciate humor. The study, led by Prathiba Shammi, measured responses to jokes and cartoons. Half of the study group had injury to the prefrontal lobes caused by stroke, tumor, or surgical removal. The responses of this group were compared to a control group similar in age, gender, and education. The study found that damage to the right anterior frontal lobe was disruptive to the ability to appreciate jokes and cartoons (Shammi, 1999).

Peter Derks conducted a study of laughter using electrodes attached to the brain. The electricity observed in the entire cerebral cortex indicated that most of the brain is actively engaged during laughter. Laughter can be just a simple physical response to the nonhumorous stimulus of tickling, while positive social interactions usually evoke a smile, laugh, or chuckle and can be thought of as eliciting the laughter response (Derks, 1997).

There have been several studies of the benefits of laughter. Some research indicates that laughter increases adrenaline, oxygen flow, and pulse rate. After laughter, many people report feeling more relaxed and calm. Laughter can be observed in relationships with another person or with several others. The relatively new research on mirror neurons suggests that the brain has a basic mirroring response to emotional actions.

When parents conceive a child, their combined genetic information provides the developing embryo with the necessary body-building directions—such as gender identity, nose placement, and skin color. After the child is born, parents and others must provide cultural information about how to live in a complex social environment. They provide this mentoring through language and the brain's remarkable, recently discovered mirror neuron system.

The renowned neuroscientist V. S. Ramachandran suggested at the turn of the twenty-first century that the discovery of mirror neurons might provide the same powerful unifying framework for the understanding of teaching and learning that the 1953 discovery of DNA did for the understanding of genetics. Recent developments suggest that his prediction might be correct. Ramachandran goes on to say,

When we observe someone yawn, it activates the brain's yawning system. Adults typically override the tendency and stifle the yawn—but if we stick out our tongue at an infant who is only a few hours old, it's probable that she will immediately reciprocate, even though she had never before stuck out her tongue (or even had any conscious awareness of her tongue). Her observation of our behavior will automatically activate the mirror neurons that regulate her tongue movements.

Since she has a zillion movements to learn and therefore no reason to stifle the action, her mirror neurons will activate the motor neurons that project her tongue. Similarly, smile and she'll smile. Clap your hands and she'll clap her hands. It's like monkey see, monkey do in childhood. (quoted in Sylwester, 2006)

Research on mirror neurons as related to humor and laughter has been fascinating to study. Laughter is contagious. When someone laughs, even if the situation is not funny, it is easy to join in the laughing. How do the mirror neurons figure into this? The contagious character of laughter is caused by mirror neurons found in brain cells that become active when an organism is watching an expression or behavior that they can do. When you see someone laughing, even if you don't know what is causing the laughter, you will probably laugh too. The imitative behavior is caused by mirror neurons being activated (Miller, 2010).

> *All creatures must learn to coexist. That's why the brown bear and the field mouse can share their lives in harmony. Of course, they can't mate or the mice would explode.*
>
> —Betty White

HUMOR CREATES A NURTURING ENVIRONMENT FOR LIVING

One of my favorite "mouse droppings" involves the impact of different cage environments on rats. (See Figure 3.4.) Could positive experiences change the actual physical structure of the brain? Rats were put in three different environments. The first rats were loners raised in dark isolation with only food and water. The second set was raised with other rats in a small but social group. The third group of rats was treated to a condition called environmental complexity. These fortunate rats lived in colonies of twelve with toys and frequent

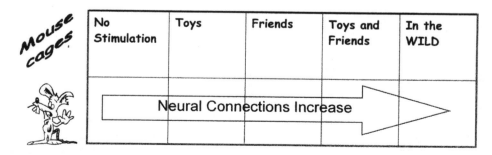

Mouse cages	No Stimulation	Toys	Friends	Toys and Friends	In the WILD
	Neural Connections Increase				

Figure 3.4   Mouse Cages

stimulation from the scientists. These lucky rats did indeed have larger brain mass and performed better on problem-solving maze tasks. A subsequent study (Volkmar & Greenough, 1972) found that the brains of rats in the wild had the most neural connections, which might lead someone to ask if schools are just cages with toys and friends!

Since personalities emerge from genetics and emotionally stored memories (LeDeux, 2002), it seems probable that humor identity comes from the experiences of joy, laughter, and fun stored in memories and from the temperament that is inherited. This is the nature–nurture theory explored in Chapter 2.

A positive emotional relationship with significant adults provides the emotional groundwork for the neurological development of a child from birth (Siegel, 1999). When a child enters preschool, the emotional response system is fairly well developed. There are people who are unable to respond appropriately in a school or workplace environment because they do not have the emotional tools necessary.

Educators notice the sad and angry kids, usually notice the kids who are depressed, and always notice the kids who act out. These kids become the adults who are dysfunctional in the workplace. Can you identify someone you have worked with who exhibits some level of dysfunction? The challenges of working with these folks are explored in subsequent chapters, but the importance of nurturing the positive emotions from an early age is well established. There is now sufficient evidence to show that positive emotions lead to well-being and increased health in both adults and children (Diener & Chan, 2010).

HUMOR HELPS PEOPLE COPE

This wallpaper is killing me. One of us will have to go.

—attributed to Oscar Wilde on his deathbed

Talk about facing the most difficult challenge of life—death—with a sense of humor! As defined in Chapter 1, a sense of humor is the capacity of a human being to respond to life challenges with optimism (Morrison, 2005). The goal is to increase optimistic response patterns along with positive emotionality experiences. There is often "dark" or "sick" humor in response to life tragedies. This topic is explored further in Chapter 4. "Humor can provide the healthiest and most powerful method of providing a perspective on life's difficult experiences" (Sultanoff, 1994).

Humor is often shared during extreme pattern disruptions or crisis experiences. After the events of 9/11 there were concerns for the ability of the nation to find its sense of humor. Our perceived ability to cope was dependent on the ability to respond to a new trauma. Millions tuned in to the late-night shows to see how comedians would handle the painful events. David Letterman took a week off and came back with a tribute to New York. As comedians tried to balance the grief and the need for the normalcy that humor has to offer, it was a time when humor (or the lack of it) was in the forefront of the lives of the citizens of the United States.

> *Can we be funny? Why start now?*
>
> —New York Mayor Rudy Giuliani, responding to a question from *Saturday Night Live* producer Lorne Michaels during the show's first telecast after the terrorist attacks of 9/11

> *Tom Ridge announced a new color-coded alarm system. Green means everything's okay. Red means we're in extreme danger. And champagne-fuchsia means we're being attacked by Martha Stewart.*
>
> —Conan O'Brien

> *This thing is so confusing. Yesterday the alert went from blue to pink; now half the country thinks we're pregnant.*
>
> —Jay Leno, on the color-coded terror alert system

Would you believe that age improves a sense of well-being and the ability to respond to challenges with humor? There is hope that aging may actually improve the positive thinking of the brain. Psychologists Mroczek and Spiro (2005) surveyed 2,727 men and women ages 25 to 74 to determine how age, gender, marital status, education, health, and other factors impact well-being. They found that the aging process itself predicted a more positive mental state.

> The older the person was, the more he or she reported positive emotions like cheerfulness, life satisfaction, and overall happiness within the past 30 days. And, surprisingly, the younger participants reported more negative emotions, like feeling sad, nervous, hopeless or worthless. (Mroczek & Spiro, 2005)

Although elderly white males have the highest suicide rate of any group, Mroczek and Spiro found that older men in the study, especially those who were married, reported being the happiest and having the least amount of negative emotion. Older women also reported more positive emotions than younger women. How do Mroczek and Spiro account for this increase in happiness among people nearing the end of their lives?

From research, it is noted that older adults regulate their emotions more effectively than younger or middle-aged adults. It is thought that older individuals seem to be able to know, through their years of experience, what kinds of external events increase or decrease their positive and negative emotions. Therefore, they achieve a better "emotional balance" by selecting people and situations that will minimize negative and maximize positive emotions (Mroczek & Spiro, 2005).

Once humor is established as a hardwired response pattern, a sense of humor can become a finely honed skill that enables an individual to consistently respond with optimism and humergy. When humans persist at increasing the fun in their lives, they become increasingly skilled at developing their own individual humor craft. So this story is in honor of the joys of aging!

> Four old retired guys are walking down a street in Yuma, Arizona. They turn a corner and see a sign that says, "Old Timers Bar—ALL drinks 10 cents." They look at each other and then go in, thinking this is too good to be true. The old bartender says in a voice that carries across the room, "Come on in and let me pour one for you! What'll it be, gentlemen?" There seems to be a fully stocked bar, so each of the men orders a martini.
>
> In short order, the bartender serves up four iced martinis—shaken, not stirred—and says, "That'll be 10 cents each, please." The four men stare at the bartender for a moment. Then look at each other. They can't believe their good luck. They pay the 40 cents, finish their martinis, and order another round. Again, four excellent martinis are produced, with the bartender again saying, "That's 40 cents, please." They pay the 40 cents, but their curiosity is more than they can stand. They have each had two martinis and so far they have spent less than a dollar.
>
> Finally one of the men says, "How can you afford to serve martinis as good as these for a dime a piece?" "I'm a retired tailor from Phoenix," the bartender says, "and I always wanted to own a bar. Last year I hit the lottery jackpot for $125 million and decided to open this place. Every drink costs a dime. Wine, liquor, beer, it's all the same."
>
> "Wow! That's quite a story," says one of the men.
>
> The four of them sip at their martinis and can't help but notice seven other people at the end of the bar who do not have drinks in front of them and hadn't ordered anything the whole time they were there. One man gestures at the seven at the end of the bar without drinks and asks the bartender, "What's with them?"
>
> The bartender says, "Oh, they're all old retired people from Florida. They're waiting for Happy Hour when drinks are half price."

HUMOR AND PAIN MANAGEMENT

Hob Osterlund (2011) and her team recently completed a five-year study on the use of comedy in people undergoing chemotherapy. This was the first study of its kind and did have significantly positive results. The following results of this groundbreaking study are printed with permission of Osterlund.

Impact of Humor on Outpatients Receiving Chemotherapy
The COMIC Study: Corresponding Author: Hob Osterlund.

We compared cancer and chemotherapy-related symptoms as well as immune and endocrine function between participants who watched either a humorous or non-humorous DVD. Participants who watched the humorous DVD described an overall decrease in cancer and chemotherapy-related symptoms as well as decreased anxiety. They also exhibited physiologic changes consistent with improved immune function as compared to their baseline.

Cancer and chemotherapy-related symptoms, as well as anxiety decreased more in the humor intervention group than in the non-humor group but were of borderline significance. These findings merit further study. In conclusion, humor has the potential to be a low-risk complement to pharmacologic therapy in oncology practice. Further studies are needed with larger numbers of participants in order to determine to what degree humor and laughter might positively affect both immediate and long-term health outcomes.

Conclusion: Pilot study findings support the use of humor as a low-risk intervention that may complement pharmacologic therapy for management of symptoms related to cancer and chemotherapy. Additional study is recommended to more fully assess the efficacy of humor in cancer and other health conditions.

For more information on this study, watch "Humor Rumor," a YouTube video that details this research in a memorable comedy format. More information about Osterlund's journey is found in Chapter 6 of this book. In another overview of the research studies, positive emotions were associated with lower pain or a greater tolerance for pain (Diener & Chan, 2010).

PROMISING RESEARCH CONTINUES

Dr. Lee Berk, a Loma Linda University academic medical researcher, has become a special mentor and friend through AATH. His work has continued to focus on the positive power of laughter and humor. The intuitive foundation that was laid down by Norman Cousins intrigued him in the 1980s. In his earlier work, Berk and his colleagues discovered that the anticipation of "mirthful laughter" produced surprising and noteworthy effects. Two hormones—beta-endorphins (the family of chemicals that elevates mood state) and human growth hormone (HGH, which helps with optimizing immunity)—increased by 27 percent and 87 percent respectively in study subjects who anticipated watching a humorous

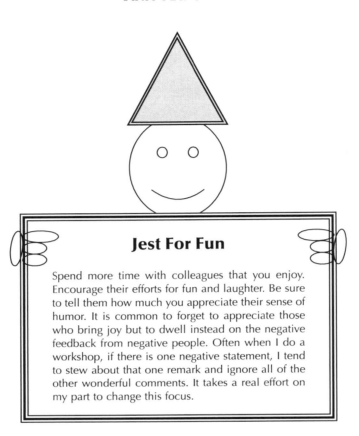

Jest For Fun

Spend more time with colleagues that you enjoy. Encourage their efforts for fun and laughter. Be sure to tell them how much you appreciate their sense of humor. It is common to forget to appreciate those who bring joy but to dwell instead on the negative feedback from negative people. Often when I do a workshop, if there is one negative statement, I tend to stew about that one remark and ignore all of the other wonderful comments. It takes a real effort on my part to change this focus.

video. There was no such increase among the control group who did not anticipate watching the humorous film.

Another study found that the same anticipation of mirthful laughter reduced the levels of three detrimental stress hormones. Cortisol (termed "the steroid stress hormone"), epinephrine (also known as adrenaline), and dopac (the major catabolite of dopamine) were reduced 39 percent, 70 percent, and 38 percent respectively (statistically significant compared to the control group). When chronically released, high levels of these stress hormones can be detrimental to the immune system.

Another Berk and Tan Research Study

Lee Berk and Stanley Tan (2009) examined the effect of "mirthful laughter" on individuals with diabetes. Diabetes is a metabolic syndrome characterized by the risk of heart attack, blindness, and other neurological, immune, and blood vessel complications. They found that mirthful laughter, as a preventive adjunct therapy in diabetes care, raised good cholesterol and lowered inflammation.

A group of twenty high-risk diabetic patients with hypertension and hyperlipidemia were divided into two groups: group C (control) and group L (laughter). Both groups were started on standard medications for diabetes (glipizide, TZD, metformin), hypertension (ACE inhibitor or ARB), and hyperlipidemia (statins). The researchers followed both groups for 12 months. The patients in the laughter group (group L) had lower epinephrine and norepinephrine levels by the second month, suggesting lower stress levels. They had increased HDL (good) cholesterol. The laughter group also had lower levels of inflammation.

At the end of one year, the research team saw significant improvement in group L: HDL cholesterol had risen by 26 percent in group L, and only 3 percent in group C. Harmful C-reactive proteins decreased 66 percent in the laughter group versus 26 percent for the control group.

Berk and Tan Research Study Conclusion

The study suggests that the addition of an adjunct therapeutic mirthful laughter prescription (a potential modulator of positive mood state) to standard diabetes care may lower stress and inflammatory response and increase "good" cholesterol levels. The authors conclude that mirthful laughter may thus lower the risk of cardiovascular disease associated with diabetes mellitus and metabolic syndrome. Further studies need to be done to expand these findings.

In describing himself as a "hardcore medical clinician and scientist," Berk says, "the best clinicians understand that there is an intrinsic physiological intervention brought about by positive emotions such as mirthful laughter, optimism and hope. Lifestyle choices have a significant impact on health and disease and these are choices which we and the patient exercise control relative to prevention and treatment" (Berk, 2009).

POSITIVE PSYCHOLOGY FLOURISHES

As mentioned in Chapter 1, the Positive Emotions and Psychophysiology (PEP) Lab at the University of North Carolina Chapel Hill wants to understand and share the significance of positive emotions. This is a study of the relationship between emotion and the autonomic nervous system activity in people who flourish. Martin Seligman, former president of the American Psychological Association, uses the term *positive psychology* to identify what makes people thrive. Traditionally, psychology has focused on deficit characteristics such as anger, anxiety, and sadness. Seligman, along with Mihaly Csikszentmihalyi, who originated the concept of flow, has changed the paradigm to the study of human strengths and sources of happiness (Seligman & Csikszentmihalyi, 2000).

Psychology previously focused on studying what was wrong with people. Humans often center on what they are not able to do—on what they do not know. What happens when research changes the paradigm of study to strengthening the positive attributes? A hypothesis called broadening studies states that "distinct, discrete positive emotions broaden the scopes of attention, cognition, and action, widening the array of percepts, thoughts, and action presently in mind. A corollary narrowing hypothesis states that negative emotions shrink these same arrays" (Seligman & Csikszentmihalyi, 2000). "The positive emotions actually widen the opportunities for learning whereas the negative emotions narrow the options," say the folks at the PEP Lab (http://www.unc.edu/peplab/.

The implications of this research are critically important to leaders in the field. It gives credence to the concept of joy-flow and the humergy concepts I've identified, and it provides the impetus for further research on humor.

The positive emotions are more difficult to study than the negative ones since they are comparatively fewer in number and relatively undifferentiated. The optimistic emotions of joy, amusement, and humor are not as easily "read" as anger or fear. As mentioned in the research on fear, folks attend quickly to the negative emotions because they alert the attentional system to the worry about immediate survival. The positive emotions, while important for personal growth and emotional stability, do not pose this urgent need (Fredrickson, 2003).

A relatively new option for the treatment of a variety of disorders is the use of either laughter therapy or humor therapy. Mostly investigational in nature, this option is based on the use of humor as a deliberate attempt to provide symptom relief, and it is practiced for both physical and emotional disorders. As previously mentioned, some therapists are experimenting with the use of humor as a treatment option for depression and mental illness. Clowns, toys, and humor resource rooms are available in some hospitals as a focus on the healing benefits of humor. There is mounting scientific evidence that humor reduces the natural stresses of illness and distracts the patient from pain.

The psychology instructor had just finished a lecture on mental health and was giving an oral test. Speaking specifically about manic depression, she asked, "How would you diagnose a patient who walks back and forth screaming at the top of his lungs one minute, then sits in a chair weeping uncontrollably the next?"

A young man in the rear raised his hand and answered, "A basketball coach?"

PLAY

There has been some information on the research about play in previous chapters. Play does play (pun intended) an important role in the study of humor and laughter. Play therapy has long been used with children as a vehicle for working through emotional challenges. The Association for Play Therapy defines play therapy as "the systematic use of a theoretical model to establish an interpersonal process wherein trained play therapists use the therapeutic powers of play to help clients prevent or resolve psychosocial difficulties and achieve optimal growth and development." (http://www.a4pt.org/ps.playtherapy.cfm)

A lay definition might be "a form of counseling that uses play to communicate with and render assistance, especially to children whose natural language is play" (http://en.wikipedia.org/wiki/Play_therapy). Play involves multiple centers of perception and cognition across the entire brain. Depriving animals of play disrupts their brain maturation (Panksepp, 2003).

Two professors who are members of AATH have been pioneers in teaching a course on play at Western Michigan University. Kay Caskey and Laurie Young have a course titled "Holistic Approaches to Play across Life Span." They see play as an optimal way to reduce stress, increase productivity, enhance learning, and improve coping skills for people of all ages.

An article in *USA Weekend* titled "Where the Playgrounds Are: America's Most Playful Cities" (USA Weekend, 2011) begins by saying that play is serious business. The article reiterates that children need play. They announce the top five of America's most playful cities for kids. KaBOOM! is a national nonprofit dedicated to building and renovating America's playgrounds. It researches the best communities for offering children access to vital playground space (USA Weekend, 2011).

I'm grateful that the interest in play and humor research is growing. Future mouse droppings will be revealing to those who might think humor research is just a bunch of "crap." Leaders in every field can be most effective when they are aware of the cognitive implications of humor research and feel confident in applying this knowledge to their practice.

For many of the folks in AATH, it is difficult not to be "high on humor." There is not only an abundance of play, there is a search for playfulness. In fact there can be a passion and fervor among those who believe so strongly in the healing power of humor that it clouds their thinking about the research. Attendees at the Association for Applied and Therapeutic Humor conference in Chicago in 2003 witnessed a strong negative reaction from the audience when Rod Martin presented an overview of the research that challenged some popular theories about humor. Humor quackery is difficult to overcome, but AATH is dedicated to understanding the hard science of humor. Research on humor is increasing, but many of the mouse droppings are scattered and inconclusive.

As mentioned previously, there are few organizations dedicated to scientific research on humor. One such organization is the International Society for Humor Studies, which publishes *Humor: An International Journal of Humor Research*.

Jest For Fun

Do a happy dance! Jump for joy! Laugh for no reason! Get out of your comfort zone!

Some journals that occasionally cite humor research in their publications include the *Journal of the American Medical Association* and the *Journal of Physiology*. For a great overview of the many facets of humor, take a look at *The Encyclopedia of 20th-Century American Humor* (Nilsen & Nilsen, 2000). And once again, for the lay practitioner who wants a quick, reliable overview of the research, the Association for Applied and Therapeutic Humor maintains a highly recommended website at http://www.aath.org.

> *To steal ideas from one person is plagiarism. To steal from many is research.*

SUMMARY

A staggering amount of data emerging from biological research and from imaging technology provides compelling evidence linking humor and optimal living. While it is clear that fear and stress inhibit well-being, the research on humor and joy is more complex. An increasing number of studies confirm the relationship between positive emotions and using humor to maximize living. The good news is that the research indicates that humor can:

- Maximize learning
- Build relationships
- Create a nurturing environment

- Relieve stress
- Manage pain

Emotions drive attention and attention drives learning. The emotion of fear has traditionally driven workplace culture. Fear is the most frequent basis for evaluations, policies, and accountability. This fear is harbored in cultures that reflect stress and burnout in both employers and employees. Extreme stress is not only detrimental to a healthy lifestyle but also decreases productivity and increases anxiety.

Positive emotionality (including humor) can act as a hook, line, and sinker in memory retention. Humor has the power to capture attention (hook), manipulate this information with repetition and practice in the working memory (line), and provide feedback and reflection as part of a response system (sinker). Humor can become a component of the automated response system.

Laughter and humor research is difficult to quantify because each individual finds humor in different ways. Laughter is contagious and reflects human connections. Mirror neuron research is giving insights as to why humans laugh with others and why humor is an important part of relationships.

Humor contributes to a healthy environment that reduces stress and increases coping capacity. It is an indicator of the ability to survive tragedy and adapt to change. Research on humor is in the pioneering stage, but as MRI and other technologies continue to advance, further insights will be gained into the complex issues of the relationship between positive emotionality and learning. Humor research is in the pioneering stages, and there is often a healthy debate about the research presented in this chapter, but the research seems to indicate enormous benefits from the inclusion of laughter and humor for everyday living.

> *Until the scientists get all the details worked out, get as much laughter as you can.*
>
> —Robert Provine

POWERFUL PRACTICE—STRATEGIES FOR LEADERS

- Identify current staff professional development needs to find ways to keep up to date on the fast pace of cognitive and humor research.
- Find a way to share resources and expertise from workshops and conferences.
- Encourage creative and humorous insights.
- Link cognitive research and humor practice into an action plan for staff development. Involve all employees, inviting their insights for practical application.

- Facilitate a discussion on the prevalent emotional forces at work in your system. What negative emotions are narrowing thinking and limiting opportunities for personal growth and development? What emotional impact does your accountability system have on the opportunities for positive emotionality?
- Encourage staff to come to consensus on one area of humor research. Brainstorm possible ways of increasing the positive emotionality for all with the purpose of expanding thinking and increasing flow experiences.
- Stress relief strategies can be shared on the staff bulletin board. There are numerous articles and ideas available in the popular press.
- Pair different colleagues each month (month mates). Focus on building relationships based on fun and providing support for that person in their quest for humergy. Choose one playful or fun activity to do with that person during the month. This can be as simple as taking a walk, eating lunch together, or sharing jokes.
- Give each staff member the gift of a tennis ball with his or her name on it. A powerful self-massage can be experienced when the ball is positioned between an individual and a wall or preferably the floor. This is especially relaxing for the upper back and neck muscles that can become tense during the day.
- If you do not have a staff exercise facility, ask for donations of good used exercise equipment to be placed in a designated exercise room (if space and your insurance plan allows it) in your building. Encourage members to work out in the morning before work or after work with each other.

STUDY GROUP FOCUS

- Review and discuss the research on positive emotionality at the PEP Lab at the University of North Carolina Chapel Hill. For details see the website at http://www.unc.edu/peplab/.
- List your fears about using humor. Do others share your concerns?
- How can you use humor to help you learn? Share any memory hooks that you use. Begin to develop humor hooks for what you need to remember. Look for humor everywhere. Increase your strategies for fun with purposeful attentional humor tools.
- Discuss how you use humor to keep focused. Keep track of how often you "change state." Incorporate purposeful movement into your day. Take frequent "laughter breaks."

CAFÉ CONVERSATIONS

- Review the research of the PEP Lab from the University of North Carolina Chapel Hill. Discuss the implications of this research in relationship to your goals.
- Explore ways that you can use humor as a hook for increasing your own productivity. Share the benefits of your insights with trusted colleagues.

Since you were dying for the research, I am finishing this chapter with tombstone humor.

Having a great time—wish you were here!

I told you I was sick!

Here lies Ann Mann, who lived an old maid, but died an old Mann.

Here lies Johnny Yeast. Pardon me for not rising.

Why me? Albert J. Krispel.

I was somebody who is no business of yours.

Sir John Strange. Here lies an honest lawyer, and that is Strange.

Here lies the body of our Anna. Done to death by a banana. It wasn't the fruit that laid her low. But the skin of the thing that made her go.

What are you looking at?

In memory; from your sons, except Ricardo who did not pay any money.

Looked up the elevator shaft to see if it was on its way down. It was!

"Always go to other people's funerals, otherwise they won't come to yours."

—Yogi Berra

4

HURTFUL HUMOR IS NO LAUGHING MATTER

No sense being pessimistic. It wouldn't work anyway.

Humor often emerges as a response to transitions, change events, pain, and tragedy. It's an invaluable coping response to the complex difficulties humans face. Most people rely on their sense of humor to survive workplace challenges and increased demands placed on them.

There are moments in history when nations wonder if the ability to use humor has been lost to an extraordinary tragedy. During these times there appears to be a fear of laughter and of the ability to use humor.

A difficult economy often generates a focus on a work ethic that marginalizes humor and in some instances banishes it altogether. Political mandates and increased demands on productivity have been reflected in less fun, laughter, and joy in many workplace environments. This phenomenon, rooted in deep fear, is reflected when there exists a joyless workplace culture.

HUMORPHOBIA

Humorphobia is the fear of fun, laughter, and humor. Humorphobia exists as a transparent thread often woven into the fabric of people's lives. Most leaders are passionate about creating a happy work environment yet are hampered by unspoken belief systems that permeate organizations. These fear factors include:

- Fear of not having time for humor because of accountability expectations
- Fear of being perceived as silly, unproductive, an airhead, and unprofessional
- Fear of losing control

- Fear of inadequacy or inability to tell a joke coupled with inexperience in the use of humor (because humor is not taught or modeled in most training programs)
- Fear of punishment or retaliation in an environment that is hostile or unaccustomed to humor
- Fear of being made fun of or being the brunt of jokes

Humorphobia is often barely perceptible but has a tremendous impact on humor practice. The fears that generate humorphobia create substantial barriers for creating and sustaining humergy.

Many fears are well founded because fun and play have been under attack for several decades. Political and economic forces have demanded accountability for tax dollars spent in most organizations. The focus is on the bottom line and getting the most work from employees, which can drain worker energy and motivation. Increasing demands generate increasingly stressful conditions for the workplace.

> *Most of the time I don't have much fun. The rest of the time I don't have any fun at all.*
>
> —Woody Allen

We often have a culture that reflects deep fears and limits the capacity to support joyful workplaces. After each workshop that I have facilitated on humor and stress, people have shared their distressing stories with me. One woman told of not being able to even take a sick day because she was the only person working in that office and her boss demanded she be there every second. There were no lunch breaks out of the office, no laughter, no smiling, and no appreciation for her work. One person told me that parties were never allowed and that birthdays were not to be acknowledged—much less celebrated.

Humor Paradox

This is the humor paradox. Many claim to place a high value on humor, but the reality is that fears keep people from initiating and sustaining humor practice. (See Figure 4.1.) Let's take a closer look at some of the fear factors that inhibit humor practice.

Limited Time

Wasting learning time is a firmly established, well-founded fear. It is a struggle to find the time necessary to implement mandates, and supervisors often have

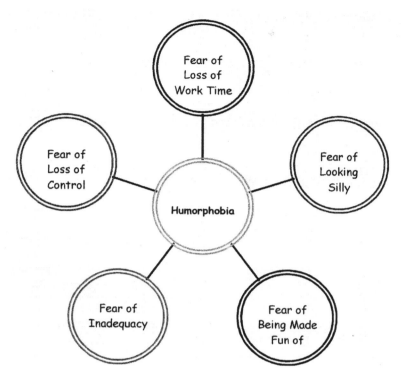

Figure 4.1 Fear Factors

deep concerns about their ability to increase productivity and cut costs. Managers who believe in humor use it with caution because of their very real concerns about public accountability issues. Several employees have expressed the worry that if they are seen "goofing around," the perception will be that they aren't working. Employees often worry that if they are joking and laughing with each other, they are not being productive. The message is strong and clear: there is no time for fun.

Unprofessional or Childish Perceptions

There is a general societal perception that play, laughter, fun, and games are for young children. Unless working with children or in the entertainment business, professionals are generally not expected to be playful, enthusiastic, energetic, fun-loving individuals.

Play is considered something to be done outside of the job. People who try to incorporate a little fun can be accused of "goofing off." One person told me during a workshop that she was told to "quit acting like a two-year-old."

He is not only dull himself, he is the cause of dullness in others.

—Samuel Johnson

Losing Control

Humor can be noisy, energetic, and loud. In a culture that values quiet and order, it may appear that employees are out of control. Managers may think that employees will not take them seriously if they are joking and having fun.

A boss with a good sense of humor can motivate and encourage collegiality and networking. Humor and laughter, when skillfully used, have been shown to enhance communication.

Inadequacy and Inexperience

Humor is often considered an inherited trait rather than a skill that can be nurtured and developed. Humor skills as a part of training programs are virtually nonexistent. In fact, since many have been programmed to believe that play and fun are immature activities, the ability to practice humor effectively has been limited. The benefits of humor as outlined in previous chapters should be convincing that there is a need to develop humor confidence through humor practice. Chapter 5 explores a variety of ways to improve humor skills and abilities. The study of humor is complex and deserves recognition as an integral part of employee preparation programs.

Being Made Fun Of

One of the greatest fears is the fear of being laughed at. Speech classes usually begin with the recognition that many people would rather die than give a speech. No one likes to be the brunt of ridicule, and cruel teasing is prevalent in many workplace environments. The dark humor of sarcasm, mockery, and ridicule are controlling tactics used by bullies to manipulate their victims. Many people have been ridiculed for attempts to have fun and use humor.

The challenges of addressing humorphobia cannot be overestimated. When these fears are deep seated in an individual and firmly rooted within an organization, a few fun activities will not begin to address the complexity of the issues. The benefits of humor (Chapter 1) must be reviewed for possible inclusion in employee preparation programs and supported in mentoring programs. Novice employees desperately need the benefits that humor can provide for them in their first years at a challenging new job. Awareness of humorphobia and identification of these fears are crucial in the ability to create a culture that supports humergy.

Jest For Fun

Cherish the people in your workplace who have a sense of fun. You may have a Robin Williams, Richard Pryor, or Lucille Ball in your workplace. Invite them to start a staff meeting with jokes or stories. Better yet ask them to organize some fun activities to celebrate workplace accomplishments.

ADDRESSING HUMORPHOBIA

Observe and record the evidence of humorphobia in your workplace. Over time, humorphobia can become an integral part of the negativity of individuals and impact the entire system. Awareness of fears, commitment to change, and focused staff development are preliminary steps in building the confidence needed to revive the energy of humor. The level of trust in an organization can be measured by the amount of humergy that exists there. As mentioned in previous chapters, fun is an indicator of trust. An environment of trust is critical for optimal productivity to occur. Listening for the language of humorphobia is a helpful step in becoming more aware of how fears are verbalized.

- We need to be professional here. What will the public think if there is fun and laughter?
- We cannot measure humor. It's "soft data" and not meaningful in the workplace. Solid research is the only tool of value.
- There is no time for fun and games. Let's just get this meeting over with.
- I don't do "touchy feely."
- I've tried humor before and it didn't work!

Humorphobia gives some powerful insights into the resistance encountered by enthusiastic leaders trying to nurture a positive climate. If you've heard the above statements, if you've ever been called a "Pollyanna" or a "Mary Poppins" or labeled as an "unrealistic optimist," you have encountered humorphobia.

Some cause happiness wherever they go; others, whenever they go.

—Oscar Wilde

Strategies to Combat Humorphobia

A commitment to the change process is required to address the deep-rooted issues of humorphobia. Skillful leaders will

- Hold a passionate belief that humergy facilitates productivity and encourages trusted relationships
- Provide the groundwork to analyze and learn from fear factors
- Offer ongoing staff development opportunities for systemic change

Various ideas to combat humorphobia include:

- Staff development days. Watch the FISH video (Lundkin, 2000) and form four focus groups based on the tenets—play, choose your attitude, be there, and make their day. Have each group focus on fun ways their group can improve workplace climate throughout the year.
- Study groups that meet on a regular basis to read and plan activities to address culture issues. Suggested resources are *Fun Works* by Leslie Yerkes (2001), *Making Humor Work* by Terry L. Paulson (1989), and the book you're holding right now.
- Study groups or café conversations, which are included at the end of each chapter.

Things are going to get a lot worse before they get worse.

—Lily Tomlin

HUMORDOOMERS

Humorphobia breeds humordoomers. Humorphobia impacts both the administrator and employee by undermining confidence, stifling creativity, and sabotag-

Jest For Fun

Give the gift of humor. For birthdays, holidays, and special occasions give a joke book, perform a skit, or provide another humorous present. Comic strip newspaper makes great gift-wrap.

ing humor practice. Working long and hard seems to be the societal norm for proving commitment and effectiveness. Time is a precious commodity, and the increased demands require employers to make every minute count.

A humordoomer is a person who consistently uses negative humor to control and manipulate others. Humorphobia breeds humordoomers, skilled crafters who use subtle techniques to suppress humor in the workplace. Humordoomers are usually unhappy individuals stressed by the dual demands of accountability and limited time constraints; they're pessimistic leeches who can suck the humergy right out of you.

Grown in a Petri dish of fear and anger, these folks are threatened by joyful energy and enthusiasm. They often use humor to manipulate others and to maintain a level of control of their world. Their negative humor reflects their unhappy immersion in the confining straits of a workaholic world. Often their techniques are so woven into the fabric of a culture that not only are they unaware of their own webbing effect, their unsuspecting prey are oblivious as well.

In an article in *School Administrator*, Michael R. Weber (2003) addresses the "draining effect" that negative people have on everybody and everything. As Weber says, they consume the energy of the entire staff, negating new ideas and programs. He thinks that any effort to convert these malcontents is extremely difficult because you cannot force people to change. Note: recognize that anyone can exhibit humordoomer behavior at times as a result of anger or fear and stress.

An angry workshop participant confronted me about the icebreaker activity used at a regional curriculum meeting. "Please do not use your cutesy kindergarten stuff at our meetings. We just do not have time." I was genuinely puzzled. This activity was designed as a pair/share networking task to introduce members to each other. The majority of the group visibly enjoyed the purposefully planned games and activities; however, even after carefully defining the goals of the activities, this encounter was the beginning of my understanding of the impact of humordoomers.

Although it is evident that it is essential to laugh and possess a sense of humor, humorphobia creeps into the culture. Administrators are stressed and concerned about their abilities to meet accountability mandates while budgets continue to be cut. People are expected to work harder for less money. When resources are scarce, anxiety increases and the resulting stress boils over into the culture, increasing the rising plague of burned-out employees. Cognitive research clearly demonstrates the detrimental impact excess stress has on productivity, networking, and workplace culture.

A focus on quality has generated various techniques to try to "improve" employee effectiveness. Entire books are written with step-by-step instructions on evaluation techniques meant to change employee behavior.

The beatings will continue until morale improves!

Punitive measures originally designed to force improvements increase the toxins in the culture. Perceived punitive measures intensify feelings of fear and anger, while anger that is unresolved intensifies into bitterness, rage, and even violence. Deep-seated anger manifests itself in many ways. Negative humor may be used to express frustration, hostility, fears, and anger. If one feels inferior, laughing at others becomes a way to feel superior and can become a weapon in the hands of stressed, unhappy individuals. Control and power are the goals of those who use humor to evoke feelings of fear and distress in others. Humor that is sarcastic, cynical, or mocking results in the recipient feeling helpless and vulnerable.

There are two indicators of unresolved anger that can be identified and observed in workplace behavior. Managers familiar with these categories can view these behaviors through the humor lens:

1. Bullying
2. Victimization

It can be a struggle to teach employees about the roles of bully and victim, but it behooves leaders to become aware of these practices. Numerous insights emerge when looking at these characteristics through the lens of humor.

> *To laugh 'til you cry, and cry 'til you laugh—cleansing your body of tension and washing your emotions clean.*
>
> —Karyn Buxman, *Amazed and Amused*

Bully Humor

A bullying type of humor can be used to control what happens in relationships. When making fun of others, bullies are usually expressing internal fears because they are unable or unwilling to recognize their own emotional needs. Humor becomes a weapon of the bully when used with the intentional purpose of wounding another.

Bully behavior is frequently portrayed in the media as an acceptable method to express frustration, hostility, fear, and anger. The use of mockery and sarcasm allows the venting of anger. Jokes with the express purpose of making fun of others abound on television, in movies, and on the Internet. Fears about difference in culture have often been expressed in jokes about Italians, Jews, Mexicans, gays, and religious entities. While often clever, these jokes perpetuate the bully mindset that it's okay to make fun of individuals or groups. There is research to suggest that this type of humor can lead to violent behavior. "The devaluation of racial, ethnic or religious groups, sometimes disguised as humor, is a major contributor to violence and aggression against these groups. It was found that emotional empathy was negatively correlated only with the humorousness of negative ethnic stereotype jokes" (Forsyth, Altermatt, & Forsyth, 1997).

My local congressional representative recently posted this joke on Facebook:

> Father Daughter Talk . . . My daughter just walked into the room and said, "Dad, cancel my allowance, rent my room out, throw all my clothes out, take my TV, IPhone, IPod and my laptop. Please sell all my jewelry. Then sell my car, take my house key. And then write me out of your will." Well, she didn't put it quite like that . . . she actually said . . . "dad this is my new boyfriend, Mohammed from Iran."

The response to this was quite mixed, with several people protesting that he was profiling and discriminating against Muslims. There have been several editorials in the paper. However, many of his followers claimed that "this was only a joke." His supporters gave responses such as, "It is just humor," "Lighten up," and "It's a joke people, geez." This is an example of blatant bullying. It is not really funny unless deep down you fear or dislike Muslims. It is also an instance of folks trying to "blame" those voicing objections by asserting that the disapproving comments were from people who did not have a sense of humor. One of the worst things someone can say about a person is that they do not have a sense of humor. If it follows bullying, this is bully humor.

The Victim

The recipient of bullying feels powerless. The fear of being made fun of can strip away confidence and the ability to make positive changes, and legislative mandates and funding inequities have resulted in loss of power and hope for many employees. Victims emerge who blame others for difficulties, acquire a learned response of helplessness, feel they have no control over their lives, and operate out of deep fear and anxiety. They do not appear to enjoy life and constantly remind others of their own difficulties.

One of my vivid memories is a dreary January day when I thought it would be fun to brighten the week and suggested having a Hawaiian luncheon. I shared ideas about baking an upside-down pineapple cake and playing Hawaiian music. A few others chimed in with additional ideas. One unhappy woman looked at me with disgust and said, "Sure must be nice not to have anything to do!" It was obvious she had so much "important" work that she had no time for anything fun, and she didn't approve of others wasting their time on such frivolous things as a party. This use of sarcasm can be a powerful negative force within a system.

Jest For Fun

The inside doors of the staff restroom stalls are an ideal place for jokes, reminders, and stories. One community college called this restroom informational marketing tool "The Flush."

Blessed are the cracked for they are the ones who let in the light.

Uncovering the Transparent Language of Humordoomers

The bully:

- "Do you think you're in this place to have fun?"
- "Wipe that smile off your face!"
- "Stop fooling around and get to work."
- "You could do it if you didn't play around so much."
- Name calling: "You're so (stupid, ugly, white, fat, etc.)."
- Mockery, exaggeration of a behavior such as walking or speech
- Ridicule of clothing (for example, too-short slacks: "You expecting a flood?" or a sports coat: "You going to a funeral?")

The victim:

- "Great. I have the worst job here."
- "I have no reason to be happy."
- "People today have no respect."
- "Do you have to be so perky?"
- "Quit being a Pollyanna and get real. You can't make this place any better."
- "Don't do so much, you'll make the rest of us look like couch potatoes."
- "Oh sure, now they want us to use humor? Like we don't already have enough to do."

If challenged, the humordoomer usually responds with, "Can't you take a joke?" or "I was just playing with you." Often a clever ruse is the blame technique, in which the humordoomer accuses the challenger of having no sense of humor by saying he or she can't take a joke. This is intended to excuse offensive behavior while putting the recipient on the defensive.

If you find yourself in a hole, stop digging.

—Will Rogers

Coping with Humordoomers

While humordoomers are difficult to deal with, there are some strategies that you can use to stimulate humordoomer reform. Attempt to identify the cause of the negative behavior exhibited by humordoomers and follow this with

suggestions for change. This requires a loving attitude and skillful communication. (Note: these negative patterns of behavior are usually hardwired after years of repetition.) The following are strategies to combat stressed humordoomers (who are fearful and overwhelmed):

- Kill them with kindness and understanding. Often people need someone to listen to them and empathize.
- Identify the strengths in these people and tell them how much you appreciate this quality in them. It really helps if you have several staff members doing this.
- Ask them what they are going to do to make things better. Encourage any attempts at improvement.

The following are strategies for pessimistic humordoomers (who are habitually negative):

- Smile and say "If you tell me something awful, I need you to tell me three positive things. I just can't handle negativity today!"
- Do the broken record routine: "So what's the good news?" Just keep repeating this with a laugh. If they come up with something positive, cheer and do cartwheels!

And the way to combat angry humordoomers, who are resentful and frustrated with a lack of control in their life and who are unable to express their feelings in positive ways, is to recognize that these folks may actually need more help then you are able to give. If you have the opportunity, suggest that they seek counseling and/or therapy.

It is common to think of something clever to say after an encounter with negative people. Here are some one-liners that you can experiment with:

- "I resemble that statement."
- "Start today with a smile and get it over with."
- "There's no time like the pleasant."
- "If you don't learn to laugh at trouble, you won't have anything to laugh at when you are old."—Ed Howe
- "In life, pain is inevitable, but suffering is optional."—Hedy Schliefer
- "Life is wonderful, without it you're dead."—Red Skelton
- "When does the fun start?"
- "Don't take life too seriously; you'll never get out alive."

If you find one that you like, use the broken record routine. Use the same response every time negative humor is encountered. Several of my AATH colleagues shared ideas with me about how they deal with humordoomers. Chris Balmer is a counselor and says, "don't try to push humor" on humordoomers. From Allen Klein:

When I lived in New York City, everyday I would walk my dog. And everyday I would pass a neighbor who would tell me about all the robberies, attacks, and fires in the area. I nicknamed her "The Voice of Doom." It took me a few weeks to learn this, but one day I realized that I could walk in the opposite direction and get the Voice of Doom out of my life. You can do it too. Walk in a different direction and get those humordoomers out of your life.

Deb Hart is well known as the nurse who can get even the most difficult patients to laugh with her. However, she admits it is more difficult with closer family and friends. She agrees with Allen to avoid humordoomers if possible and if not to say positive things to them. Let them know that you only have so much time to listen to negative comments.

Kris Harty tries to involve them:

There will always be people who are not on board. Leave them be. Play with the folks who play back. They're the ones who will be receptive to your message. Along the way, sometimes those humordoomers find themselves unwillingly and unwittingly laughing, too. And that opens doors, minds and experiences for everyone involved! Learning flows naturally from laughter.

There have been numerous instances in workshops when people have said they are married to a humordoomer. That has to be a difficult challenge as you can hardly avoid them. You may find that your humor differences are irreconcilable. As one person told me: "It's better to have loved and lost than to live with a humordoomer the rest of your life."

DESTRUCTIVE GAMES PEOPLE PLAY

- *Clue.* Folks who are passive-aggressive play this game very well. They don't give many clues as to why they are angry, they just say and do things to let you know they aren't happy with you. You haven't a clue!
- *Outburst.* The purpose of this game is to control what others say and do. The object of this game is to instill in others a fear of their temper. They threaten folks with their well-known quickness for an angry tirade or outburst.
- *The Blame Game.* This is the game where people are unable to take responsibility for any of their own behavior, but blame their spouses, their fellow employees, administrators, their own friends and family, the government, the media, and so on for their deficiencies.

Jest For Fun

Share the list of destructive games at a staff meeting. Ask the staff which game they would most like to plan or play. Group staff members according to their game choices and have them actually come up with rules, game pieces, and the winning strategies. Share the ideas with other staff. Hopefully the laughter generated can initiate a serious look at existing negative tendencies.

- *Troubles.* The rules of this game are simple. Think about every possible thing that can go wrong, exaggerate the possibilities, and live in fear and worry that big troubles will happen "right here in River City."
- *Scrabble.* Victims also play this game. Whatever suggestions are offered as possible solutions to their litany of difficulties, they say, "Yes, but I cannot do that because . . ." or "Yes, but I know someone who tried that and it made it worse . . ." They scramble their word options to always spell the word *no.*
- *Monopoly.* Victims who think they have it worse then anyone else play this game. They have a monopoly on difficulties. If you ever mention that you're tired and have to work late, their response is: "You're lucky you don't have my job. I have to work late tonight, and then I have to meet with the boss and practice for the administrative review. When I go home I need to make a casserole for the church supper. My mother has to have bunion surgery, my car is out of gas, and we have to go to Florida for winter break again this year." Whatever your own difficulties, these victims let you know that they have it much worse.
- *Taboo.* Folks who avoid facing problems and consider it taboo to discuss their anxieties with you play this. Most topics are taboo, including their bullying behavior and their offensive humor techniques of mockery, sarcasm, or ridicule.

There are actually some individuals who are adept at playing several of these games at the same time.

It's what you learn after you know it all that counts.

—John Wooden

Even if the intent is not to harm,
if the impact is harmful,
it is inappropriate humor.

Figure 4.2 Intent versus Impact

INTENT VERSUS IMPACT

When the impact of humor is hurtful, the humor is inappropriate even if the intent was not to harm. Thus, the impact of the humor on the recipient is more important then the intent of the relater. (See Figure 4.2.)

The impact of humor on a group is less damaging than that of humor targeted at a person as an individual. There is a difference between Jay Leno offending those of your gender on national television and having a significant person in your life tell you the same thing. Read these quips, first as heard from Leno on national television and then again as if your spouse was the speaker.

- "I just got a dog for my wife. Best trade I ever made."
- "I still miss my ex-husband, but my aim will improve."
- "If we can put a man on the moon, why not all of them?"

The change in focus is significant. There are moron, blond, Polack, and fat people jokes that are usually not taken seriously; however, an awareness of their impact on the targeted population is an essential humor skill.

> *When used as a weapon, humor can wound, corrupt, and humiliate. Yet, when used as a tool, humor can establish rapport, educate audiences, and empower people.*
>
> —Jessica McCann

JUST ON THE EDGE: DARK HUMOR

Sarcasm, mockery, and irony can have a purpose, when skillfully used, to cope with stress, challenge beliefs, and criticize the behavior of others without offending. This type of edgy humor does capture attention and can cause reflection and rethinking beliefs. Don and Alleen Nilsen have written *The Encyclopedia of 20th-Century American Humor* (2000), a great resource for humor research. They state that several comedians and humorists have achieved popularity by using ethnic humor and stereotyping—even vulgarity—to win an audience. African American comedians like Richard Pryor, Eddie Murphy, Whoopi Goldberg, and Chris Rock use comedy to tease listeners about their prejudices. Jay Leno and David Letterman use the daily news and politics as the basis for their opening monologues with jokes laced with satire and irony.

Don Nilsen and Aileen Nilsen identifies political correctness as avoiding any language or action that could offend one's political sensibilities. He says that political correctness stunts the many positive opportunities that humor has to offer. It is censorship that bans all stereotyping, ethnic jokes, religious humor, and vulgarity. Censorship from the conservative right says there must not be the use of profanity or jokes about body parts, bodily functions, or religion. Censorship from the liberal left spells out a whole different set of taboos, making gender issues and ethnicity entirely off limits.

Ethnic humor and stereotyping can vary from playful teasing to more hostile humor. The difference between humor intended to seriously wound and purposeful humor used as a skillful tool to facilitate change can be subtle. When trying to decide if humor is appropriate, use the following guideline: even if the intent is not to hurt, if the impact is hurtful, it is not appropriate.

It infuriates me to be wrong when I know I am right.

KIDDING AND TEASING

One day the five-year-old twins were eating breakfast in the kitchen when their grandmother sang a silly song. At the end, she said: "Ben, you have purple teeth, and Tyler, you have green ears!" One of them responded that it was not nice to tease. Obviously their kindergarten teachers were doing a great job of making sure that there was no harmful teasing in their classrooms. A discussion ensued about bad teasing being the kind that hurts a person's feelings and how it's different than fun kidding when someone is trying to make you laugh or

Jest For Fun

Looking for a fundraiser? Have a roast for the administrators in your system. Make sure they understand they will be the recipients of this type of humor.

have a good time with you. This is an example of a discussion about impact versus intent on an elementary level.

Teasing is often used by folks to help others laugh at their own behavior (a fundamental skill). It is a highly developed ability. Remember the impact versus intent rule. If the other person is really able to enjoy the humor then the teasing is okay. It takes careful observation techniques to determine if others are okay with gentle kidding and teasing.

GROUP SURVIVAL HUMOR

Group survival humor emerges from coping with someone who is hostile toward the group or from unwelcome change. Hostile jokes target those in power who have caused difficulty for the group. This group survival humor seems to relieve stress and ease a group sense of loss of control. This humor often strengthens group bonds and further alienates the authority figure. Numerous jokes found on the Internet target people in positions of power.

Doctor Jokes

All of them surgeons, they're highway robbers. Why do you think they wear masks when they work on you?

—Archie Bunker

I told my doctor I had suicidal tendencies. He said that from now on I have to pay in advance.

—Rodney Dangerfield

Employer Jokes

She brings a lot of joy whenever she leaves the room.

If you gave him a penny for his thoughts, you'd get change.

She doesn't have ulcers, but she is a carrier.

He sets low personal standards and constantly fails to achieve them.

Politician Jokes

If ignorance is bliss, then Congress must be paradise.

It's 98 percent of politicians that give the rest a bad name.

The trouble with political jokes is how often they get elected.

Lady Astor once told Winston Churchill, "If you were my husband, I would put poison in your coffee!" Churchill is said to have immediately responded, "If you were my wife, I would drink it."

You know why a banana is like a politician? When he first comes in he is green, then he turns yellow and then he's rotten.

I think Congressmen should wear uniforms like NASCAR drivers so we could identify their corporate sponsors.

LAUGHTER AND TEARS

Comedy is tragedy plus time.

—Carol Burnett

There is a delicate balance between laughter and tears. Can humor be effective when coping with death, sickness, depression, anxiety, and other life challenges? Humor usually emerges during a healthy healing process. Forced laughter or contrived humor is often inappropriate, so great caution must be exercised in using humor during tragic situations. Having said this, humor is a great healer during times of disaster and grief.

At Maple Elementary School in Loves Park, Illinois, a sixth-grade teacher, Andrea Sweet, was diagnosed with cancer and underwent chemotherapy. Her situation was obvious due to her loss of hair and wearing of hats. She encouraged her students to join in her coping strategies by laughing with her. Her room is often permeated with this laughter. When Halloween came she read a story about witches, listing ways that people can identify witches. One of the items was loss of hair. When I first met Andrea, she had just read the book and was laughing that the students were now sure that she was a witch. The principal of the building, Becky Girard, stated that for the school picture, all of the teachers wore hats as a tribute to this teacher who had inspired everyone in the building with her infectious laughter and sense of humor.

A school bus driver in my workshop told me that he tries to get the kids to laugh before they leave his bus, especially the ones who climb onboard with tears or sadness.

Several of my colleagues are hospital clowns who work in programs with kids who are very ill. It is so important to get those kids to laugh. Pain is eased and joy increased when laughter combats life challenges.

> *Life does not cease to be funny when someone dies, anymore than it ceases to be serious when someone laughs.*

> —George Bernard Shaw

SUMMARY

An awareness of humorphobia is necessary to begin to integrate humergy into the workplace climate. The fear factors that impact humorphobia are concerns with time, professionalism, lack of control, inexperience, and being made fun of. These fears contribute to the challenges of administrators trying to integrate humor into the culture.

Resistance to change is often exhibited as humorphobia. Humordoomers are negative folks who sabotage efforts to infuse fun and laughter into the culture. Positive efforts by visionary leaders can assist most in the change process, so staff development focused on creating play, laughter, and fun to optimize learning is an effective tool. However, often bully and victim negativity needs to be confronted by identifying specific behaviors and concerns accompanied by suggestions for improvement. Change for the most dysfunctional individuals might only be achieved through counseling.

Humor is an integral component of living emotional and intellectual lives, at both the individual and organizational level. Humorphobia and humordoomers create a no-fun, restrictive learning environment. These barriers need to be addressed in order to create the positive emotionality and relational trust necessary for optimal learning.

POWERFUL PRACTICE—STRATEGIES FOR LEADERS

- Recognize that effective leadership can jumpstart humordoomer recovery. The fear of using humor stems from the fact that it is not a controlled substance. To practice humor, one has to be willing to let go and enjoy some degree of chaos. Humor requires risk taking. It involves not just acceptance of change but actually searching for the excitement that change generates. A person using humor often seeks the unexpected and reveres uncertainty. As the workplace has become more and more demanding, it has not only inhibited humergy but also has created a hostile environment for humor practice.

- Generate staff discussion on how your organization can cultivate the risk taking required to support humor practice. Some effective strategies might include theme weeks, which can generate creativity among all of the staff, such as Hawaiian Week or Childhood Games Week (hula hoops, jacks, tiddlywinks, checkers, or tic-tac-toe contests), and a Fourth of July in January party.

STUDY GROUP FOCUS

- What can you do when confronted with someone who constantly uses humor to control and manipulate others?
- Give an example of how humor helped you in a crisis situation. How can you intentionally use humor to help you cope with a crisis?
- What strategies do you think would be the most helpful for you in dealing with humordoomers?
- Keep a journal for one week of the type of humor observed on television. Discuss any insights relative to the information found in this chapter.
- Share any strong reactions you had to the information in this chapter. Relate past experiences that illustrate something that triggered this reaction.

CAFÉ CONVERSATIONS

- One of the greatest fears humans have is a dread of being laughed at. Bullies often manipulate others through this fear by threatening with sarcasm and ridicule, and most avoid these people. A discussion question might be: what observations have been made about humor used as a vehicle for bullies?
- Attempts at humor during a crisis situation can be experienced by those immersed in that crisis as insensitive and even hurtful. There is a belief that the use of humor in a crisis will hurt rather than help others. This was well documented during 9/11, when talk show hosts, normally skilled humorists, were painfully uncomfortable in using humor immediately after this tragedy. How have you used humor in a crisis?
- Discuss the impact of negative humor. What impact does the humordoomer have on the culture of a workplace? What are the options for changing the behavior of a humordoomer?

I am not pessimistic, I am optimistically challenged.

5

THE HUMOR WORKOUT: PUMPING UP WITH PRACTICE

My grandmother started walking five miles a day when she was sixty.
She's ninety-five now, and we don't know where the hell she is.

—Ellen DeGeneres

Jest do it. Determination and resolution are all you need to start your humor workout. The actual decision to pump up your humor practice can be similar in scope to the decision to include more physical fitness in your life. This is a powerful choice that can improve your sense of humor and increase your capacity for reaching the joy-flow state. Do not let anything deter you from your goal to have more fun. Let the workout begin!

GATHER BASELINE HUMOR DATA

The first step for your humor workout is an awareness of your current humor practice. What is your sense of humor? There are several resources available for you as you begin your analysis. Some have already been mentioned in previous chapters. Review one or several of these tools to help determine your humor strengths, humor techniques, and humergy needs. The instruments will give you some insights into your preferred humor style and your humor belief system. They are intended to help you assess the condition of your current humor health.

It is advantageous to improve your humor practice beginning with a study of humor styles. Fortunately there is ongoing research on the topic of humor styles. Ed Singer recently completed a study on individual humor style characteristics and the "Big Five" personality traits (Singer, 2010). The purpose of the study was to establish the validity of a new projective test, the Singer Multidimensional Humor Inventory (SMHI). Humor may come more naturally to some individuals; it is nonetheless a learned behavior and can be modified when it impedes well-being.

Singer's (2010) completed research is titled "Individual Humor Style Characteristics and the 'Big Five' Personality Traits." Here is the conclusion from Singer's PowerPoint presentation at the April 2010 AATH conference:

> The relationship between personality and humor style is highly complex. While it is true that humor comes more naturally to some individuals, it is nonetheless a *learned* behavior . . . and thus, like any other, can be modified when it impedes wellbeing. By identifying adaptive and maladaptive humor patterns in individuals, clinicians can help their clients improve their social interactions, alleviate stress, and raise self-esteem. Further study is recommended. (Singer, 2010)

Kim Edwards and Rod Martin (2011) also review the multifaceted personality as it is related to mental health. They say that a sense of humor can be thought of as "a *customary behavior pattern* (e.g., tendency to tell jokes and amuse others, tendency to laugh frequently), an *attitude* (enjoyment of humor), a *coping strategy* (use of humor to cope with stress), an *aesthetic response* (enjoyment of particular forms of humor), or a *skill* (ability to create humor)" (Edwards & Martin, 2011, 197). It is recommended that you start with a self-analysis of personality and humor style before beginning humor practice. Your humor style will have a significant impact on your humor practice. There are numerous tools in this book to assist you with this process.

Assessment Tools

- Appendix 1: Humor Terminology and Categories
- Appendix 2: Humor Styles Inventory
- Appendix 3: Identifying Your Sense of Humor
- Appendix 4: Comedian List
- Appendix 5: Humor Reflections
- Appendix 6: Humor Belief Inventory
- Table 1.1: Developmental Humergy Characteristics of Individuals

Here are a few additional resources that you might want to explore:

- Additional list of famous comedians at http://www.buzzle.com/articles/list-of-famous-comedians.html

- The Humor Styles Questionnaire assesses four dimensions relating to individual differences in uses of humor (Rod A. Martin, Department of Psychology, University of Western Ontario, rmartin@uwo.ca).

The last resource, the Humor Styles Questionnaire by Rod Martin, refers to four dimensions and different uses of humor and is well worth exploring. Martin hypothesizes that there are four main dimensions of humor styles (two healthy or adaptive and two relatively unhealthy and potentially detrimental):

1. *Affiliative humor* is described as a propensity for saying funny things, telling jokes, and making an effort to amuse others to facilitate relationships. This style is affirming of self and others.
2. *Self-enhancing humor* refers to a humorous outlook on life. These folks always seem to see the sunny side of life and are able to use humor to cope.
3. *Aggressive humor*, also described as humordoomer behavior (Morrison, 2008), is used to criticize or control others. It advances oneself at the expense of others.
4. *Self-defeating humor* or self-deprecating humor is making fun of oneself. This can become excessive when used to ingratiate oneself with others or when used to hide underlying negative feelings (Martin, 2007).

Observe Humor Practice

Efforts to become aware of your own humor practices will give you invaluable information. Start with reflections on when and how you play, laugh, and have fun. It may feel awkward at first, but keeping a humor journal is the best way to record what tickles your funny bone. Jot down on a daily basis what you found humorous that day. After a month of making a conscious effort to increase your fun, reread your entries and reflect on your humor practice again. Are you laughing more now? What makes you laugh most often? Is your humor positive or negative in nature?

Humor practice often involves overcoming your own fears of feeling silly or inept. As mentioned in previous chapters, humor requires a certain amount of risk taking. A lot of people practice "safe humor." They feel safe laughing only in the following situations:

- With children
- With animals
- With strangers

- With drugs or alcohol
- With sarcasm or hurtful humor

A review of each of these categories can increase your awareness of your own comfort level with humor practice.

With Children

Many people choose to work with children in their chosen career because being with young people brings joy to their lives. Children allow us to experience the inner child, delighting with their language innocence and honest appraisal of situations. Teachers sharing the innocent word twists of their students will cause others to be doubled over in hysterical laughter. Children invite us to experience humor by looking through their naïve eyes.

> *Teacher: "What do you call someone who keeps talking when people are no longer interested?" Susie: "A teacher!"*

With Animals

The playful antics of pets have been shown to increase the laughter in a household. Pets provide unconditional acceptance and tremendous comfort to their owners. The ability to laugh and find common ground with others through the activity of animals creates bonds that are strengthened through stories and conversation. Several recent articles in the popular press have indicated that animals add to the quality and length of life.

> *My dog can lick anyone!*

With Strangers

Have you ever been on an airplane with a complete stranger and laughed about experiences that you might never be able to relate with family or friends? There is a degree of safety and comfort in talking with people that you know you will never see again. Strangers are great secret keepers. You can tell them anything and may share the bizarre behaviors of your friends and family. This is all done within the safe comfort of the airplane seat or wherever those conversations with strangers occur.

> *Time's fun when you're having flies!*

> —Kermit the Frog

With Drugs or Alcohol

Alcohol or substance abuse is readily accepted by society as an excuse for silly or uninhibited behavior. As detailed in Chapter 2, play is generally not an acceptable outlet for teenagers and adults. People frequently seek approval or permission from peers in order to have fun. Societal language that revolves around drugs and alcohol reflects the perceived need for a substance in order to let go of inhibitions enough to indulge in silly behavior. One often hears the phrase, "I couldn't help it, I was wasted!" or "I can't wait to get bombed!" There is a subtle language revolving around alcohol use that includes a purposeful loss of responsibility for one's actions as a result of excessive imbibing. Alcohol is often seen as a necessary ingredient in order to have fun: "I need a drink!" The underlying societal pressure to drink in order to "loosen up and have fun" leads to questions about this cultural phenomenon: Why do youth and many adults think that a "good time" is associated with getting drunk or binge drinking? Does the extinction of play among young people lead to increased risk of substance usage?

This author has not found anything in the literature about the correlation between alcohol consumption and the extinction of play (as defined in Chapter 2). Binge drinking and partying are viewed by many young adults as the ultimate kind of fun. It is probable that the opportunity during the preteen years for healthy fun with free time for play has essentially been extinguished. The relationship between humorphobia and substance abuse would be an intriguing topic for further research. Is it possible that risk-taking patterns of youth, including substance abuse, are a direct result of the early extinguishing of play and fun? The hope is that this topic will be a focus of future research.

With Sarcasm or Hurtful Humor

Making fun of others, or *aggressive humor*, can become a habit at an early age, and this form of safe humor is readily accepted in many cultures. Ridiculing others is pervasive in the media. Many schools and workplace organizations have implemented programs to teach about bullying behavior because one of the most frequent and accepted forms of humor is cruel teasing and harassment. Laughing at other people can become habitual and indicates unhealthy patterns of behavior. As mentioned in Chapter 4, this form of humor is really not funny and is often malicious and controlling. It is usually practiced by humordoomers, people who are insecure with others who are optimistic and joyful .

When used by comedians or via the web, this type of humor can be incredibly funny. The following quotes are from the *Malcolm Kushner Museum of Humor Newsletter*, June 15, 2011:

- "His ignorance is encyclopedic"—Abba Eban
- "All modern men are descended from wormlike creatures, but it shows more on some people."—Will Cuppy
- "I'm going to memorize your name and throw my head away."—Oscar Levant
- "He can compress the most words into the smallest idea of any man I know."—Abraham Lincoln
- "Nature, not content with denying him the ability to think, has endowed him with the ability to write."—A. E. Housman
- "He has the attention span of a lightning bolt."—Robert Redford

If you practice safe humor, you might want to try expanding your humor experiences. Although there are benefits to several aspects of safe humor, you can benefit from a humor workout that is outside of your comfort zone.

Review Nature and Nurture Elements

Humor involves making the most of what has shaped you as a humorous being. The following personal elements contribute to the nature and nurture of a sense of humor (Figure 5.1):

- Physical characteristics
- Gender
- Culture
- Temperament
- Life experiences: childhood, parenthood, health and aging, and work and career

Let's examine each of the nature and nurture elements.

Physical Characteristics

Most people are not completely happy with their body size, shape, or other characteristics. Each unique physique lends itself to the ability to create humor highlighting a person's individuality. Not too many people have a Lady Gaga or Brad Pitt type of body. Body type gives us a unique opportunity for self-deprecating humor. Several comedians have used this as a starting point for their monologues, including Jay Leno, who takes advantage of his long chin, and Phyllis Diller, who demeans her body type, shape, and hair color. The humor categories of slapstick, pantomime, and impersonation can be phys-

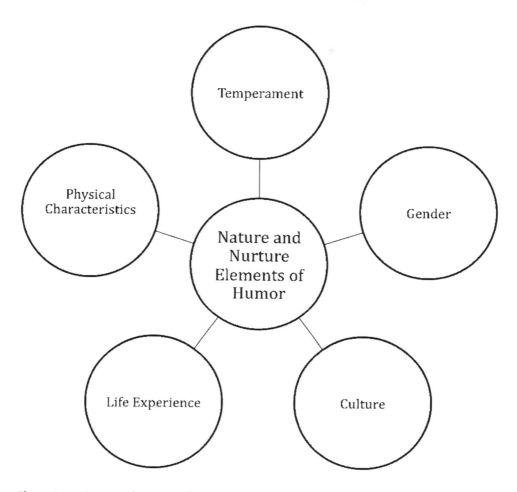

Figure 5.1 Nature and Nurture Elements of Humor

ically demanding and require an athletic build. Clown personas are often de-veloped based on body build and type. This is a favorite quote from Dolly Parton illustrating self-deprecating humor: "I am not offended by all of the dumb blond jokes, because I know I'm not dumb. I also know I'm not blond."

People with disabilities have the unique chance to use their "handicap" as an advantage. Kathy Buckley is a popular comedian who uses her hearing impair-ment as a part of her comedy routines. When I heard her at an AATH confer-ence, she integrated her school experiences as a part of her material. In second grade she was put in a school for retarded children because of her speech and hearing loss. It took nearly a year to diagnose the auditory impairment. After telling this story, her quip is, "And they called me slow?"

Gender

Men and women respond differently to humor. Males score higher than females
on aggressive and self-defeating humor when using the Humor Styles Questionnaire (Martin, 1996). Gender differences are apparent in some of the emerging
research on humor perceptions and usage (Martin, 2007). It has been perceived
as more difficult for women to succeed as comedians and humorists because of
traditional gender roles and expectations.

   Most of us frequently receive the male- or female-bashing jokes that travel the
e-waves and reveal the depth of feelings about gender differences and relationship issues. You may not find jokes about your gender very funny.

- He said, "What have you been doing with all the grocery money I gave
  you?" She said, "Turn sideways and look in the mirror."
- Get a new car for your spouse. It'll be a great trade.
- Sometimes I wake up grumpy, other times I let her sleep.
- I still miss my ex-husband, but my aim will improve.
- A man's got to do what a man's got to do. A woman must do what he can't.
- Don't be sexist. Broads hate that.

   There are two theories to arguing with a woman. Neither works.

   —Will Rogers

Culture

Humor can reflect cultural and ethnic differences. Laughter transcends cultural
boundaries when the humor is universal in nature and part of all human experiences. Many jokes have been targeted toward ethnic groups (Polish jokes) or
religious groups ("Have you heard the one about the minister, the rabbi, and
the priest?"). There are times when stereotypes are used as an advantage to
poke fun at traditional prejudices, for example because it's more acceptable for
an Asian comedian to poke fun at Asian culture than for someone of another
ethnic background to do so. Another example is Ole and Lena stories, which are
frequently told by Norwegians as well as recounted on the *Prairie Home Companion* live radio broadcast, which originates in Minnesota, home of many of
Norwegian descent. This is an example of how a culture pokes fun at itself.

- Ole and Lena went to the Olympics. While he was sitting on a bench, a
  lady turned to Ole and said, "Are you a pole vaulter?" Ole said, "No, I'm
  Norwegian . . . and my name isn't Valter."

- Ole bought Lena a piano for her birthday. A few weeks later, Lars inquired how she was doing with it. "Oh," said Ole, "I persuaded her to svitch to a clarinet." "How come?" asked Lars. "Vell," Ole answered, "because vith a clarinet she can't sing."

There are numerous jokes about "rednecks," including the "Top Ten Etiquette Tips":

1. Never take a beer to a job interview.
2. While ears need to be cleaned regularly, this is a job that should be done in private using one's OWN truck keys.
3. It's considered tacky to take a cooler to church.
4. If you have to vacuum the bed, it is time to change the sheets.
5. Even if you're certain that you are included in the will, it's still rude to drive the U-Haul to the funeral home.
6. If you are the groom, at least rent a tux. A leisure suit with a cummerbund and a clean bowling shirt can create a tacky appearance.
7. Establish with her parents what time she is expected back. Some will say 10:00 p.m. Others might say "Monday." If the latter is the answer, it is the man's responsibility to get her to school on time.
8. A centerpiece for the table should never be anything prepared by a taxidermist.
9. Be assertive. Let her know you're interested: "I've wanted to go out with you since I read that stuff on the bathroom wall two years ago."
10. When approaching a four-way stop, the vehicle with the largest tires does not always have the right of way.

Temperament

In Chapter 2 there is an overview of some of the inherited characteristics that affect humor, including intensity, adaptability, and approachability. Each trait creates a different quality of humor in individuals. These temperamental traits are reflected in common terminology used to describe someone as having a "dry" sense of humor or being a prankster or practical joker. Individual temperament is the underlying basis for humor style, but it also might create a gulf of separation between people who have completely different responses to a joke or story.

Have you ever been laughing hysterically at something and then noticed that no one else is even smiling? Differences in temperament probably contribute to widely diverse humor responses and a clear preference for certain categories of humor (Appendix 1). It behooves us to understand temperament in order to complete the database analysis of humor practice.

When sending out jokes via email (yes, I do), I automatically eliminate some people that I think will not appreciate the joke. One day I tried to figure out why I was eliminating certain people—and I think it has to do with their temperament and humor style. One person always sends me blonde jokes—and she is blonde, so I love that she is laughing at herself! The following joke, "Replacement Windows," is from a blonde:

> Last year I replaced all the windows in my house with that expensive double-pane, energy-efficient kind, and today I got a call from the contractor who installed them. He was complaining that the work had been completed a whole year ago and I still hadn't paid for them. Helllooo, . . . just because I'm blonde doesn't mean that I am automatically stupid. So, I told him just what his fast-talking sales guy had told me last year, that in ONE YEAR these windows would pay for themselves! "Helllooooo? It's been a year!" I told him. There was only silence at the other end of the line, so I finally just hung up. He never called back. I bet he felt like an idiot.

Life Experiences

Life experiences contribute to your humor workout. Each database needs to include your core life experiences (such as parenting, friends, and hobbies), which have enriched your sense of humor. Your humor style has its foundation in your lifelong experiences.

Childhood. My father, Bill Wiltz, enjoyed laughing with others. Whether he encountered friends or strangers, he was laughing within a few minutes, and so were the other people. He didn't really tell jokes but just visibly enjoyed life, often repeating many of the same lines over and over again, always followed by his own hearty laughter. Many of those lines involved gentle inclusion of my mother, Ruth, who admirably tolerated his quips. She was the love of his life, and he was especially delighted when he made her laugh. The laughter experiences from my childhood were a powerful force in my own humor development. Many of the Wiltz clan shared this infectious laugh. Now I am on Facebook with several of the Duncan cousins who share their own unique humor perspectives.

If you experienced a lot of fun, play, and laughter during childhood, your humor style will be different than if you grew up with humorphobia or with an absence of fun and laughter.

The cognitive emotional responses of childhood become part of one's humor being. If lifelong experiences include a tendency to blame others or to feel victimized, helpless, and angry, it will be a challenge to move toward humergy.

Self-awareness and acceptance of all feelings require intensive work, perhaps even therapy. Understanding one's own painful feelings of fear and anger are much more likely to result in a healthy humor workout. This self-analysis requires forgiveness of those who have hurt us as well as a forgiveness of ourselves. Often dark, negative humor emerges from anger when forgiveness has not occurred. Incredible strength is needed to understand one's own emotional reactions because it requires positive emotionality and a high level of self-confidence to make light of feelings of fear or inadequacy. Overcoming fears might be the most difficult part of the humor workout experience. (Some of you might think sit-ups are easier!)

> *I got nothin' against mankind. It's people I can't stand.*
>
> —Archie Bunker

> *There's nothing wrong with revenge—it's the best way to get even!*
>
> —Archie Bunker

Parenthood. During workshop sessions, a teacher (who was not a parent) noticed that jokes about parenting were funnier if you were a parent. If you are not a parent, you will not have the experiences to make these particular humor connections. Here are a few examples of parent humor:

- We childproofed our homes, but they are still getting in.
- If you have a lot of tension and you get a headache, do what it says on the aspirin bottle: "take two aspirin" and "keep away from children!"
- Insanity is heredity! You get it from your children.

Kids often provide unexpected challenges and laughter. This was on the web from an anonymous mother in Texas:

1. A king-size waterbed holds enough water to fill a 2,000-square-foot house 4 inches deep.
2. If you spray hair spray on dust bunnies and run over them with roller blades, they can ignite.
3. A three-year-old's voice is louder than 200 adults in a crowded restaurant.
4. If you hook a dog leash over a ceiling fan, the motor is not strong enough to rotate a 42-pound boy wearing Batman underwear and a Superman cape. It is strong enough, however, if tied to a paint can, to spread paint on all four walls of a 20- by 20-foot room.

5. You should not throw baseballs up when the ceiling fan is on. When using the ceiling fan as a bat, you have to throw the ball up a few times before you get a hit. A ceiling fan can hit a baseball a long way.
6. The glass in windows (even double pane) doesn't stop a baseball hit by a ceiling fan.
7. When you hear the toilet flush and the words "Uh-oh," it's already too late.
8. Brake fluid mixed with Clorox makes smoke, and lots of it.
9. No matter how much Jell-O you put in a swimming pool, you still can't walk on water.
10. Pool filters do not like Jell-O.

Health and aging. Anxiety about the aging process and health are eased when humor is experienced to help us cope with the loss. As age creeps up on us, so does the frequency of jokes about health and the aging process. Humor about getting old will not be nearly as funny to someone in his or her twenties as to those in their fifties.

- When I was younger I wanted a BMW. Now I don't care about the W.
- I asked my wife if old men wear boxers or briefs. She said "Depends!"
- Old age comes at a bad time.
- How you can tell you are getting older:

  - When people tell you that you look great, they add "for your age."
  - Everyone whispers.
  - You forget names, but other people forget they even knew you.

The following are some stories about the aging process

Friendships

Two ladies in their nineties had been friends for many decades. Over the years, they had shared all kinds of activities and adventures. Lately, their activities had been limited to meeting a few times a week to play cards.

One day, they were playing cards when one looked at the other and said, "Now don't get mad at me—I know we've been friends for a long time, but I just can't think of your name! I've thought and thought, but I can't remember it. Please tell me what your name is."

Her friend glared at her for at least three minutes. She just stared and glared at her. Finally she said, "How soon do you need to know?"

Red Lights

Two mature women were out driving in a large car—both could barely see over the dashboard. As they were cruising along, they came to an intersection. The stoplight was red, but they just went on through.

The woman in the passenger seat thought to herself, "I must be losing it. I could have sworn we just went through a red light."

After a few more minutes, they came to another intersection, and the light was red. Again, they went right through. The woman in the passenger seat was almost sure that the light had been red but was really concerned that she was losing it. She was getting nervous.

At the next intersection, sure enough, the light was red and they went on through. So she turned to the other woman and said, "Mildred, did you know that we just ran through three red lights in a row? You could have killed us both!" Mildred turned to her and said, "Oh, crap, am I driving?"

The Benefits of Aging!

Silver in the hair
Gold in the teeth
Crystals in the kidneys
Sugar in the blood
Iron in the arteries
   And
An inexhaustible supply of natural gas

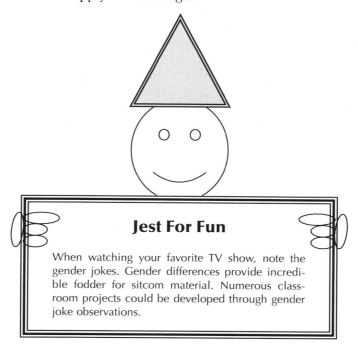

Jest For Fun

When watching your favorite TV show, note the gender jokes. Gender differences provide incredible fodder for sitcom material. Numerous classroom projects could be developed through gender joke observations.

Along with the humor about health and aging, weight is a huge societal concern. The popular press constantly bombards us with the dangers of being overweight. A result is that there are numerous jokes about eating. If weight gain is a worry for you, these may seem funny:

- Eat right, exercise, die anyway.
- I keep trying to lose weight, but it keeps finding me!
- If we are what we eat, I'm cheap, fast, and easy.
- Health nuts are going to feel stupid someday, lying in the hospital dying of nothing.

My favorite quote on exercise has to be the one created by my cousin Beth Duncan-Eller: "Why is it that when I exercise to prevent an early death, I feel like I am going to die?"

Work and career. Career choices greatly influence the connections to humor style. Nurses, police officers, and construction crews all have their own humor workout styles based on the unique events that occur in their work. There is a special sense of humor that middle school teachers possess that seems foreign to many others. Some say these teachers have been warped after working with hormonal creatures for several years. Maybe the field just attracts a certain humor type. Anyway, there are certain jokes that middle school teachers find really funny that may be just slightly humorous to the rest of us.

Hamish Boyd works as a standardized patient and trainer for the faculty of medicine at the University of Calgary. He does many things, including training first- and second-year students on how to do a proper prostate exam—yes, that includes bending over. He shares how he brings humor to this job: "I am at the age where it is recommended that men have their prostate examined yearly. I don't need to worry. I get mine examined a minimum of 26 times a year."

Hamish continues to share how his humor practice impacted not only his professional life but transitioned into his personal life with his wife Fif, who is also a Laughter Yoga leader.

One of the doctor preceptors we work closely with took our Certified Laughter Yoga Leader Training. She requested Laughter Yoga sessions for the first and second year student doctors as part of their module on Alternative and Complementary Medicine. The medical profession is beginning to take laughter seriously! The students were more than ready to laugh with me. The students were stressed. The laughter yoga helped them personally and also has helped them to engage with patients.

One of the patients I role-play is a heart attack case. One would assume that having played a heart attack patient hundreds of times, I would call 911 when I actually had one. Not so.

I had told Fif that I was not feeling well and thus could not attend a soiree with her. I am usually a party pooper, and she assumed that once again I was making excuses. I felt the tingling down my arm, knew I was having a heart attack, and then fell asleep. When I woke up the next morning I told Fif I thought I had had a heart attack. Thinking I was making up more excuses, she was furious and sent me off to the clinic, saying, "Don't tell me you had a heart attack, go check it out." So off I drove to the neighborhood walk-in clinic. Once there, I described my symptoms to the doctor, and she said in a thick Scottish brogue, "Sounds like you had a heart attack, dear." She sent me off to the lab for tests. I was feeling fine and I looked great. Fif was packing up so we could go camping. I had not returned home for 10 minutes and the phone rang. It was the doctor. "You need to get to the hospital immediately, and do not drive." I don't know who was more shocked or grey—Fif or me. Fif, immediately bouncing back, said, "You look great. I'm sure it will be fine." Then it dawned on us, it had been a full moon. Emergency would be packed. Prepping me so we would be seen quickly, Fif cautioned me, "Don't tell them you are feeling fine. Be a bit frail or we'll have to wait for hours." Fif coached me in how to appear sicker so that we could be seen quicker and ultimately hit the road sooner.

Within minutes of arriving I was called up to triage. My doctor called ahead and had sent the paperwork. "How are you feeling, Mr. Boyd?" said the nurse.

"Great!"

Fif promptly kicked me and gave me the hairy eyeball.

After a few more questions, I asked, "Will this take long? I'd like to go out and have a smoke."

In spite of looking and feeling great, within a few minutes, I was on a gurney, IVed, oxygened up, with leads plastered onto my chest to monitor my heart monitor. The attending emergency doctor came in, took one look at me, and there was a moment of recognition. He had been one of the medical students I had trained. "I am assuming that this is not a mock case." We chuckled. He then called in the cardiologist. He took one look at me—again that moment of recognition, "I am assuming this is not a mock case!" Over the course of my stay at the hospital I was not allowed to smoke. This was a bit stressful for someone who has smoked for over 35 years. Peals of laughter poured from my room as we stuffed bendable hospital straws with cotton batten and soaked them with peppermint essential oil for flavour. When the healthcare team was doing rounds we would ask for a light and then pretend to smoke the cigarette.

The heart monitor leads were at best five feet long, and the toilet was my bedside companion, tucked away in a small cupboard right beside the bed. When the little door was opened it folded out like a sideways jack in the box. It was so small that when I sat on it I was afraid the whole cupboard would tip over and pin me to the floor. I could see the headline: "Heart patient crushed by killer commode."

Fif read bad jokes. I told a great joke but she is a bit daft and rarely understood the punch line, which would send us into more reams of laughter.

Hamish and his wife are a great example of how a spouse can support your humor practice!

> If it weren't for laughter, a sense of humor, and taking ourselves lightly, rehabilitation wouldn't have been nearly as much fun or fruitful for me, Fif, and the healthcare team. Fif and I have been laughing since we first met twenty-five years ago. This is key to relationship. We employ it personally and professionally.

Nurses have a unique humor appreciation that is foreign to those of us in other fields. Jokes about catheters, bedpans, and call buttons permeate their humor practice. Mark Clarke is a nurse educator who shares his "moving" sense of humor to introduce the GI system. Here is his description:

> Just completed a day-long course for 40 Nurse Assistants on the GI system—anatomy, physiology, pathophysiology, bias and obesity, gastric bypass, C-difficile, and a little interlude I titled: Tout de Suite. Working in table groups of 4, they were given 20 minutes to come up with all the euphemisms for "flatulence" they could think of. Smartphone use was allowed (very young group on average). Posted all phrases on dry erase board—1 point for each unique term. (Always have to include a cultural component in these classes.) They came up with 50 words in 4 languages. Used 2 repetitions of a musical found on YouTube. Top 2 scoring groups rec'd Whoopie cushions. It was a good day. Also convinced a brand new visiting educator to open her talk with her grandfather's favorite phrase: "A fart is just a turd honking for making the world a better place."

Wonderful examples of nursing humor are found in the free *Journal of Nursing Jocularity* at http://www.journalofnursingjocularity.com/. While you are there, check out the interview, "Go with Your Strengths" (http://www.journalof nursingjocularity.com/2010/05/03go-with-your-strengths-jnj-talks-to-mary -kay-morrison/).

Chances are that you share a common humor perspective with those in your field. See if you can determine which employees would appreciate the following:

- Technology is dominated by those who manage what they do not understand.
- A meeting is an event at which the minutes are kept and the hours are lost.
- The primary function of the design engineer is to make things difficult for the fabricator and impossible for the serviceman.
- Computers are unreliable, but humans are even more unreliable. Any system that depends on human reliability is unreliable.
- Under the most rigorously controlled conditions of pressure, temperature, volume, humidity, and other variables, the organism will do as it darn well pleases.

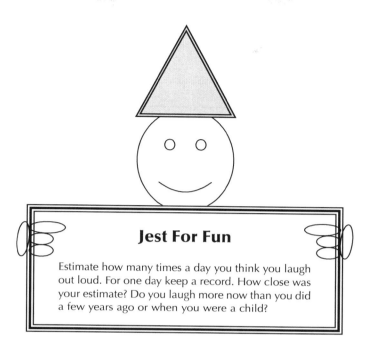

Jest For Fun

Estimate how many times a day you think you laugh out loud. For one day keep a record. How close was your estimate? Do you laugh more now than you did a few years ago or when you were a child?

SEARCH FOR HUMOR TRAINERS AND COACHES

It's important to have the support of others when beginning humor practice. Determine the people in your life who support your optimism and positive energy. Spend increasingly more time with them and limit the time spent with humordoomers. Seek out the funny people in your life and those with whom you laugh. Try a buddy system. Practice your humor with those you trust. Ask your friends to help you in your goal of increasing the laughter in your life—most are very willing to do so, as their laughter meter will also escalate. These laughter friends will last a lifetime.

Human laughter, derived from primate antecedents, becomes heavily "corticalized" and associated to language, fully incorporating in this new form of social grooming as the *social brain* hypothesis has described. Laughter participates on the neuromolecular recompenses of the linguistic virtual grooming, but "augmenting" them, as it now comprises a heavy physical massage (absent in languaging) and a new form of cognitive reward throughout its "automatic" problem-solving minimization. The behavioral consequence of both the real message and the extra endorphin reward is that the laugh signal becomes eagerly looked upon in social interactions—mainly in those where some bonding or positive memory outcome is desirable. The bonds of laughter, probably more robust as more laughter episodes accumulate upon them, will accompany the individual all along his/her life cycle: babies & toddlers, children play, adolescent groups, courtship, parenthood, grandparents, social coalitions, small-talk partners, social sharing of food. . . .

An intriguing consequence associated to the bonding function of laughter is the conveyance of individual "identity." That's what the bonding is about: a shared cortical memory about positive interactions between *specific* individuals. (Edwards & Martin, 2011)

REVIEW YOUR HUMOR WORKOUT FACILITY

Analyze your current environment to see if it will nurture your humor development. A negative environment can make it difficult, if not impossible, for you to succeed. Take a look at the differences between a fear-based culture and a culture of humergy as shown in Table 5.1. You might decide that a new workout facility is the answer. (Yes, you might consider a job change.) A humorphobic environment with assertive humordoomers will severely limit your humor workout. Of course, often it is not possible to make a job change. In that case, here are a few suggestions for you.

- Review all possible adaptations you might make within your work environment.
- Find one or two other people in your organization who can support your humergy.
- Make sure you find stress management techniques that assist you in your life outside of your job.
- Review the research on humor and laughter, and find a time to share the information with your boss or manager. The research on fun increasing productivity is a good start!

Table 5.1   Cultural Indicators of Humergy

Fear-based	Joy-flow
No choice	Opportunities for choice
Quiet atmosphere	Music, conversation, laughter
Criticism	Affirmations
Administrator centered	Service centered
Reward system	Intrinsic motivation
Intense	Reflection
Threatening	Challenging
Low trust/low fun	High trust/lots of fun
Boredom	Engaged
Low energy	Enthusiasm, excitement
Stressful	Challenging
Fearful	Joyful

- Check out blogs and websites that support your work and are positive in nature. Check out Michael Logan's blog, *Ask Mike the Counselor*, and belong to the positive psychology listserv. There is a list of web resources in the references and resources at the end of this book. For an online list, go to the Humor Quest website, also listed in the references. You can find me on Facebook, LinkedIn, and Twitter.

Whenever I feel blue, I just start breathing again.

SET YOUR HUMOR WORKOUT GOALS

There are several aspects of physical fitness training that create a nice analogy for developing a humor workout. These include:

- Strength training
- Flexibility training
- Aerobics
- Stress management
- Cool down

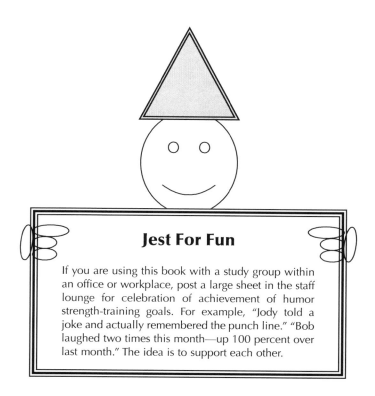

Jest For Fun

If you are using this book with a study group within an office or workplace, post a large sheet in the staff lounge for celebration of achievement of humor strength-training goals. For example, "Jody told a joke and actually remembered the punch line." "Bob laughed two times this month—up 100 percent over last month." The idea is to support each other.

Strength Training

Strength training will enhance the strength of your own humor style and build on your techniques. Here are some practical suggestions.

The ability to laugh at oneself when faced with events beyond one's control, to admit to blunders with humor, and to find humor in all situations is a critical life skill. This skill is one that can be developed at any age; however, since moral and ethical development escalates in the frontal lobe of the preadolescent brain, this seems to be an ideal time to build confidence in one's ability to laugh at mistakes (Sylwester, 2005). This highly developed cognitive ability is a more advanced skill than purposeful clowning and the talent of telling jokes. Since humor proficiency is not universally found in most job training sessions, many of us would welcome a course on humor skill development.

If you are teaching teenagers in any capacity or have the challenging job of parenting a teenager, you have the opportunity to nurture this self-deprecating humor in young folks. Preteen and teenage years are usually a difficult period when most teens laugh at jokes that focus on sex, food, authority figures, and any subject that adults consider off limits. Humor skill development and acquiring positive emotionality are important skills that are neglected in most work with young people.

Numerous middle school teachers already use several techniques to model humor for their students. Rachael is a focused seventh-grade science teacher, but she delights her students with occasional bursts of song or otherwise "goofy" behavior. Allowing teenagers to observe your playfulness will give them the freedom to grow their own humor beings.

The search for absurdity and unusual human behavior (especially in oneself) can initiate healthy self-deprecating amusement. Exaggeration and comparison are good ways to begin to laugh at oneself. Even slight exaggeration can tweak your perception of something and take it from difficult to funny. Some examples of self-deprecation include the following.

Overstatement

This is similar to exaggeration in flexibility training but with a focus on oneself; for example,

- "I used to have an open mind but my brains kept falling out."
- "I keep pressing the control key but it's not giving me any!"
- "To save time, let's agree that I know everything."
- "How about never, is never good for you?"

- "The face is familiar but I can't quite remember my name."
- "I took an IQ test and the results were negative."

Analogy or Comparison

- "Elvis is dead and I'm not feeling too good myself."
- "He or she who laughs last, thinks slowest."
- "Always remember that you are unique, just like everyone else."

There is a difference between being able to poke fun at oneself and the anxious humor that is a result of insecurity. If you feel like a martyr or a victim during this humor workout, the results will not contribute to the positive emotionality and humergy of a healthy humor being.

Politicians who recognize the ability to acknowledge controversial issues and steal the punch of criticism have long used self-deprecating humor. When Ronald Reagan's advanced age was used against him during the 1984 campaign, he quipped, "I will not make age an issue in this campaign. I am not going to exploit, for political purposes, my opponent's youth and inexperience."

> *To those of you who received honors, awards, and distinctions, I say, well done. And to the "C" students, I say you too can be president.*
>
> —George W. Bush accepting an honorary doctorate from his alma mater, Yale University

> *I am Al Gore and I used to be the next president of the United States.*
>
> —Al Gore, in a speech at Bocconi University in Milan after losing his close race with Bush

Students might enjoy researching famous folks who were able to poke fun at themselves. Humor seems to be a popular tool with some politicians campaigning for office. Unfortunately, some political advertisements often poke fun at their opponent in a vicious way.

Flexibility Training

Humor practice requires flexibility and the self-confidence to know you will meet the hurdles of life with optimistic amusement. Stretching is a large part of flexibility. One strategy for mental stretching is exaggeration. Stretch the truth. When difficulties occur in your life, take that challenge and use exaggeration to assist in coping. Laughing at the difficulties helps to ease the experience.

The following jokes work by first suggesting a fairly common image followed by painting a picture that is so exaggerated that it becomes nonsensical.

- "It's been so hot, the trees are whistling for the dogs."
- "Nothing makes a fish bigger than almost being caught."

Bending in new ways and stretching your abilities will increase your humor power. Start with an awareness of your emotional state after a review of your baseline data. The optimal goal is to increase your positive energy and strive for the joy-flow stage as described in Chapter 2. One's emotional state fluctuates as a continual response to the environment and to physical challenges. Healthy living integrates humor as an adaptation to the change process to achieve balance and joy in life.

Aerobics

Practice, practice, practice!

- Look for humor in everything.
- Collect humor books, emails, stories, and jokes.
- Begin with humor that you feel comfortable with and progress to humor that you have not tried before. Send humor via email. Try telling jokes, if you have not done so before, starting with one-liners. Repeat stories that you found funny.
- Practice humergy with difficult people in your life. React to them with positive energy and work toward forgiveness.
- Play every day. Try a hula hoop, Silly Putty, skipping, and chalk pictures on the sidewalk!
- Have intentional fun. Plan for it. Some people like red noses. Others like to share smiles and laughter with unsuspecting people in the grocery store or bank. It is great fun to see the responses, and this is a guarantee that your day will be brighter, too.

Play is one of the attributes that I seek in my aerobic humor practice and is why I enjoy my grandchildren so much. They bring out my capacity for play. This week I have been climbing trees, jumping on the pogo stick, riding bikes, swinging (on swings), using the hula hoop, and playing hide and go seek. It is with purpose and intention that I play, and my grandchildren give me amazing opportunities to do so. Bless them!

According to comedian Steve Allen, a sense of humor is increased by exposure to humorous life experiences. Search for the everyday humor because it's universal. The humor resources such as comedy clubs, light-hearted movies, books, cartoons, and comics are obvious; however, a concerted effort is required to practice the art of exaggeration, to experience silliness, or to choose play. Some people carry props such as puppets or clown noses to wear while trying to spread the humor. This is not a comfort zone of mine, but many find this a creative outlet for bringing humergy to others. Collecting cartoons, puns, and jokes is a common practice. Email has contributed to widespread distribution of comic material. My husband Don delights in receiving and sharing e-jokes. His chuckling lets me know that I will soon be the beneficiary of another joke. Sharing humor builds relationships and strengthens trust.

Practice, practice, practice—here is a riddle; just for practice see if you can come up with some answers to the question. Several possible answers are at the end of this chapter.

> A girl is locked in a room that is empty except for a piano, a wooden table, a saw, and a baseball bat. The door is locked, and there are no windows or other openings. How does she get out?

Stress Management

As mentioned in Chapter 3, humor has been shown to be a stress reliever. The ability to use humor in fear-laden and negative situations reflects an exceptional

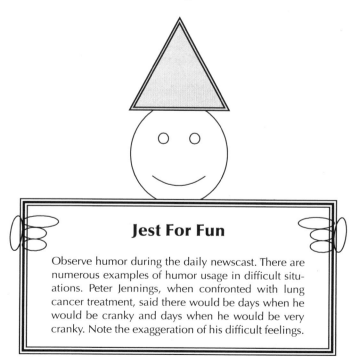

Jest For Fun

Observe humor during the daily newscast. There are numerous examples of humor usage in difficult situations. Peter Jennings, when confronted with lung cancer treatment, said there would be days when he would be cranky and days when he would be very cranky. Note the exaggeration of his difficult feelings.

level of emotional intelligence. Humor can be applied to redirect one's negative energy into a positive form—a highly developed cognitive skill. Recognizing internal frustration and learning to react with humor is beneficial for health. The ability to not only survive but also to thrive in difficult situations is reflected in humergy techniques.

Eat blueberries and salmon, try Zumba, jump rope, dream sweetly, and take care of yourself in all of the recommended ways. Subscribe to online "good news" newsletters like *Live the Joy* by Kelly Epperson, *The Humor Hotline* by Bronwyn Roberts, and *Don't Get Mad, Get Funny* by Leigh Anne Jasheway. Read newspaper columns by humorous writers like Dwayna Covey with New Season Coaching. Continue to search for ways to enhance your sense of humor. Enjoy each morsel of life, and laugh during the times when life is hard to swallow. Humor makes the medicine go down in the most amusing way.

Cool Down

It is possible to have a preconceived notion of one's personal sense of humor. For an individual to expand his or her ability to humergize, it is important to expand an awareness of how to move from the inhibitions of humor toward enjoying humor practice. After you have cooled down, head for the shower: shower yourself with accolades for completing your humor workout. Now is the time to revisit your goals and set new ones. Chat with your coach about your progress. Encourage others in their humor practice.

Jest For Fun

If at first you don't succeed, skydiving isn't for you. Be realistic about your workout goals. Don't be afraid to keep trying new things.

CHECK YOUR JOY-FLOW STATE

Humor is the vehicle that can help us return to the safety net where learning is fun. *Happiness, fun, play, mirth, comedy, joy,* and *jokes* are all terms that have been used to define humor. Humergy is a powerful mind–body connection creating a remarkable feeling of control over one's life. Fully developed characteristics are exhibited by the individual who:

- Consistently chooses a positive response pattern in life. The capacity to do this emerges from a focus on creating an affirmative environment (even a mental one) in which to operate.
- Welcomes challenge in change, incongruity, and uncertainty. Has the confidence to think outside of the box and see numerous possibilities. If a situation does not progress as planned, another option is found.
- Understands that humor is a coping skill that can be a response to change (from small annoyances to a major crisis).
- Purposefully uses laughter to ease pain and realizes that laughter is a sign of healing and health.
- Uses self-deprecating humor as an exaggerated statement of truth with the knack for laughing at one's own mistakes or difficulties.
- Empathizes with other people and is able to "read" the emotions of others. Has the ability to assist others in seeing the humor in difficult situations and elicit laughter in difficult situations. Emotional intelligence operates at full throttle.
- Listens to others and honors their feelings. Recognizes that anger in another person usually mirrors fear.
- Has the ability to use humor in communicating with others. Highly skilled humergists are able to ease the tension in group meetings by promoting laughter at the situation or at themselves.
- Plays frequently and encourages others to do so. Understands that play promotes learning, builds trust, and encourages creativity.
- Finds balance in life. Looks at work as a career and the opportunity to expand personal talents and abilities in the service of others.

SET NEW HUMOR WORKOUT GOALS

You know the routine. Start over again and practice, practice, practice! (See Figure 5.2.)

1. Write your humor practice goals after reviewing Appendix 5, "Humor Reflections"; for example, "laugh more often each day," "try a new form

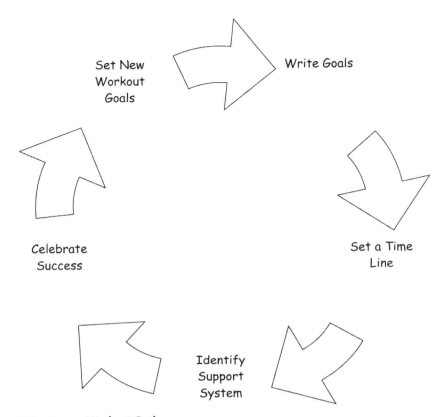

Figure 5.2   Humor Workout Cycle

of play," "tell more funny stories," "find a supportive colleague," "read a funny book," "start a humor mentor program," and so forth.

2. Set a time line. For example, "By the end of the month I will have two coaches in place and will have tried a new form of play each week."

3. Identify your support system. Who have you relied on in the past? Continue the search for colleagues who enjoy humor.

4. Celebrate your success. Party with your coaches and mentors. Be sure to enjoy the success of your humor practice.

5. Set challenging new workout goals. Start over!

Your humor improvement plan will succeed if you initiate a workout time line when you set your goals. Surround yourself with coaches and trainers who will support your humor practice. Celebrate your humor accomplishments. The Humor Styles Inventory (Appendix 2) will assist you in deciding whether to work your frontal lobes, your laughter lines, your funny bone, or all three. Although both nature and nurture contribute to a sense of humor, humergy is a skill that can be learned and practiced. Encourage others to join you in your quest for optimistic emotionality. Remember that humor is a powerful antidote for stress and will add to your quality of life. Also remember that many playful behaviors have been gradually extinguished from most lifestyles and it will take effort and practice to rejuvenate a humor being.

SUMMARY

Everybody can add fun, laughter, and play into their life. Begin with the goal of increasing your humergy level, reducing stress, and bringing your best self to work every day. Your enthusiasm, excitement, and energy are powerful forces that reflect your renewed sense of humor. This humor workout provides benefits that maximize creativity and comprehension by:

- Increasing the ability to take risks and try new things
- Expanding the ability to generate ideas
- Capturing our attention
- Increasing memory storage and retrieval

A consistent humor practice will facilitate communication both with individuals and in groups by:

- Enabling observation of one's own emotional state
- Reflecting the inner spirit of self and others
- Increasing the ability to "read" the emotions of others
- Reducing tension, fear, and anger
- Nurturing trust
- Increasing group energy and positive group dynamics

Your individual humor workout will enhance your life and bring laughter, fun, and joy both to you and to all around you.

POWERFUL PRACTICE—STRATEGIES FOR LEADERS

- Focus on your own sense of humor:

  - Review the developmental stages of humor in Chapter 2 of this book. How did you develop your sense of humor? Reflect on and even write down your own humor history.

- Take one or more of the humor questionnaires found in the appendices. Practice the skills that strengthen the humor style you enjoy. Try different forms of humor at a pace of one a month. Note the reaction of your colleagues.
- Choose a certain time each day to record or journal the times that you laughed. Try to increase your humor stats—frequency and quality of humor recorded.
- Observe the humor of those people in your life that make you jump with joy and who fill your life with humergy. Seek out those individuals and create some zest together.
- Make it a goal in your life to make everyone that you come into contact with laugh or at least smile. Sometimes it is easiest to practice with people you do not know, such as people in the checkout line or in the elevator, clerks, wait staff, or toll booth attendants.

- Play every day. Encourage your colleagues in the art of play.
- Go to the park and swing (you can be a swinger, too!).
- Play an old-fashioned game of Cahoots, Kick the Can, or Hide and Go Seek!
- Get out your hula hoop and see if you can still make it go up and down your body—okay, just around the waist a couple of times!
- Find your old yo-yo. "Walk the dog" or "go around the world."
- Dance and shout to your favorite music. Do an "ants in your pants dance."
- Sing loudly in the car, shower, or—if you're talented—in public.
- Do the Twist, the Mashed Potato, or a country line dance.
- Try something new that's a stretch for you—bungee jumping (pun intended), board games, sports, and artistic endeavors.
- Get on your neighbor's pogo stick.
- Build a tree house and spend time there making funny monkey noises.
- Play with Lincoln Logs or Tinker Toys.
- Perform karaoke with a hair brush!
- Pitch a tent in your back yard. Invite someone over for tent talk.
- Teach the kids in your neighborhood how to play one of your favorite childhood games.
- Experiment with string, kites, magnets, Silly Putty, and bubbles.
- Find old toys at garage sales and reminisce. Share the joys of these toys with anyone who will play with them too.

Note: if you do not know what some of these "play" items refer to, ask your fellow "seasoned" friends and colleagues.

Jest For Fun

Sponsor an "It Takes Balls to Relieve Stress" activity. Give each staff member a different ball (football, baseball, golf ball, bowling ball, etc.). This person pairs with another to brainstorm ways the ball can be used to relieve stress. Each week a different ball activity can be initiated by those staff members.

STUDY GROUP FOCUS

- Take the Humor Styles Inventory (Appendix 2). Use the Informational Websites resources listed at the end of the book. Share your results with the group. Discuss how different humor styles affect communication between colleagues. Small groups of those with similar styles would be intriguing.
- Use your study group as a support system for increasing the humor in your lives. Share humor resources. Do your humor workouts together.
- Choose books on humor (see references and resources section) to read in a book club format. Generate discussions on the book content with different members serving as facilitators.
- Compile a humor "recipe" book as a fundraising effort for your not-for-profit organization.
- Discuss how your temperament impacts your humor practice.
- How are you going to improve your humor practice? What are your goals?
- Form a laughter club; information can be received from Steve Wilson, founder, president, and cheerman of The Bored(tm) World Laughter Tour, Inc. (http://www.WorldLaughterTour.com).

CAFÉ CONVERSATIONS

- Review current literature on the importance of humor and stress management. How is humor practice supported for employees in your environment? Identify your colleagues who exhibit exemplary humor practice.
- How can the talents of these folks be maximized?
- How can there be increased support for a wellness lifestyle that includes humor workouts?

I was going to buy a copy of The Power of Positive Thinking. Then I wondered what the heck kind of good that would do.

Several possible answers to the riddle earlier in this chapter:

A girl is locked in a room that is empty except for a piano, a wooden table, a saw, and a baseball bat. The door is locked and there are no windows or other openings. How does she get out?

- She breaks out with the chicken pox.
- She uses the saw to cut the table in half. Since two halves make a whole, she crawls out through the hole.
- She plays the piano until she finds the right key. Then she unlocks the door and lets herself out.
- She runs around the room until she wears herself out.
- She swings the baseball bat three times. It is three strikes, and she is out.

6

HUMOR AT WORK: STORIES OF COURAGE

*To play at your work and work at your play—realizing that work with-
out meaning is death, and play without effort is pointless.*

—Karyn Buxman, *Amazed and Amused*

Yes, it does take courage to apply humor practice in the workplace. Research is the necessary foundation for both the practice *and* the application of humor in the field. However, the impact of humor practice is seen by those with the courage to actually apply their personal humor practice in their profession or their job. It is frequently a challenge to promote humor practice in the "real" world. In my humor career, I have encountered incredible examples of people from all walks of life who are making an extraordinary difference in the lives of others with the *purposeful* use of humor and laughter.

Convincing most people that humor is important is not an issue. Almost everyone will readily say that they value humor. However, persuading executives, colleagues, and community organizations to actually implement humor practice can be a challenge. Humorphobia, or fear of humor, permeates many of our organizational systems. Many humorists have persisted in their humor practice in spite of some of the obstacles of doing so.

In this chapter, it is my privilege to share remarkable examples of colleagues who have used humor and laughter to make a difference not only in their own lives but also in the lives of countless others. Many of these remarkable humorists are active members of AATH, and all are trusted colleagues and friends who purposefully use humor in their careers and in their lives. Several have been participating in the AATH Humor Academy graduate and certificate program at Portland State University. These exemplary humorists were invited to share their stories because their humergy will inspire others to find creative ways to incorporate humor into various workplace settings. Their contact information is in Appendix 9.

FACILITATING MILITARY TRANSITIONS

> *Nothing great is ever accomplished without an element of risk. There are no guarantees . . . LEAD BOLDLY!*
>
> —Chip Lutz, AATH president

Chip Lutz is a trusted friend and fellow alumnus of Northern Illinois University—go Huskies! Since cochairing its annual conference in 2008, Lutz has been an active and influential member within AATH. He currently serves as the president of this remarkable organization as well as an instructor for the Humor Academy. Here, Lutz describes his experiences with the Department of Defense Yellow Ribbon Program.

Since September 11, 2001, the armed forces of the United States have experienced an operational tempo unlike any they've ever experienced before, which includes the continual deployment of reserve employees. Personnel of the reserve forces have been deployed, redeployed, and (sometimes) multi-deployed in support of U.S. operations worldwide. This takes a toll on the service member, the family, the extended family, and the communities that support them. Reintegrating into a family and going from deployment back into the community can be a difficult task. The Department of Defense has recognized this and has put together a program, the Yellow Ribbon Program, to try and give service members and their families the tools they need to get back to nonmilitary life.

As a speaker with this program, I work with all branches of the military. I speak on stress, anger, transition issues, and (pretty much) whatever they need. I'm not a mental health professional, but I do understand the issues we deal with—both as a retired service member and as a service member's spouse. In March of 2003, I became a single parent of four children (ages 10 and under) when my wife (a Navy reservist) deployed overseas in support of Operation Noble Eagle.

In my presentations, I use a lot of humor. One reason is that it opens up what can be a hard crowd to the possibility of learning. It helps with our connection and with the facilitation of ideas and experiences between people. One program in particular that I do is about using humor to deal with stress. This program is the most popular program I provide, not only because it gets people laughing, but because it helps them refer back to many of their own funny experiences and share them. People always approach me after the program sharing their own stories of laughter and how it helped them transcend tragedy. I think that's key. Stories help us learn, transform, and see things from a different perspective—not only for the people that share them but for others that hear them as well.

I recently received an email from a Navy commander who had been in a program of mine three years ago, and he stated that, at that time, he was not ready to "hear" me. But, after time, he was able to use the skills that we had discussed about using humor and attitude. He was able to deal with stress and stay positive in his efforts to change a terrible situation he had faced due to his deployment experiences.

In the end, we impact all of our futures as military personnel. Our military workers sacrifice so very much to ensure the freedoms that many take for granted; they should not have to sacrifice their ability to laugh as well.

Chip Lutz
President, Covenant Leadership; speaker; author; retired Navy officer

SHARING MILITARY REFLECTIONS

Another exceptional member of AATH is Linda MacNeal, who also works with the military Yellow Ribbon Program. She is an AATH Humor Academy advisor and has served on AATH conference planning for many years. Linda shares her reflections on her personal preparation for a presentation memorializing the 10th anniversary of 9/11.

In the past my messages have centered on humor principles and techniques and how you can develop these new habits to help you remain resilient and light-hearted. I usually jump right into the subject as I am usually either the kick-off speaker to set an energetic tone for the day or I am used to wake them up after the audience has been a bit bored through many mandatory briefings.

However, this time, things are different. On September 11th, at 8:46, the event participants (as well as many across the U.S.) will observe silence in honor of the 9/11 tragedy. I am the kick-off speaker right after that. Sooooo . . . I can't just jump up and launch into my peppy, humorous message, I need to transition slowly from the properly somber moment into humor.

I've spent the last two days in study mode, reading all that has been written on the subject of humor or comedy in September and October 2001. It's fascinating! I have been reading about what went on on late night TV with the comic hosts as well as Mayor Giuliani appearing on *Saturday Night Live*. I don't know if you know (I sure didn't) that the publication *The Onion* played a role also in the road back to normalcy, as did many other factors.

I've finally completed my preparations and have decided on a way to get from somber to silly. It was a fabulous exercise to help me evaluate how I regard and use my humor outlook as a constant companion.

Linda MacNeal
Speaker; owner, Humor Solutions; Humor Academy advisor

CARING FOR SENIOR CITIZENS

Hamish Boyd and his wife Fif Fernandes have been doing laughter workshops in Canada in a variety of settings for several years. They are active members of the Humor Academy in AATH. Hamish describes an amusing instance where they invited the participants in a senior retirement home to try "sexy laughter."

We started by volunteering at her mother's retirement home on Sunday mornings with fourteen septo-, octo-, and nonagenarian ladies, most of them in wheelchairs. After the second Sunday, one of the ladies wheeled up to me and whispered surreptitiously in my ear, "This is better than church!" Another of the ladies would continuously pipe up during the session, saying, "You two deserve a medal." When we asked, "What do you love?" with eyelids fluttering, one ninety-four-year-old with a sultry, deep voice would invariably and emphatically state, "Men!"

Some ladies were shy and others rather feisty. Nevertheless, they would all purse their lips, roll their shoulders and toss their hair, and each in her own unique way launch into her own version of sexy laughter. Within weeks of doing the Laughter Yoga, their range of motion improved dramatically, pains decreased, they felt a greater sense of community, and in one lady's case her blood pressure was reduced by 20 mm Hg, which brought it into acceptable range. The laughter, breath work, visualization, and rhythm aided them in recalling and reminiscing their carefree younger years.

Hamish Boyd
Playwright, actor

Fif Fernandes
Therapeutic clown, Calgary Hospital; speaker; Laughter Yoga leader

CARING FOR AGING POPULATIONS

Assisting others in "aging well" has long been a passion of Kathy Laurenhue and is exemplified in her business, Wiser Now. Her newsletter and website provide invaluable information for caregivers and folks working with people with dementia. Brain games and fun strategies are included in her extensive resources. Her work with Alzheimer's patients is of special interest to all who have experienced family members with this dreaded disease.

A lot of my work has been in the field of Alzheimer's disease, and the first story I ever wrote was "What to Do When Your Mother Blows Her Nose in the White Bread." Someone wrote back to me to suggest the title was demeaning to people with dementia, but the story content was the exact opposite: how to maintain a person's dignity when she makes an obvious faux pas. The story was based on a real incident with a friend's mother who was part of an adult day program that made sandwiches for a soup kitchen. When her nose started to run, she grabbed the first item she saw resembling a handkerchief and blew. The program leader took the slice of bread from her, threw it out, helped the woman to wash her hands, gave her some fresh tissues for her pocket, and went on as if nothing happened. My friend and I definitely had a good laugh over the incident, but only when we were far removed from her mother.

When you are working with people with Alzheimer's disease or other forms of dementia it's easy to shame and embarrass them. They are always on guard against making mistakes and will refuse to do many things that might expose their growing incompetence in completing ordinary tasks. In any situation, it's important to "laugh with" rather than "laugh at" a person, but people with dementia, especially in the early to middle stages when they are aware of their losses, seem especially vulnerable. At the same time, one of the amazing gifts of Alzheimer's disease is that one's sense of humor—and ability to smile and enjoy—is among the last things that is lost.

We often talk about humor in terms of light—lightening the mood or atmosphere, making light of a mistake. That's exactly what the program director did in the case of my friend's mother, but one needn't walk on eggshells around people with dementia. It's important to encourage laughter and even joke-telling. One of my favorite stories was told by Virginia Bell. She is the founder of a long-running day center for people with dementia. One day, during a discussion of shells and other beach treasures that were being passed around the group, she said, "I wonder how sand dollars multiply." Without missing a beat, one of the participants responded, "They give birth to baby dimes."

Kathy Laurenhue
CEO, Wiser Now; trainer; author

CHANGING PERSPECTIVES, BRINGING JOY

Kelly Epperson is the current editor of the AATH Humor Connection and writes a free weekly "Live the Joy" newsletter. She is the author of numerous books and is a sought-after speaker. She founded the first Happiness Club in Illinois, providing lively and supportive free programs for members. Her Joy Beyond Your Dreams programs are effective for people dealing with life changes.

As a writer and inspirational speaker, I give keynotes, programs, and trainings to a wide variety of groups. Humor is always infused into my material no matter if the audience is a cancer support group, nurses, teachers, customer service professionals, seniors at the retirement home, or seniors in high school.

I use funny photos, quotes, headlines, and stories. A little bit of laughter can open the heart and open the mind. Most importantly, humor gives hope. Every person has a different situation and circumstance, yet the power of humor gives an improved outlook for the future. They feel uplifted and empowered.

After one breakfast meeting, a gal stated that she was off to work and no longer felt the chip on her shoulder. She had been angry with a coworker from the day before, had stewed all night, and woke up with an axe to grind. She now had a changed perspective and would not confront her colleague as she had planned.

Kelly Epperson
Author, speaker, joy giver

WRITING FUNNY

Not only does Dwayna Covey work at a college and serve as a columnist for The Bridge Weekly *serving New Hampshire and Vermont, she also provides weekly laughter sessions in her community. Dwayna serves as an advisor for the AATH Humor Academy and volunteers on the AATH conference planning committee.*

During the last night of my stay in California for the 2010 AATH Conference (my first AATH conference) I began to put into place the steps to retain my newly discovered knowledge as well as how to share it with friends, colleagues, family, and clients. Step one—I had just put my weekly column, "A Dose of Dwayna," (published in *The Bridge Weekly* newspaper, http://www.thebridge weekly.com) to bed, which replayed my conference experience and how humor and laughter are such important positive components in our lives. I have set up two Laughter Clubs; one is held at my workplace—a large academic medical center. The second is scheduled to begin at the local high schools—a free event for community members. It is essential to note that research is taking its place in the forefront and leading the way!

Dwayna Covey,
Counselor, educator, life coach

PLAYING IN THE BUSINESS WORLD

Business applications of play and fun are the focus of Leslie Yerkes's work with Catalyst Consulting. She has researched companies that find fun and has looked at their productivity levels. She has recorded this information in her book, Fun Works. *Her insights about fun as a sign of organizational trust are the foundation for many humor studies. She is the author of numerous books and an amazing speaker and coach. Leslie has been a keynote speaker for AATH, providing wisdom from her years of experience in the business world.*

I know the value of my sense of humor, my lightness in life, and my constant ability to see "the cup half full" in every situation. So strong is this sense of joy, play, and optimism that I have often been accused of being one of those "hokey pokey" kind of people.

This buoyance of mine has carried me far in life. It acts as an attractor. It has helped me to bridge into the unknown, make friends in the company of strangers, diffuse difficult transitions, and bring strength and hope into many serious situations.

I learned it from my family. I grew it stronger while being a foreign exchange student in Australia (the land of good humor). And I intentionally surrounded myself with other joyful individuals who make me laugh and remind me constantly that laughter is my best wellness strategy—and one of my strongest suits.

I have mourned the times in life when stress has deflated my ability to stay afloat with a playful approach. I can be intensely driven and sometimes discover that I have left behind the very important copilot of joy. When I am out of balance, my world tips and my relationships spiral downhill. With one breath, one smile, one laugh, everything comes back into perspective and balance once again.

I have spent the majority of my career observing and studying individuals, groups, and organizations in the context of work. Specifically, I am curious to learn when working relationships and working environments are the most vibrant, productive, and sustainable. In every instance, one of the greatest contributors to organizational well-being is the ability to take the work seriously but to lighten up on life and the process of getting there.

I know that one's humor is not a "nice to have" but a "need to have." It is a choice to rise each day and greet the new beginning with hope, joy, abundance, and laughter. Humor is a countenance and a competency.

My life and my work teach me that humor is positively contagious and contributes to a longer, healthier, and happier existence.

Leslie Yerkes
Speaker, author, management consultant, entrepreneur

SHARING YOUR TOYS

For over thirty years, Adrienne Edmondson worked in human resources and organizational development, including work with three Fortune 500 companies. The heart of her business is motivational coaching, team building, and fun-fusion (bringing humor/fun/mirth to the work environment in a fun and nonharassing way)! Adrienne is the treasurer on the board of AATH and participates in the Humor Academy.

In my work experience I have found that humor has faded from the workplace. One of the reasons is because of HR policy revolving around harassment in the workplace. Because harassment is perceived by the person it is directed toward or even by a person in the general vicinity, if a person views it as harassment, it is harassment. Therefore, the workplace has become off limits for humor/fun/mirthfulness.

The recession has had a significant impact on the workplace. It has created an environment that is less civil, overworked, and afraid. Many employees are feeling as if management does not care about them. They are concerned about their jobs and benefits. Employees have lost their civility due to ever increasing work demands on the job. Companies have learned how to do more and more with less. That is apparent when you look at the number of people who are unemployed. Those who are employed are survivors; they are suffering from employee stress disorder (ESD). They view themselves lucky to have a job. When and if the job market does improve the survivors will be the first out the door to seek greener pastures.

I have found, however, humor is the best solution for defusing hostile situations and creating a creative work environment. I kept a box of toys in my cubical. The toy box included Nerf balls, Nerf paddles, puppets, colorful clay, a paddle ball (a paddle with a ball on a rubber band), hats, funny glasses, and a magnetic dartboard. Some individuals would actually come to my area and play with the toys. Sometimes I would throw the Nerf balls over the cubical walls and get a game going. After a few minutes things would calm down and people would get back to work. What I noticed most about the calm was that people were more invigorated. I could hear the clicking of keyboards and faint phone conversations. That told me people had found new energy to get the job done.

One of the challenges about infusing humor/fun/mirthfulness into the workplace is convincing management that it does have a tangible benefit. Convincing management requires them to understand human behavior and get them to have fun themselves.

Adrienne Edmondson
President and CEO, Edmondson Associates; certified laughter leader

COPING WITH CANCER

On several occasions, I have had the pleasure of hearing Katherine Puckett, who is the national director of mind/body medicine at Cancer Treatment Centers of America (CTCA). As a keynote speaker at the AATH conference for several years, she shares her passion for promoting nontraditional healing treatments for cancer patients. Katherine has long been an advocate of using humor in her work with those patients. The benefits have been astounding.

We lead Laughter Club for our patients and their caregivers. We also offer a mini Laughter Club monthly as part of new employee orientation, which usually really catches people by surprise! Our hospital builds humor and fun into many events (holidays, staff training, contests) to help energize people and to help counteract the potential heaviness of caring for patients with very serious illness.

Most often our patients and families find this to be a welcome distraction from thinking about cancer. One young girl, at the hospital with her mother who had cancer, said, "I never thought about laughing every day, but now I know I can. Like even when I don't feel happy, I can still laugh and feel better." She went on to say she hoped she could find a laughter club near home so she could laugh all the time.

A man attending Laughter Club one day at our hospital asked me quite seriously, with a frown on his face, "Do we *have* to laugh?" I said, "No, but you may not be able to help it once we get going." He ended up being one of the most active participants, and when I saw him in the hallway the next week, he greeted me with laughter!

Katherine Puckett
Cancer Treatment Centers of America;
National director of mind/body medicine, CTCA

INFUSING COMEDY

People naturally expect that folks will infuse humor into comedy routines. So did you hear the one about three different comedians who had powerful messages for three different AATH conferences? Judy Carter is a professional comedian and a comedy coach. She thrives on sharing positive energy and optimism with aspiring comedians through her business, Comedy Workshop Productions. She teaches others to be funny! She says, "Had a poignant moment at women's event in Detroit, MI. I love making people laugh. Is it weird that I get more satisfaction making them cry?" Laughter and tears are closely related, and Judy realizes the importance of using humor to decrease stress and increase productivity as she shares her comedy skills in mentoring those entering the field.

Leigh Anne Jasheway calls herself "the accidental comic." She has her masters degree in public health and has presented to numerous conferences on using humor to relieve stress. Her newsletters and books have been an inspiration to many in our field. She has generously shared her humor styles inventory for your use; it can be found in Appendix 2 of this book.

Gina Barreca was an AATH keynote presenter for the 2011 AATH conference. Her monolog about trying on swimsuits was hysterical. By day Gina is a professor at the University of Connecticut–Storrs. Gina is also a gifted columnist writing on humor and feminism. Her books are incredibly funny and fun! I observed her warmth and nurturing nature with several who are entering the field of comedy and humor research.

These female comedians have all contributed to the idea that women can be funny and that comedians can come from all backgrounds. Check out their websites and information and try to throw a little comedy into your daily routine!

Judy Carter
Author, speaker

Leigh Anne Jasheway
Author, speaker

Gina Barreca
Professor, author, speaker

COUNSELING APPLICATIONS

Humor is an important strategy that Chris Balmer uses in counseling clients. His mission includes inviting others to embrace the power and joy of humor. Balmer does workshops on the value of humor, presenting to groups in education, business, social services, and health fields. Chris is a long-time member of AATH and was a speaker at the 2010 conference.

Humor is useful in the assessment, intervention, and support phases of my counseling work. When exploring a client's issues I always probe where, how, and with whom they involve themselves in any positive or uplifting experiences. I quickly learn where they are out of balance and learn clues about what activities they are inclined to be open to adopting.

When I am intervening to help change a nonfunctional behavior or pattern, we cocreate ways they can do things that will engage them in positive emotional experiences like joy, pleasure, and optimism. This often involves increasing their exposure to humor and laughter as we redirect their mental focus away from problem negative-focused expectations and experiences and toward more positive, empowering experiences and more satisfying emotional self-management.

One client experiencing anxiety and depression was particularly stuck in a pattern of worrying and "catastrophizing," which did not allow any room for even believing that her life could improve in the area she held out slim hope for. She couldn't tell me any examples of positive activities she enjoyed and had pretty much given up any hope of changing her life. The intervention I used was to get her to imagine the situation getting even worse and describing to me the most absurd, bizarre, and humorous turns of events as she exaggerated the various negative consequences to a most extreme outcome.

When she realized that the outcome she conjured up was totally unrealistic, she laughed and said: "I can see that worrying about this is really a waste of time . . . the worst that I imagine is unlikely to ever happen." That seemed to bring a slight perspective shift that allowed her to see how her worst-case expectations (and the habit she had developed around this) was a big part of her problem. She was able to redirect her focus of attention to the positives in her life circumstances and how much better she felt when she noticed them and began reviewing her days from a new positive mind set. As time passed she became more accomplished at doing this and became more depression resilient in the process.

Chris Balmer
Counselor, professor, researcher, administrator

OVERCOMING PERSONAL CHALLENGES

Lois McElravy is a dynamite motivational speaker who speaks about her challenges as a result of a severe brain injury from an automobile accident. Before the accident Lois was an independent contractor and sales representative for fifteen companies in twenty retail stores. The accident completely turned her life upside down. Lois has been a speaker for AATH and is a member of the Humor Academy. She describes her continuing journey of using humor to cope with her health challenges.

Hanging on with humor and learning to laugh in the midst of trying times rescued me from the distress and despair of adjusting to an abrupt life change caused by a brain injury and initiated my recovery.

At first it felt impossible that I would ever be able to laugh or feel happy again. My husband didn't know how to help me, but he knew how to make me laugh. When I laughed, something magical happened. For that brief moment, I forgot my problems and felt a glimmer of hope.

Motivated by my husband and mother, I tried to see the funny side of brain injury, but life didn't feel funny. Surrounded by chaos and confusion, I initially used hostile humor to express my frustration and release anger. Suffering from an identity crisis and shattered self-worth, I used putdown humor to express the self-loathing I felt about my "new self." Eventually I learned how to use coping humor to let go of my sadness, grieve my losses, and accept my new reality. When I needed to take a time-out from my life, humor provided my escape.

I noticed when something went wrong and I got stressed out, my ability to figure things out declined and people got uncomfortable or felt bad for me. But if I handled difficulties with a light-hearted approach, my ability to figure things out improved and people relaxed. Over time, I learned to poke fun at my flaws and blunders without putting myself down and became a master at using self-effacing humor to silence my inner critic and grow my self-confidence.

After participating in a brain injury documentary in 2005 and learning how prevalent coping humor was among brain injury survivors, I became intrigued with studying humor. In 2006, I began teaching humor workshops, which were frequently booked as conference break-outs along with my keynote speech. Averaging twenty events a year, I motivate, inspire, and entertain international audiences with personal stories that impart a heartfelt message of perseverance and hope and equip people with humor strategies they can use to cope with the unpredictable swift pace of their life.

My humor specialty is "survival humor," and my sense of humor turns darker as my frustration builds and my patience shrivels. Props are one of the humor strategies I regularly use to remind myself to lighten up and help me tame the sassy little girl who still lives inside of me. I distribute mini magic wands to others with instructions about how they can activate the magic.

I'm quoted for saying, "When life knocks you down, humor is the magic wand that cushions your fall, lifts you back up and points you in a new direction."

Lois McElravy
Founder, Lessons from Lois; speaker, author

OVERCOMING PHYSICAL CHALLENGES

A recently published book, A Shot in the Arm and a Strong Spirit, *provides a wonderful description of Kris Harty's medical challenges as a lifelong patient. It began with a diagnosis of juvenile rheumatoid arthritis at the age of seven. Living with chronic illness and disability, she now is a popular speaker who describes how humor helped her to survive.*

From the start, especially when speaking to an audience, my sheer physicality can be a barrier to being seen, heard, and accepted. People don't always know what to make of someone who is 4′6″ and walks with a limp and a walking stick! Whether on or off the stage, I immediately try to put others at ease. One way is to encourage a laugh by incorporating my self-description up front: "The Short Chick with the Walking Stick."

Humor is a great dissolver of tension and anxiety. By helping the audience laugh right away, they accept me as "one of them" much quicker, allowing us to move past barriers and toward the reason why we're there. The comical side of things (and there's almost always a comical side) lets us address the pink elephant in the room in a nonthreatening way. My clients love that sensitive subjects can be treated with respect and insight while accompanying comic relief permits all of us to enjoy a much needed release.

I use humor throughout my work and business as a writer and speaker. Sometimes I'll use amusing lines or words that I know from previous experience will resonate with my readers or audience. Sometimes it's something funny that comes to me on the fly. Either way, humor helps break down barriers and pull readers or listeners more deeply into my message of hope, perseverance, and how to "Stick to It—No Matter What!" Sometimes that message is weighty, especially when dealing with examples and stories involving serious medical issues and loss. Humor brings the energy back up and allows for a positive, lighter note that helps us all digest the content before diving back into the meat of the matter.

Kris Harty
Author; speaker; CEO, Strong Spirit Unlimited

EDUCATING TEACHERS AND STUDENTS

Sharon Olds recently completed a fascinating dissertation on how humor is used by administrators in schools. Sharon is a colleague from my job at the KIDS arm of the Regional Office of Education in Boone and Winnebago counties in Illinois. As you can imagine, her school is filled with laughter and joy. I am especially honored that she used the term humergy *to describe her work (Morrison, 2008).*

I recently completed my doctoral research surrounding the topic of humor and its use by female school superintendents or district administrators. Through the use of interviews and observations, I gathered data that described the motivation/rationale behind the use of humor by women in school district leadership roles, qualified the use of humor and developed a hierarchy of strategic uses through an analysis of interview and observation data, described the use of humor in various leadership roles and the relationship between leadership style and humor, described the use of humor as it related to gender, and explained how humor is used throughout all job responsibilities.

How?

A phenomenological study design approach was utilized to analyze the verbatim transcripts and observation notes. With this type of methodology, a researcher recognizes her own perceptions regarding humor and purposefully identifies and brackets out these ideas. This allows a common portrait to emerge based solely on the gathered data.

Transcripts and notes were analyzed and significant statements were identified. These extended statements were simplified into fewer words, called formulated meanings. The formulated meanings were clustered into common strands and five overriding themes arose that were discussed as the primary findings:

Theme 1: The decision to use humor is highly dependent on one's audience and must be strategized.

Theme 2: Humor is usually purposefully strategized and pre-planned with motive.

Theme 3: Humor in a tense, intense, or contentious setting is consciously strategized but spontaneous.

Theme 4: Humor use is variable along the lines of gender and familiarity of relationships while tending to be individualized by personality.

Theme 5: Humor for the self (internal) is socially evaluative and of a different nature than humor for a group (external) which is always strategic.

The final truth of this research seemed to be that all humor is strategic and serves an immediate strategized purpose. While a witty remark may seem spontaneous or off the cuff, it is in reality a quick innate response or quip based on a history of patterned responses and reactions. The strategy is also affected by the calculated characterization of a person or group of people. There are many contradictions that have arisen regarding the strategic nature of the use of humor. In reality, there are no constants that typify the use of humor among a group of female superintendents. There are many thoughts about with whom one feels more comfortable—a female leader may believe that she identifies more with male humor but in reality may tolerate typical male humor only as a method towards acceptance.

A contrast is evident between the use of humor that is self-sustaining and the nature of external humor. Internally sustaining humergy acts as a self-preservation coping tool in the strenuous world of school superintendency.

Sharon Olds
Elementary school principal, researcher, author

COMPILING HUMOR RESOURCES

Don and Alleen Nilsen are the authors of the *Encyclopedia of 20th-Century American Humor,* freely sharing their insights and resources through Power-Point slide shows. They have sent flash drives with their informational Power-Points to folks around the world. They are members of the International Society for Humor Studies (ISHS) and are recently retired professors of English from Arizona State University. Their work includes compiling extensive bibliographies of those in the field of humor. As professors at Arizona State University their work will continue to impact thousands of lives with their dedication to humor research.

INITIATING INTERACTIVE INSTRUCTION

Information about improving college teaching was the project of Tony Trunfio. He designed the Laugh First Project as a way to create "faculty instruction that reinforces silly teaching." Trunfio is a member of AATH and has served as the Humor Connection *editor.*

I created the GOTCHA method of teaching to demonstrate how humor and other fun strategies can animate a stagnant class and make it more interactive.

The Laugh First Project was founded in April 2008 as a way to create "faculty instruction that reinforces silly teaching." Since then, its mission has expanded to "edu-tain" not only professionals but the lives of everyone from children to senior citizens.

Tony Trunfio
Speaker, professor

EDUCATING ONLINE

Enid Schwartz's work on humor is well known in the field. She has authored works that range from children's humor development to surviving cancer through humor. She is a fellow advisor in AATH, and her expertise in the AATH Humor Academy is invaluable. Schwartz is not only an author but also a nurse, a professor, and currently teaches an online course using humor.

As to how I use humor in teaching my online classes, I've actually thought about this to help add to your book. How do I express the incidental humor that occurs? Much of the humor I use comes from working off of someone else's posts. I put lots of :-) on my comments and have been known to use "LOL" when something the student says really tickles me. I also talk about the importance of humor in our nursing practice. I share funny incidents that happen as a means of trying to teach a point, such as my story about developing rapport with a pre-surgery patient who had been tagged as "difficult" by handing him a hospital gown and telling him to put on one of our Paris originals. If I think of anything else, I'll let you know.

I would add about humor in online environments that it is important to be sensitive to the fact that there is no nonverbal clues so presenting something humorous could more likely be misinterpreted, so smiley faces are helpful. There is also a delicate balance between trying to be professional online and being relaxed enough to let play in. Humor is important to help decrease the tension students feel and to build rapport without diminishing the instructor's position. I honestly don't know how I do it. I just try to be me online as well as offline, and I try not to be too distant from my students. I like to tell funny stories that are true, but have a point. I also tend to embellish a little so that humor sneaks in but the story isn't diminished.

Enid Schwartz
Nurse, educator, author, researcher

SURVIVING GRIEF

Fif Fernandes has done remarkable work as a clown at the Calgary Children's Hospital, as described previously. Her work with the children and their families has often had unexpected results.

I was at the Houston Airport on route to Chicago when "Alexander's" dad contacted me requesting Jumpa visit his son. I am on staff working as a therapeutic clown at the Alberta Children's Hospital. The children named me Jumpa (Tibetan for "special, loving friend"), Napi (Blackfoot for "trickster") and Satara (Farsi for "morning starlight"). I journey with kids, families, and staff in emergency, oncology, pediatric, intensive care, and palliative.

I had played with Alex a few days earlier, and things were going well. He had been in remission from cancer. Now his dad was struggling to hold back the tears, "He may not live till the end of the week."

Even if I was to fly back to Calgary, I would not be able to see Alex for a week since this was at the height of H1N1, I had been on a plane, and our hospital adheres to strict infection prevention control.

"May I speak to Alexander?" I quivered as tears silently streamed down. I heard the rustling of the sheets and finally a barely audible, "Hello."

"Hey Dudester, its Jumpa! Wanna laugh?"

"OK."

Have you ever tried to find a private place in an airport? Covering my hand over the mouthpiece of my iPhone, trying not to look or sound conspicuous, I started to laugh like a horse, then a monkey, then drew in a long inhalation and longer exhalation as I smelled polka dotted and striped flowers with Alex. Laughter Yoga. People around me were smiling. Well at least they are not calling 911 to haul me away. In less than two minutes, Alex was exhausted but happy.

"Would you like me to phone you again tomorrow?"

"Sure, yes please."

And thus Alex and I embarked on a beautiful journey of love and laughter. For the next three months we laughed everyday. The two minutes stretched to seventeen. Within three months he was going home on day passes! We eased off on the daily visits and calls. However, all too soon he was back at the hospital; our daily dose of laughter and breathing resumed.

Hamish, my husband and fellow Laughter Yoga leader, and I were enjoying my birthday dinner when my pager went off. It was 10:00 p.m.—Alexander's dad. He was in PICU. The team had tried everything. It was time to allow Alex to go with dignity and peace. Within fifteen minutes I arrived at PICU. Alex's eyes were closed, breathing steady. He looked very peaceful. I knew he knew I was there. As we did with every laughter session we shared, I asked, "Whom should we invite today?"

He always responded, "The Buddhas!" This evening, I responded for him and continued our Laughter Yoga ritual. Once the entire retinue of Buddhas of every color filled the room, he would offer them juice, pizza with black olives and pepperoni—vegetarian, of course!—and chocolate chip cookies. Then we would laugh and breathe. When we were done we would always, always, always share the laughter and joy we had created with everyone in the hospital, the whole world, and all the universes in all the times, including all beings—creatures of the land, sea, sky, and space.

The following evening, Hamish and I had been invited to facilitate a Laughter Session for a Buddhist community. I shared Alex's story and how we would do Laughter Yoga together. At sunset, we laughed him into the Buddhafield. Just at that time Alex passed away peacefully between his mum and dad. In his nine years and five days he shared vast joy and laughter with all who he met.

His parents requested that I be part of his memorial service. They further surprised me by asking me to MC the event. Because of the joy Alexander and I shared with laughter, his parents also wanted me to start the memorial service with Laughter Yoga. The response from the over 300 attendees was nothing short of wonder and joy. Though bittersweet because of the death of a beautiful nine-year-old boy, the Laughter Yoga created a connection between people that allowed for both grief and laughter. Even now, people I don't know who attended the service will approach me and talk about their experience of how the Laughter Yoga helped them to find the joy amidst the profound pain. Even in death, Alexander continues to bring joy and laughter.

Fif Fernandes
Therapeutic clown, Calgary Hospital; speaker; Laughter Yoga leader

Note from Fif Fernandes:
The names have been changed to protect privacy. I have permission from the family to share this story. And I give my permission to Mary Kay Morrison to use this story in this book.

SURVIVING DEATH

When Allen Klein's wife was diagnosed with cancer, there were a few moments when laughter lightened the mood and eased the pain. But those few moments had a profound impact on Klein, who wrote about these experiences in his best-selling book The Healing Power of Humor. *He has authored several other books in which he describes how people can find more joy and laughter in life. Klein is a past president of AATH and has been a frequent keynote speaker.*

In my workshops, I go through the letters L.A.U.G.H. Each stands for something and reminds the audience how to get more laughter in their life and their work. For example,

> L is for Let Go: If you are angry or upset about anything, you can't laugh about it.
> A is for Attitude: I tell people that our attitudes are the crayons that color our world. What color are you choosing?
> U is for You: Only you can let go. Only you can change your attitude.
> G is for Go Do It: Find out what makes you laugh and go for it.
> H is for Humor Eyes and Humor Ears: Open your eyes and ears and look for something to laugh about. It's all around us.

Everyone in my presentations gets a red clown nose to take home.

The stories of how people use these always amaze me. One mother, for example, told me that she wears one when trying to get her kids out of bed on school mornings. It starts the day off on a happy note. And another couple told me they plant clown noses all around the house and put them on as a signal to head off an impending fight. For them, it is like an instant red light to stop what might turn into a heated argument.

I advise people to remember to keep things light. I suggest they either carry around a feather as a reminder to do that or to put on a clown nose when things get stressful and turn those Maalox moments into more mirthful ones.

Allen Klein
Speaker, author

CARING FOR STRESSED HEALTH CARE PROFESSIONALS

Joel Schwartz calls himself "the stress-less shrink!" He retired from being chairman of the Department of Psychiatry at Abington Memorial Hospital and continues his work as an author and speaker. He currently serves on the board of directors of AATH, cochaired the AATH 2010 conference in Orlando, Florida, and works as a Humor Academy advisor.

Health care is stressful for both the professional and the patient. Dealing with life and death on a daily basis without relief will eventually take its toll on the care-givers. Facing a procedure, even a minor one; dealing with an acute or chronic illness; or watching a loved one deteriorate are just a few of the medical and emotional situations that confront patients and families everyday. Although there are many avenues available to help both the patient and the caregivers deal with stress, one of the most underutilized is humor, laughter, mirth, and wit.

For example, a young physician, four days out of medical school and into his internship, finds himself working in the emergency room on July 4th. The atmo-sphere is electric, the situation chaotic, with patients with heart attacks, strokes, broken bones, diabetic shock, automobile accidents, cuts, and sprains. Amidst the turmoil a nurse rushes over to the doctor and informs him that a black widow spider bit the patient in room 5. There were many things the young doctor learned in medical school, but the treatment of black widow spider bites was not one of them. Fortunately there was a shelf of reference books close at hand and in one was the treatment of black widow spider bites. It said the following: If a black widow spider has bitten someone, do the following:

1. Wrap the patient in a warm blanket.
2. Put a tourniquet above the bite.
3. Immerse the area in ice.
4. Rush the patient to the nearest hospital.

The irony of the instructions broke the tension, and the doctor started to laugh. The story spread like wildfire, bringing smiles and laughter to everyone who worked in the ER and helping reduce the tension of the day.

An older woman went to a new gynecologist for her first visit. It was the doctor's custom to joke with his patients, but this woman would have none of it. "Doctor," she proclaimed loudly, "I do not appreciate your humor." The doctor, of course, got quiet and proceeded with the history taking in a serious manner and then asked his nurse to prepare the patient for the examination. Later when he came into the room, the patient said, "Doctor, I hope you weren't offended by what I said to you before." "I wasn't," he replied. "I'm not a doctor." The patient broke out laughing, and the rest of the visit was tension free.

The timing of humor is critical and must wait until the patient or the profes-sional can and is willing to hear it. It should never demean, degrade, or embar-rass the person and should be sensitively politically correct.

Joel Schwartz

Chief of staff, Department of Psychiatry,

Abington Memorial Hospital; speaker; author

CARING FOR STRESSED HOSPITAL PROFESSIONALS

At the age of five Amy Robbins began practicing humor. Later in life as a physician and cardiac anesthesiologist in the Bronx, she had to prepare the sickest patients for surgery. What she found was that the physicians, nurses, students, and technicians needed to care for each other during stressful times, and humor was her path to help with that! She describes her method.

I think a lot of my humor came out in order to "break" tense moments or to "gently" let my surgical colleague know that I might have noticed something in the operative field (from my vantage point at the "north" end of the table) that she/he did not see (or frankly, might have missed). Instead of admonishing . . . humor often worked. That's not to say that there were really, really tense, sometimes very frustrating instances. I've seen some very angry people in the operating room over the course of several decades. But, in the middle of the night during your *ninth month* of pregnancy—when you know that *after* you've pulled your patient away from the edge of the abyss, there's *yet another* urgent patient waiting in the wings and you cannot *possibly* imagine how you'll be able to start another case at 4:30 in the morning after a *ten hour* surgical marathon . . . you've simply *got to* laugh and practically snort the coffee out of your nose when you turn around and three of your male colleagues (an anesthesiologist and two perfusion technologists) have quietly let their O.R. scrub pants drop to the ground, exposing their boxer shorts!

I would've done the exact same thing, but I was wearing a thong.

In another situation Amy instituted a "Bring your cello to work day."

Since I was the only one who played the cello, there were several of those days and no one argued with me. I'd park myself and my cello near the sickest patient who'd been on a mechanical ventilator for the longest period of time. And then I would play something "hemodynamically appropriate." For example, I'd play something adagio (slow) if the patient's heart rate was too fast—or something allegro (fast) if the patient's heart needed speeding up. A therapeutic serenade. Worked nicely most of the time. I was in my fifth year of post-graduate training for goodness sake! Let my medical student do the "scut" work and pick up the x-rays and run and get the lab results and transport patients to CT scan!

Enlisting help from some colleagues, we'd often write song parodies (especially as tributes to the patients who were "in the running" for Longest ICU

Stay With No Discernible Improvement). Bringing in our guitars, these activities were best done after midnight when patients often suffered from "ICU psychosis."

Amy Robbins
Anesthesiologist, Internal Medicine, Critical Care Medicine (ICU)

CLOWNING WITH PATIENTS

Clown noses bring laughter to those lucky enough to be in the path of Deb Hart. Deb has recently traveled to Peru to share her noses and laughter with people in need. In her work with the homeless and with those in pain, Deb Hart is generous with her time and talents. Deb is a long-time member of AATH, serving on the board of directors and volunteering as a Humor Academy advisor. She served as conference chair for many years. She shares her insights on techniques that served her as a nurse.

In the hospital, I often walked around with puppets. If a particular patient seemed or actually expressed that they had no control in their environment or seemed disengaged from their environment I would ask if I could put a puppet on their foot. Always, they moved their foot. I then would laugh. I would call in another nurse or health care worker and say "Look at this. He/she is making the puppet dance" . . . this would make the patient move more. This in turn gave back some element of control to the patient, and then they would be more engaged with the health care worker. Although I never measured "how long" this positive reinforcement lasted, the health care worker and patient would talk many times about "Remember when you made the puppet dance?" and easier and less argumentative compliance to the med regime was talked about and became antidotal evidence.

Deb Hart
Nurse, certified laughter leader, therapeutic clown

LAUGHING FOR LIFE

There are several organizations that promote and provide training for laughter therapy. Several groups provide Laughter Clubs and laughter training. Dr. Steve

Wilson has been in the forefront of the therapeutic laughter movement, providing training to over 5,000 laughter professionals. He explains the programs that he has created as his life work.

In the World Laughter Tour (WLT) model of therapeutic laughter, great care is given to creating a particular psychological environment (humanistic) in which therapeutic laughter activity will take place. In the WLT method, Certified Laughter Leaders (CLLs) expose participants to the therapeutic potential of mirthful laughter through a systematic, repeatable, and educational program. More or less, the fun comes first, last, and if we can manage it, in a manner of speaking, always.

Fun, mirth, attentiveness, support, encouragement, and proper information are the heart of the experience in the laughter therapy circle, along with the invitation to examine and adopt a healthier lifestyle through healthier attitudes. This is done systematically and is quite advantageously repeated until the participant can carry on the process independent of the formal laughter therapy session, with self-education and, perhaps, occasional returns for "booster shots."

Albeit quite fun, the WLT CLL has training, education, and support for creating the environment most likely to engage the participants in corrective emotional experiences. Techniques, including specific attitudes and group leadership, are used by CLLs to help participants be amenable to enthusiastic participation.

The CLL training has three overriding objectives. Successfully completing the basic training course, the CLL will be better able to

- Use information from many sources, including gelotology (laughter science), positive psychology findings, knowledge of ancient practices, and modern clinical, counseling, healthcare, educational, consulting, corporate, and volunteer work.
- Help their clients use life energies to choose and modify their life and work directions and bring mirthful laughter to life.
- Identify emotional and attitudinal factors that improve health and increase happiness and life satisfaction for clients, patients, residents, and students.

Based on the anecdotal evidence provided by more than 6,000 people already trained in laughter therapy, I believe that a well-founded, systematic, humanistic therapeutic laughter program can successfully address concerns of humor/laughter trauma and health and happiness, and bring about improvement in a wide variety of conditions. I eagerly await and encourage the gathering of scientific evidence as well.

Steve Wilson
Psychologist, humor/laughter therapy; CEO, World Laughter Tour

SHARING LAUGHTER YOGA

Dr. Madan Kataria is credited with starting the Laughter Yoga movement in India and has trained many people who are currently conducting laughter sessions all over the world. He was recently featured on the cover of New Yorker *magazine. Laughter Yoga teacher Pat Conklin, a member of AATH, has been trained by Dr. Kataria and shares these thoughts.*

In Orlando, Florida, silliness and play paved the way to a bolder, more fulfilling professional life for a laughter and fitness enthusiast. At age fifty-three, I became a first-time entrepreneur, something I'd never dared to even contemplate before coming across Laughter Yoga in 2009. Although no stranger to reinventing my career when circumstances dictated, I had always sought more conventional (and "serious-minded") employment in my chosen field of biology—working as a researcher in biotech labs, then a personal trainer in a fitness facility, then a grant writer for a large hospital system. For me, laughter was a change agent of a different color, propelling me to found Laughter Yoga Orlando, a business that provides mobile Laughter Yoga, motivational speaking, and laughter life coaching services.

If humor is perceived as risky, imagine how threatening the expression of spontaneous silliness might be to someone whose childhood experience had taught her to be quiet and serious, follow the rules, and fear failure. But Laughter Yoga had quite the opposite effect on me: it provided a safe space for me to lighten up and step outside of myself, play and flex my creative muscles, overcome self-imposed and self-defeating resistance to the new and unknown—and take formerly unthinkable risks.

Just five months after experiencing my first laughter session, I began my adventure into entrepreneurship by earning certifications as a Laughter Yoga Leader and Teacher from Dr. Kataria's School of Laughter Yoga. Within the next fifteen months, I had become the Levity Institute's first certified Laughter Life Coach in Central Florida. As such, I now specialize in lifestyle and weight management coaching—and use coaching practices and laughter exercises in combination to help my clients envision what they want for themselves, break through barriers, and create new possibilities.

Pat Conklin
Certified Laughter Yoga leader and teacher

STANDING UP FOR MENTAL HEALTH

David Granirer is, quite simply, an inspiration. He is the founder of Stand Up for Mental Health. He teaches stand-up comedy to people with mental illness as a way for them to build confidence and to fight public stigma from this disease. His program has found worldwide success as he brings joy and often a career to those suffering from mental illness. David has inspired participants at several AATH conferences as a keynote speaker. His message is a powerful example of how humor can help those most in need.

The process involves a series of classes where I teach them how to write, edit, and perform an act. Once everyone has a 3–5 minute act we go out and perform a debut show.

Clients indicate that taking the class helps them to see humor in their daily life, increases their sense of optimism and hope for the future, and also increases their ability to handle stressful situations in their daily lives. They also say that they are more able to achieve closure on bad things from their past by seeing the humor in them and using this ability to cognitively reframe these situations, that is, from being bad things to great comedy material.

I have used this process to train groups across North America. The format involves using Skype to deliver weekly two-hour classes at the end of which I fly in to perform a showcase with the students.

I got the idea for Stand Up for Mental Health from watching students in my Langara College Stand-Up Comedy Clinic course in Vancouver. Though Stand-Up Comedy Clinic isn't intended as therapy, I've had students overcome long-standing depressions and phobias, not to mention increasing their confidence and self-esteem. There's something incredibly healing about telling a roomful of people exactly who you are and having them laugh and cheer.

David Granirer
Author, speaker, CEO, Stand Up for Mental Health

COMBINING THE MAGIC OF MUSIC AND HUMOR

When it comes to replenishing overextended and underappreciated nurses from around the globe, singing nurse Deb Gauldin believes funny music is the best medicine. Gauldin has realized through her extensive experience that music and laughter transcend language barriers and cultural differences. She has joyfully played her guitar to entertain non-English-speaking nurses in remote areas of Vietnam, China, and Nepal. Gauldin is one of the most charming, energetic, and loving people that I know. She is an active member of the Humor Academy and incoming AATH president. It is an honor to serve on the AATH board of directors with her.

Though she would rather "be funny" than talk about it, Gauldin never misses an opportunity to share science-based research that supports the therapeutic application of both humor and music. She concludes that happy, valued nurses ultimately result in happier and healthier patients, families, and communities in every corner of the world. Without support, Gauldin worries the very nurse she may one day need might exit nursing entirely. With a wink, she reminds nurses they can never really leave the profession. "It's like the mafia," she quips. "You can't get out. You know too much!"

Regardless of where I appear, nurses assume I am there to cheer up patients. The most serious medical practitioners begin to giggle when they realize this guitar-strumming professional humorist has come to celebrate them instead! Though everyone enjoys the laughter, I feel music has an even greater ability to tickle the funny bone and tug at the heartstrings. I have used this effective combination to entertain, educate, and rejuvenate health care audiences for over fifteen years, and I believe the need today is greater than ever.

Nurses continue to experience frustration and disillusionment when they are unable to practice the ideal care they were trained to deliver. They are powerless to change much of what they face each day. A funny lyric or prop reframes stress and helps caregivers focus on what they do accomplish.

Deb Gauldin
Nurse, musician, speaker

FORMING HAPPINESS CLUBS

Kelly Epperson, mentioned above as an author and speaker, also started the first Happiness Club in northern Illinois.

As founder of the Happiness Club of Loves Park, I teach that a bit of whimsy is wise. A bit of playful humor has greatly improved the happiness quotient of members. "Joy Assignments" are taken seriously, and attendees report back with glee and photos of swinging in the park, snow angels in the yard, and putting a touch of humor in the cubicle at work. After another program, a woman was laughing through her tears. "This is the first time I have laughed since my daughter died last year. I think maybe now I can be okay again." A high school boy said, "You're really funny and really smart. I learned a lot." I believe if I was not funny, he would not have listened at all and not learned anything. It is true: humor helps.

Kelly Epperson
Author, speaker, joy giver

DISPENSING MIRTH

Many of the quotes in this book are taken from Nick Hoesl's work titled *Laughter: The Drug of Choice.* As a pharmacist, Hoesl shares that he has poked fun at himself by calling himself a "mirth dispenser" and that he is proud to have received the "Pill of the Year" Award. He says that our five senses are not complete without the sixth sense—which is, of course, our sense of humor. Nick claims that the drug of laughter has not been reviewed by the FDA as either safe or effective, but he advocates the benefits of using humor as the first drug of choice. Nick is a long-time member of AATH and has served on the membership committee.

Nick Hoesl
Author, pharmacist

RESEARCHING PAIN AND CHEMOTHERAPY

Hob Osterlund is one of the few people who infused humor while actually doing the research on humor! Osterlund was a keynote speaker for the 2011 AATH conference. She has worked in a hospital setting in Hawaii for many years. Hear her remarkable story on her website and learn about her research with the YouTube video "Humor Rumor"!

I've used humor as part of clinical practice since nursing school, much to the consternation of my undergrad instructors. Sometime in the early 1980s, laughing with patients went from being a sin to being a strength. I don't know what happened, but you can bet it was something funny.

For the first few years, humor was just part of my natural way of communicating: find absurdity, share a laugh, move on. This was never meant to be disparaging or a detriment to serious conversation; in fact, it was always meant to encourage it. I mean that word literally: to inspire courage.

In 1982 I published my first national article about humor in nursing and was invited to speak at the national Oncology Nursing Society Congress. For the next fifteen years I gave presentations about funny things that happen in hospitals, again emphasizing the absurdity of it all . . . things that nurses are asked to do, things we document in charts, the hospital culture itself, notions that the general public has of health care providers. Nursing invisibility. Expectations of the Deity. Shrinking budgets and the simultaneous demand for the most expensive and high-tech options. Pretending we can keep everyone alive indefinitely.

In 1997 I produced a film of my alter ego, Ivy Push, RN. Performing, writing, and producing comedy allowed me to reach much larger audiences than my one-at-a-time clinical practice in pain and palliative care. I performed Ivy for many large events; in addition, when I was at work at the Queen's Medical Center, Ivy Push could travel as a film. In 2006 I produced *When Ivy Push Comes to Shove*. That same year I launched the "Chuckle Channel" concept at Queen's, using a closed-circuit television channel strictly for uplifting comedy.

From that experience I discovered what it meant to patients to have friendly, funny programming, especially in the middle of the night when they were scared and in pain. The TV was no longer an inanimate object on the wall but a living, breathing relationship, and an intimate one at that. Patients sleep with it, spend the night with it, are naked with it. I was so touched by what I learned that I founded "Health, Humor & Hospitals, Inc.," became a television producer (who knew how to do that?) and took the Chuckle Channel to a new level, offering it by subscription to all hospitals in North America.

Realizing that virtually all previous randomized controlled trials in humor research had studied healthy people who had a painful stimulus imposed upon them, I then—along with a team of astounding professionals—proposed, found funding for, and conducted the COMIC (comedy in chemotherapy) Study, looking at the impact of comedy on the symptoms of cancer and chemotherapy. We found some significantly positive results and look forward to publishing them. I then produced a comedy about comedy research called "Humor Rumor." It can be found on YouTube.com, along with clips of Ivy Push. What have I learned about using humor to maximize learning? That I would not be smart without the ability to laugh, nor the old-dog courage to try new tricks.

Hob Osterlund
Clinical nurse specialist, researcher, author, Chuckle Channel creator

ASSESSING THE IMPACT OF HUMOR

Enid Schwartz, previously mentioned, completed her dissertation on "The Use of Humor in Coping with Breast Cancer." She found that a diagnosis of breast cancer can lead to emotional stress that challenges a person's ability to handle it. However, in her research, women reported that when they were able to use humor, it allowed them to cope by changing perspective and allowing them to distance themselves from the experience for at least a period of time.

Also, in her dissertation, she used a humor assessment that may be beneficial to anyone who might be thinking about doing humor research, trying to assess personal humor, or learning about the humor in the workplace. She generously shared it for this book. You may want to use this as a strategy for working with groups.

Humor Assessment Questions*

1. What importance does humor play in your life?
2. What makes you laugh?
3. Who makes you laugh?
4. Since your illness do you find yourself using humor more, less, or about the same?
5. What is one area of your life to which you would like to add humor?
6. Do you find humor a source of relaxation?
7. What kind of jokes do you like?
8. What does the phrase "laughter is the best medicine" mean to you?
9. What type of humor offends you?
10. What is your favorite sitcom? What is it about that show that makes you laugh?

Enid Schwartz
Author, educator

*Printed with permission (Schwartz, 2006).

RESEARCHING THE ELUSIVE

Ed Singer recently completed research on individual humor style characteristics and the "Big Five" personality traits as mentioned in Chapter 5. He discussed the difficulty of doing this type of research with so many of the variables that come into play (pun intended) with humor studies. A lot of credit goes to the people doing the "hard" research as it is difficult to conduct with so many variables.

Lee Berk from Loma Linda University has made tremendous impact on the field of humor research. He continues to explore the field of mind–body medicine. He continues to look at eustress and the ability of humor to lower the levels of cortisol, increase endorphins, slow heart rate, and reduce blood pressure. His work has made inroads into the mainstream media with appearances on CNN and numerous articles in the mainstream media. He has been a mentor and supporter of AATH for a number of years.

Ed Singer
Researcher

Lee Berk
Researcher, professor, speaker

LEARNING FROM NATIONAL TRAGEDY

David Jacobson had a unique and challenging opportunity when he was manager of the Social Work Department at University Medical Center, Tucson, on January 8, 2011. Congresswoman Gabby Giffords was seriously wounded at a Congress on Your Corner event in northwest Tucson on that day. The lone gunman shot several others at the scene; some were killed, and many were hospitalized.

David's role was to ensure that his department was meeting the psychosocial needs of the victims and families. This included crisis intervention, community resource referrals, preparation for hospital discharge, assistance with postdischarge counseling arrangements, and other needs. David serves on the board of AATH and is a member of the Humor Academy. He gave an awesome presentation at the 2011 AATH conference on using humor in his role during the aftermath of this tragedy. He wrote about his experiences with crisis intervention for this book. A highlight for him was a visit from President Obama and Michelle Obama, who thanked him for his work.

The purpose of using humor post trauma is to give the victims another psychological shield they can use to arm themselves against the posttraumatic stress that is sure to come. Creating humor is more psychologically protective than appreciating another's humor, though appreciation of humor will also help with psychological adjustment. My role in the Tucson tragedy was to help guide people towards generating their own humor. That is the most therapeutically beneficial.

Humor can be used to broach sensitive topics such as trauma and guilt. There are conditions peculiar to each trauma and its circumstances that will contribute to the type of humor used, if it is used at all. There were many instances and interactions where humor would have been very inappropriate.

One way I used humor was as a cognitive behavioral therapy technique. This evidence-based therapy uses cognitive restructuring to identify and change negative thinking patterns. The technique involves altering negative automatic thoughts that occur in anxiety-provoking situations.

One example would be when the victim enters a grocery store in the future. The shooting took place outside a grocery store. The victim going to the store may think, "Oh no, what if there is a gunman in here?" This triggers a stress response, which will prevent the victim from entering the store. Those negative thoughts need to change.

One suggestion may be to help them with finishing the thought in a different direction. "What if there was a gunman in here and he forced us all to form a conga line and dance through the store?" A cognitive reaction would be, "That's silly and odds are I'll never see anything like that." The question to follow may be "What are the odds of being shot twice outside of grocery store on two separate occasions?" The humor helps bring the person back to more rational thinking. There are many examples of how this was used in the weeks following the tragic shooting that space does not allow for here, but that's it in a nutshell. Believe me; I've never been in a nutshell before.

David Jacobson
Social work administrator, speaker, author

BRINGING HAPPINESS TO GROUPS

It has been a joy to connect with and meet speaker, laughter leader, and AATH member Bronwyn Roberts from Australia. Roberts writes a free Happiness Hotline Newsletter *as part of her mission to share laughter throughout Australia. Her Facebook posts delight readers with humor that describes her everyday life. She is an active member of the AATH Humor Academy. More information about Roberts and her work is found in Chapter 7 about her intriguing humor practice with prisoners in the Land Down Under.*

As the Chief Happiness Officer of Australia's leading "Health and Wellbeing through Laughter and Humour" organization I provide a range of flexible workshops and presentations designed to assist individuals and organizations discover the proven and wide ranging benefits of having a little more fun, humor, and laughter in their every day. My clients range from the smallest community groups to the biggest multi-national corporations and include those in the health, education, and even the prison sectors.

Research shows that we learn more effectively when we're having fun, and humor forms the base for everything I do. There's nothing better than getting a group laughing and learning as soon as the program begins; they're immediately engaged and they give me so much humor energy.

People love to feel engaged, to be acknowledged, to feel they are a part of what's going on, that they aren't just there to listen. Audience participation is a big part of my programs (there are even prizes for the best answers or comments shared during our time together). My favorite response is when a client tells me how surprised they were to see everyone participating. Humor is just so engaging. A recent review read, "You had them eating out of the palm of your hand, and this group are normally too distracted to give speakers the time of day." My only marketing tool is "word of mouth" recommendations and a full diary of bookings is the best reaction a presenter can get.

Not everyone agrees with what I have to share so I make sure I have the facts on hand, know the research, can respond effectively and with respect and humor, and that I acknowledge the place even the most difficult humordoomer is in. Dazzle 'em with science and be respectful—it usually works.

The greatest asset I have is the network of the AATH. AATH gives me a chance to learn and grow from some of the best in the laughter and humor fields. Whether it's humor presentation skills or laughter and humor research, there is no better place to be than AATH.

Bronwyn Roberts

Australia Corporate Health Programs, Laughter Yoga leader

SPEAKING OF HUMOR

Kathy Passanisi will make you laugh so hard that you will cry. She is past president of AATH, a keynote speaker at several conferences, and a Life-time Achievement Award winner. Kathy is recipient of the National Speakers Association Council of Peers Award of Excellence (Speaker Hall of Fame). She is an author who is passionate about bringing laughter and joy to others. Her business, New Perspectives, reflects her enthusiasm, as does this commentary that she wrote for this book.

I have been into humor and laughter from the time I was a young kid. I never wanted to be Miss America—I wanted to be Lucille Ball or Carol Burnett. Comedy, humor, and laughter are just built into my nature.

I have been a licensed physical therapist since 1972. In all my years as a clinician, I used humor with my patients, the doctors, families, and staff. It was a great stress reliever as well as team builder. I used to put on a show at Shriners Hospital every year and dress all the doctors as bridesmaids or fairies (big hulking orthopedists). It was the great humanizer for all levels of staff to come together and laugh.

In my role as physical therapist I had to do painful things to kids. In order to get results, I had to hurt them for weeks on end. Making the experience fun and funny was the motivation to keep them coming.

I started my speaking business, New Perspectives, on April Fool's Day, 1987. I have been a professional presenter ever since, working in quality of life issues. Although I speak on "Life Balance," the "Science of Happiness," "Stress Management," "Coping with Change," and "Surviving the Sandwich Generation," I can say that the programs I do involving the therapeutic benefits of laughter, humor, and mirth have been my greatest joy.

I usually work as a keynote speaker. An auditorium with 1,000 people laughing is as good as it gets. But sometimes, it is just me and 50 aerospace engineers or pothole repair crews. I have taught the therapeutic use of humor to rocket scientists, the Department of Defense, the FBI Forensic Crime Lab directors, major medical centers, universities, thousands of health care professionals, educators, the National Institutes of Health, the military, mortgage bankers, attorneys, patient groups, insurance companies, the travel industry, married couples, and cattle vets. The list is endless. My target audience is "adults who are still breathing." My favorite field is women's health (but don't tell my male clients).

In addition to keynoting I also offer breakouts and workshops. I have done some corporate consulting regarding improving morale and service. I've written two books and am a contributing author to a third.

No matter what topic I am speaking on, I use humor and laughter to engage the audience and connect to whatever stressors they are dealing with. Although I never tell jokes from the platform (they probably already heard them—and I can't remember them anyway), I use stories to help me make my points and make sure they are memorable. It puts the audience at ease and helps them let down their barriers. I find they are much more receptive to my advice because they can relate to me. Humor and laughter humanize me and make me seem more approachable to them.

I have had people tell me the most incredible things over the years. Last spring, a woman came up to me with tears in her eyes. I couldn't tell if they were "happy tears" or "sad tears." She said it was a combination of the two because this was the first time she had laughed in two years since her 19-year-old daughter was killed in Iraq. Wow! I worked with people dealing with the aftermath of hurricanes Katrina and Ike, people who have lost homes, people who are really ill, and some who are dying. They all need and want to laugh. It's such a great coping skill.

I have to say, I also use humor with my clients as we work together to plan their events. I want to be a walking advertisement for my product and I want them to enjoy the process. It's great for business.

Kathy Passanisi
Speaker, medical professional, author

MINISTERING WITH GRACE

Susan Sparks writes about her journey in using humor as a minister in her book *Laugh Your Way to Grace.* Susan has a great blog and website. Her story is one of using humor in her ministry and from the pulpit. She is a former lawyer and comedian. She shares her uplifting experiences with her congregations. She has been invited to be the first AATH Humor Academy Commencement speaker. She has been a popular keynote speaker for many organizations including AATH. As shared on her website,

> The theme that runs through my work is humor and healing. I believe laughter is the GPS system for the soul. Humor offers a revolutionary, yet simple, spiritual paradigm: If you can laugh at yourself, you can forgive yourself. And if you can forgive yourself, you can forgive others.

In this personal and funny look at humor as a spiritual practice, Rev. Susan Sparks—an ex-lawyer turned comedian and Baptist minister—presents a convincing case that the power of humor radiates far beyond punch lines.

Susan Sparks
Minister, author, lawyer, comedian

TRANSFORMING LIVES THROUGH THERAPEUTIC CLOWNING

Have you ever met a therapeutic clown while in a hospital setting? Of course you have already met Fif Fernandes (Jumpa), who works with Cheryl Oberg (Sparkles) as a therapeutic clown at Alberta Children's Hospital in Canada. They both are involved with the AATH clowning program. Oberg and Danny Donuts organized the AATH 2011 Clown on Down, a therapeutic clown outreach program. Becky Cortino has also volunteered for this program in AATH and is a caring clown who has worked with Charlie Chaplin's volunteer hospital clowning program. She has written numerous articles about applied humor in the health care setting. All of these folks are serious about bringing the laughter of clowning to those in pain.

Kathy Keaton is "Piccolo the Clown" and a favorite speaker in Texas. In 2003 Kathy started the first Hospital Humor Therapy Program in West Texas. Weekly she delivers her caring and compassionate clowning throughout the halls of San Angelo Community Medical Center. "Piccolo" also makes monthly visits to the Children's Miracle Network children at Shannon Medical Center and often volunteers time for hospice and other nonprofit organizations. Kathy is a member of AATH and of the Humor Academy.

The Therapeutic Clown/Hospital Humor Therapist is a specialty area of clowning, more calm and gentle type of clowning than that of the circus clown or birthday clown most are familiar with. I recently performed my clown presentation "Clowns Cry Too" for eighty-five children at a grief camp near Austin, TX. Each child had lost someone they love—(some were military children from Ft. Hood). Doing activities and sharing with others brings normalcy to their lives. My presentation isn't humorous but a gentle sharing of feelings associated with loss.

I do have a time to be interactive with fun before and after the presentation. "Clowns Cry Too" helps the children view their feelings through the eyes of a clown. They observe we all have sadness in our lives—no matter who we are or what we do. They also learn their feelings are normal and similar. The counselors are able use my examples throughout the week of camping to help the children share and identify their feelings of loss and sadness.

I entertained children at our local rehabilitation camp—it was 105 degrees! The children are all outpatients of the rehabilitation center and swim, paint, fish, and so forth each day for five days. I ride on a hay wagon along with a guitar player and singer. I play my kazoo-za-phone while the children sing familiar songs on their way to the horse barn. I also do magic, sight gags, and improv and just play around with the children while they are waiting to ride horses or pet goats and other baby animals. I've done it since 1980.

Finally, I make regular weekly hospital visitations and a visit to the children's cancer clinic. During my "clown rounds" I discovered the father of one of my favorite cancer patients had been admitted with a heart attack. I was able to entertain him for a change—the family was happy to see me there—like I was an old friend. He has recovered and is doing much better.

Kathy Keaton
Therapeutic clown, humor therapist, author

SUPPORTING WOMEN IN POVERTY

Heather Wandell is founder of Another Way to See It *and provides workshops to "transform the way we see things." She has extensive experience in older-adult day programming and actively pursues the science of mind teachings through the Center for Spiritual Living. AATH has benefitted from her generous volunteer work. She has written several books and articles on humor. Heather is currently living in Abu Dhabi and shares some of her humor and laughter experiences from that country.*

I have found humor to help me through some of the darkest moments of my life. The timely intervention of humor, when I feel like a situation is just unbearable, gives me the strength and courage to carry on. It gives me hope that I will be able to get through it. I have seen it work for others, as well. It doesn't have to be a joke that invites laughter.

Just the other day, I was at the Indonesian Embassy in Abu Dhabi, where there are several Indonesian women living because they were battered by their bosses. They are not able to leave the country because the boss is still holding on to their passports. These women have suffered through some horrible situations and are living in very crowded quarters. They cannot leave the embassy itself until their situation gets sorted out. I was one of a group of four volunteers that day who did some exercises and dance movements with them. The laughter and the smiles that came from us all just having fun together and making silly faces when we couldn't quite get a move right was incredible. We didn't even speak the same language. We were just knowing that life was humorous and fun at that very moment. It appeared that suffering had vanished from that room, at least for the time we spent together.

Heather Wandell
Speaker, author, laughter leader

Humor is universal. Numerous organizations around the world serve others by building playgrounds, clowning, and working in a variety of fields. It has been an invaluable experience to teach students from Brazil, Canada, Venezuela, Mexico, Australia, and the United States in the AATH Humor Academy classes. Teaching workshops in the United States, Canada, Mexico, and Turkey has been a privilege. People around the world are sharing humor research and applications of humor to benefit others. There are cultural differences, of course, and it behooves one to research and understand the folklore of other countries when working with their residents. One of our AATH speakers from China told stories about being punished as a child for having a sense of humor. His mission in attending the AATH conference was to bring humor back to China.

These folks are making a significant difference in the world. You can too!

For you to experience success, it's imperative that you clearly understand and articulate your goals when initiating humor in your place of work. Remember humorphobia and humordoomers do exist. When you focus on the purpose of humor applications, it makes it easier to assist others in the process. Please feel free to incorporate these research-based rationales for why humor can and should be integrated into your living. Here is a quick review of the benefits of humor that were highlighted earlier in this book. Think about how humor can be applied in every career and job situation.

Imagine how you can use humor to:

- Increase productivity
- Create a healthy work environment
- Expand the opportunity for comprehension and memory retention
- Build relationships with colleagues
- Lubricate communication
- Help people cope with life challenges
- Support organizational leadership

The next chapter is devoted to those who serve as leaders in their organizations and in their workplace. It will give additional ideas on ways to implement your humor practice as a facilitator and guide.

Don't be discouraged if your initial attempt at integrating humor feels strange or doesn't go very well. As mentioned throughout this book, many workplace cultures often don't encourage humor initiation and practice. In fact, you may fear being reprimanded for having fun. Because of these obstacles, your organization or place of work might limit the feasibility of initiating humor practice. For instance, if there is a rule against office parties, you probably won't be able

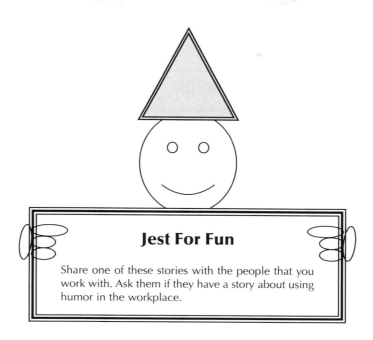

Jest For Fun

Share one of these stories with the people that you work with. Ask them if they have a story about using humor in the workplace.

to organize a Hawaiian day. However, I strongly encourage you to try on your humor persona, be as daring as possible, and play and have some fun.

SUMMARY

Humor is at work everywhere. Thanks to my colleagues for the stories of people using humor in counseling and with trauma victims, at funerals and with the mentally ill, with those who have been abused, and with those who have suffered incredible loss. The courage of those who have been willing to share their humor journeys for this book is inspirational. As you read about these experiences, connect with your courage and bring your spirit of humor, laughter, play, and fun to your world of work. Feel free to use this book as a study guide for your colleagues who also want to create a trust-filled environment that is both productive and fun.

POWERFUL PRACTICE—STRATEGIES FOR LEADERS

- Have an office garage sale in connection with spring cleaning! Make cleaning fun by offering prizes for the oldest item found, the most gross, or the funniest. Give the proceeds to a favorite charity.

- Bumper sticker bombardment: study the language usage of bumper stickers to convey a message. Create vanity bumper stickers for your organization as indicated by your programs or goals.
- Have a theme party, like a cruise to Hawaii, and bring food, music, and games to spice up lunchtime.
- Review the humor stories and share them with your leadership team. Discuss how your organization handles difficult times or crisis. Is humor used? If so, how? What practices could be put in place to encourage more humor and fun?
- When there is a lot of change going on in your workplace, play the Owl Game. Ask the employees to formulate a list of questions about the change. When the question is asked, the entire group hoots: "Whoooooo knows?" This is a great opening for a serious discussion about the changes. Thanks to Jim Crow and the Rockford teachers for this suggestion.

STUDY GROUP FOCUS

- Gather data on the current use of humor in your place of work and the implications for the entire community. Discuss ways to integrate humor in your organization or office. What messages will be given to your colleagues about the integration of humor? What can be done about those who disparage fun and humor?
- How can your humor be used when your organization is faced with change?
- Which humor story did you find the most closely aligned to your current work situation? How can you integrate humor into your workplace?
- Implement a search for the comedians in your organization. Begin by looking for the office clowns. Many comedians began laughing because of the personal difficulties in their lives. How can these people be honored for their creativity? What challenges might they present for administrators?

CAFÉ CONVERSATION

Discussion questions: How can positive emotionality become embedded in your culture? If the leadership in the organization changes, what implications will this have for a focus on humergy? How can positive changes be sustained?

> *I've learned that I still have a lot to learn. . . . I've learned that people will forget what you said, people will forget what you did, but people will never forget how you made them feel.*

> —Maya Angelou

7

LEADERSHIP IS A
FUNNY THING

*If you're riding ahead of the herd, take a look back every now and then
to make sure it's still there.*

—Will Rogers

HUMOR AND LEADERSHIP

As mentioned previously in this book, it is an honor to be the designer and
creator of the Humor Academy graduate and certificate program for
AATH. Level 3 of this program is designated as the leadership module and is
being written in conjunction with writing this book. Through collaboration
with colleagues Karyn Buxman and Chip Lutz, it was realized that there is
scant research on humor in the context of leadership. Both *leadership* and *humor* are terms that are tricky to describe and understand.

My personal experience comes from working with administrative certification
programs for educators in the state of Illinois and from completing my own administrative certificate program in education. The Illinois State Board of Education approved two of my humor classes for administrator academy certification.
I have conducted a variety of staff development workshops on humor for numerous groups of administrators and leaders.

Since the research on humor and leadership is scarce, the opinions here are
often just that—I do know that while the passion for using humor is found all
over the world in all walks of life, it is not usually taught in leadership classes.
I know it was not mentioned in my administration classes. Hopefully this will
change soon as more research becomes available on the benefits of humor and
quality information becomes part of the mainstream media.

One of the most difficult tasks for a leader is to facilitate positive change in the culture of the organization. Most leaders do not consider the purposeful inclusion of humor as a strategy for building their leadership skills. However, as reflected throughout this book, the benefits of using humor have far-reaching results.

Several aspects are explored in this chapter, including a visual framework created and adapted for school administrators (Morrison, 2008). The model depicts how humergy can impact a culture on three levels—context, process, and content—and how the emotions are integrated in each component. Since trust is a crucial ingredient in an optimal workplace culture, it is vital to consider the relationship between humor and trust. Humor practice and service are intertwined; thus there is extensive inclusion of the servant leadership model in this chapter.

> *Don't confuse being a leader with being a comedian. Use humor to lift people up, not to put them down.*
>
> —Mike Myatt

There has been a welcome change in the typical workplace on views about humor. In the past, many have held a negative attitude towards fun, play, and laughter in the organization. Leaders across the world of work are accepting and even embracing the idea that humor and laughter play an important role in productivity and in building a culture of trust. If you look at the benefits of humor as described in the stories in Chapter 6 and as identified throughout this book, there are definite advantages for leaders choosing to increase their humor practice (Hernsath & Yerkes, 2001).

When you enter the world of Pixar, chances are that you will hear laughter. Humor is prominent there and begins with senior management:

Group leaders set the tone. Much like John Lasseter's or Bob Petersen's approach at Pixar, successful humor breaks down the power structures that tend to inhibit tighter social bonds and interactions. This is precisely the type of environment Pixar seeks to create. They have established that, at Pixar, hierarchy and positional status are of less relevance than at most companies. The dominant hierarchical work environment supports the fallacy that the most experienced or senior person in the group will have the answers.

People around Google and other corners of Silicon Valley often refer to this as the HiPPO phenomenon. That is, the highest paid person's opinion (HiPPO) usually dominates how people make decisions inside most organizations. People look to the HiPPO to make decisions. People equate status and money with intelligence and insight, when often there's little correlation. (Sims, 2011)

The leader is the person who brings magic to the moment; it is a matter of behavior. The leader is a person who listens carefully, helps others frame the issue, brings a sense of urgency, and creates confidence in the next steps (Conant & Norgaard, 2011).

LEADERSHIP THEORIES

Just for fun, Google "leadership"! You will find a gazillion books about leadership and, as with all popular topics, there are countless ideas about how to "be a leader." It was enlightening to review the information about systems leadership, architect leaders, visionary guidance, analytic styles, and architectural leaders. There are articles written about different types of leadership according to traits, skills, and styles. Leadership can also be examined by gender, diversity, or culture (Northhouse, 2007).

When it comes to the specific study of humor and leadership, John Morreall has identified three benefits of humor in leadership, which include health, mental flexibility, and smooth social relations (Morreall, 1991). Most who study humor and leadership emphasize the importance of the last benefit that Morreall has identified as that of humor supporting communication and relationship-building skills (Crawford, 1994).

Humor can be designed as a strategic skill that is purposefully used to make change, improve communication, and build relationships. It can be used to contrast incongruent ideas. Stress reduction though humor is another specific strategy that can be used to bring work-related problems under control (Crawford, 1994).

There have been a few military studies (Priest & Swain, 2006), and several people include it in presentations that they provide, but most studies look at leadership style.

LEADERSHIP STYLES

Management is doing things right; leadership is doing the right things.

—Peter F. Drucker

The numerous philosophies and resources that are available on administrative styles do not usually mention humor except in passing, such as leaders keeping or having a sense of humor. However, the significance of relational leadership is woven through most of the books on the topic. The distinction among authoritarian, laissez faire, and participatory/collaborative leadership is a case in point. Most administrators have a combination of these styles with varying degrees of humergy evident.

> *You do not lead by hitting people over the head—that's assault, not leadership.*
>
> —Dwight D. Eisenhower

Authoritarian

This is a controlling and demanding type of management style. These bosses believe in a "convertible" (top-down) style of management based on an organizational chart with rigid rules and regulations. Authoritarian managers are usually very serious about a focus on the bottom line, increasing productivity, and getting the job done efficiently. Humor is often seen as frivolous and a waste of time. Remember that humordoomers equate humor with being nonproductive.

Often, when I do a workshop, participants ask how to survive in an authoritarian type of environment. I am not sure how to answer this question. I have experienced this type of administrator firsthand in several jobs that I have held. I actually quit a job because the management style was so stifling and stressful. Not all people have that option. If you are in an organization that espouses this style, feel free to give your boss a copy of this book, but only if you think he or she has a sense of humor!

> *Tell your boss what you think of him and the truth will set you free.*
>
> —Hoesl, *Laughter: The Drug of Choice*

Laissez Faire

Laissez faire is a lenient and tolerant style of management that is "hands off" in nature. Employees may waste company resources by playing games on the computer or try to avoid work by chatting with others for long periods of time. There may be a lot of laughter but little productivity. This type of administrator may seem to advocate a "fun" work environment, but in reality there is a lack of focus and purpose. Productivity can suffer. The laissez faire boss often thinks it is more important to be a "good ole boy/girl" rather than a leader. There is a big difference between integrating and employing one's sense of humor and spending vast amounts of company time on video games, social networking, and persistently avoiding "getting the job done."

> *Leadership involves finding a parade and getting in front of it.*
>
> —John Naisbitt

Participatory/Collaborative

The highest priority for collaborative leaders is to encourage, support, and enable employees to maximize their full potential and abilities. It begins with viewing those employees as associates and colleagues instead of as subordinates. Teamwork is an integral component of participatory leadership with delegation of responsibility and shared decision making. Humor is integral to this type of workplace. All within the organization take the work seriously and themselves lightly.

LEADERSHIP PHILOSOPHY

> *It's hard to lead a cavalry charge if you think you look funny on a horse.*
>
> —Adlai Stevenson

Servant leadership best describes my own personal philosophy. I think this approach fits well with the idea of using humor to make positive change in the workplace and in organizations. Having worked in numerous job situations and having experienced many leadership styles, I have found that I have been most energized by administrators who were caring, dedicated, and fun!

Caring for persons is the rock upon which a good society is built (Greenleaf, 2002). The basic assumptions for servant leadership have been touted by many leaders in the field, including Ken Blanchard, Steven Covey, Peter M. Senge, and Margaret Wheatley. The tenets are as follows:

- Leaders have a responsibility for followers.
- Leaders have a duty towards society and those who are disadvantaged.
- People who want to assist others do this best by providing caring leadership.

Simply put, the servant leader serves others. This service to others involves multifaceted commitment to supporting others in their efforts to improve. It benefits those who are least advantaged in society.

The following principles of servant leadership are adapted from the Alliance for Servant Leadership at Indiana State University.

- *Transformation* as a vehicle for individual and institutional development
- *Personal growth* as a route to serve others
- *Enabling environments* that empower and encourage service
- *Service* as a primary goal

- *Trusting relationships* as a basic platform for collaboration and service
- *Creating commitment* as a way to collaborative engagement
- *Community building* as a way to create environments in which people can trust each other and work together
- *Nurturing the spirit* as a way to provide joy and fulfillment in purposeful work

Let's take a look at how humor may impact each of these areas.

Transformation

The practice of humor can reduce depression and nourish a healthy mind–body balance, which supports both personal and organizational growth. Humor relieves stress. Humor also supports the ability to be flexible during change. As mentioned previously, humor practice can change the culture of a company and organization. Many organizations and groups struggle with managers who are authoritarian and who usually have a severe case of humorphobia.

Many years ago when I attended my first state board meeting, it quickly became evident that this was a very serious event. Everyone sat in a circle at tables and no one talked. When the administrator began the meeting with announcements, I interrupted and asked if we could at least do introductions since I did not know anyone.

I was crazy enough to add that maybe everyone could tell something fun that they had done recently. You could sense a visible wave of disbelief engulf the room. Maybe they thought that I had asked for a golden goose! The administrator sternly said that we really did not have enough time but we could do quick introductions.

At the end of my years at those meetings with me asking for and encouraging fun, we were at least smiling a bit more and sharing ideas. When I was invited by this same agency to do No Child Left Behind (NCLB) training, I said that I would only if I could make the training "fun!" They reluctantly agreed because they also must have known that I would accomplish the goals that were needed. Our group did have a great time collaborating (we still get together), and we did have an awesome training program. I felt that I was instrumental in the implementation of a beneficial and creative training program that was used extensively to transform ideas about NCLB and train the educators in our state. And it was fun!

> *Gags and practical jokes should only be used when those on the receiving end find them funny.*
>
> —Mike Myatt

Personal Growth

Reflecting on one's humor practice will strengthen leadership skills by reducing stress and improving communication with others. Daily journaling on humor leadership practice will build powerful insights into what kind of humor strategies work in various situations. Initiating humor in leadership involves taking a risk and reflecting on the results. Humor practice is a part of a purposeful routine that can improve personal growth and become a habit (Morrison, 2008).

Humorous leaders find that their ability to use humor often reflects their own personal happiness level. Encouraging personal growth among your employees will be difficult if you are not feeling energized and excited about your work. Your attitude shows. I was just at a family reunion. I had on one of those shirts that said, "Life is good!" One of the relatives had on a shirt that said, "Life is crap!" I'm trying to think of a slogan for my t-shirt for the next reunion. Email me your suggestions!

Enabling Environments

A humor-filled environment is one that recognizes the strengths and talents of the workers. As emphasized throughout this book, humor has the capacity to empower leaders to build a culture of optimism and joy. This will increase productivity, reduce stress, and retain employees. If you are having fun and being productive in your job, you are not likely to do a job search.

Happy people work harder, according to an article in the *New York Times*. Managerial actions and practices can impact employee work conditions and employee perceptions of these conditions, thereby improving key outcomes at the organizational level (Harter, 2010). Lower job satisfaction results in poorer bottom line performance. When people don't care about their jobs or their employers, they don't show up consistently, they produce less, and their work quality suffers.

The research shows that inner work life had a profound impact on workers' creativity, productivity, commitment, and collegiality. Employees are much more likely to have new ideas on days when they feel happier. It does depend on the leadership of the company and does not have to be expensive. Leaders can ensure that people feel engaged and valued (New York Times, 2011).

A lot of humor comes from unconnected thoughts, which is a process similar to the process that is vital for creativity. Studies looking at how humorous interaction between coworkers encourages innovation suggest that keeping workers laughing may jump-start their creative faculties. Humor stimulates the brain's reward center and raises circulating levels of dopamine, the chemical that is linked to motivation (Carter, 2009). Find the creative or fun employees and encourage them.

When I was a counselor at a Girl Scout camp, the director announced to the entire group of campers that I was an expert in toad training. She had organized a competitive toad race for one of the final activities of the camp, and she knew that I was not overly thrilled about handling toads. Of course all of the kids brought their toads to me to ask how they should be trained. I made up some fantastic stories—of course all of them utter nonsense.

For those of you who would like to try a toad race, you create a circle, put all of the toads in the middle, and see which toad makes it to the outside of the circle first. The point here is that the director encouraged my creativity and story telling. She was an expert at getting people to laugh and have fun. I am frequently reminded of that story because I now have several granddaughters who really love toads. Whatever kind of environment you have, you can encourage creativity with your own kind of "toad races."

> A young executive was getting ready to leave the office one evening when he saw the CEO standing in front of the paper shredder with a piece of paper in hand. As the CEO had a confused look on his face, the young executive went over to the CEO to see if he could be of help. The CEO said, "Listen, this is a very sensitive and important document and my secretary has gone for the night. Can you make this thing work?" "Certainly," said the young executive. He turned the machine on, inserted the paper, and pressed the start button. "Excellent, excellent!" said the CEO as his paper disappeared inside the machine. "Now, I just need one copy, please."

Service

Positive humor is generous in nature. What greater service is there than to share fun and laughter with others by bringing joy into their lives? Many organizations exist to ease the pain and suffering in the lives of others. This can be accomplished through smiles, laughter, and the gift of humor. Flourishing organizations can be readily identified through their employees who are joyfully involved in serving others. Several of the AATH Humor Academy participants have shared their outreach as an aspect of their service to others. Bronwyn Roberts from Australia has done laughter workshops for the women and staff at a Victoria-based women's correctional center (women's prison). Roberts sent this lively description of her service to those most in need:

> The prison workshops are organized through the Melbourne City Mission, http://www.melbournecitymission.org.au/, who assist vulnerable individuals, families

and communities and provide assistance to help people avoid or escape disadvantage, economic exclusion and social isolation.

Melbourne City Mission offer a number of support services in the prison sector and one of these services is what is known as the "Return to Work Expo." The expo is available to those due for release within 6 months and those on remand and provides a range of information for the women. Guests include employers, employment counselors, a company that provides corporate clothing for interviews and as a return to work wardrobe and clothing advice, and other relevant speakers. Discussion during the expo includes resume writing, relevant return to work training, searching for work, interview skills and services available to the women prior to and after release. The presentations include whole room presentations and smaller working groups (normally these might be called "break-out" groups—but perhaps not when you're in a prison). Discussion and questions are welcomed and encouraged.

The laughter program was first introduced in 2008 at the expo at the Lodden Prison (medium security) near Castlemaine as a bit of fun. It was so well received by the women and staff that it was decided the laughter should, if possible, be a part of future expos. The laughter leader who ran the Lodden Prison session was invited to run the program at the Dame Phyllis Frost Centre (maximum security) in Deer Park in the outer western suburbs of Melbourne. As this would be more than a 3 hour drive each way for her she chose to refer the organizers to me. Never one to turn an experience down I accepted their offer of petrol money only and discovered that, as I live in the outer eastern suburbs of Melbourne and the session check in time at the prison is 9 am, meaning I would be travelling across the top of Melbourne during peak hour, my travel would be 2.5 hours to get there, but less than 1.5 hours to return.

I developed a laughter program that would focus on self-esteem and presentation skills. The laughter was well received from the start. The women, staff and visitors interacted easily with each other, laughing together and shaking hands, chairs were moved to make more space to move around in, and to everyone's surprise, everyone joined in. There were some women and staff who it was thought might not choose to participate for varying reasons but they too had to give in and at the very least smile and giggle.

The first session was so well received that the program has been included in three return work expos, and I have been told, due to the popularity of the laughter and the effect it has on the remainder of the day, it will, funding permitting, continue to be included. Simple laughter movements were introduced during the laughter, and a few times, when the discussion became intense, someone would share a laughter movement and the tension would settle.

Following the first session at the Dame Phyllis Frost Centre in May in 2009 I was invited to share the program with the staff only at the Barwon (men's maximum security) Prison near Geelong. This is the feedback from that session.

"I was a little worried leading up to the event that staff would be hesitant to participate, but after a few warm up exercises and some interesting and funny facts about laughter from you, the staff were enjoying themselves and more than happy to participate. You had a great warmth and staff were quickly comfortable letting their playful side shine through and having a laugh at themselves. After the session I felt great for the rest of the day and am now a firm believer of the 15 minutes of laughing every day. I have had a lot of positive feedback from staff after the program and they were happy to have tried something a little different and a little bit out of their comfort zone! Thank you again for a fantastic program, we look forward to having you again in the future."

Realistically, running a laughter session in the prison sector is no different than running a session anywhere. Although I must admit that the joke about having a "captive" audience is running a little thin! Apart from the technicalities of entering the facility, police check, bring nothing but ID, and a few other minor rules required for the protection of the visitors, the women and the staff, there is really no difference, and it makes me smile to be able to say to others, "I'm sorry, I can't do that for you on that day, I'll be in prison" before I explain the full reason. (Roberts, 2011)

Trusting Relationships

Trust is frequently mentioned as the most important ingredient in creating a collaborative culture. Is there trust in your organization? Just look for a high level of humergy. Trust is the critical component necessary for supporting a collaborative culture. A high level of trust is reflected in a high level of fun, laughter, play, and humor. All stakeholders can work together to create a systemic culture of humergy and a positive learning environment. It is rare to find an organization where humor is identified as a key ingredient that needs to be nurtured and practiced. Yet the energy, enthusiasm, and hope generated by humergy are a visible sign of trust. This sense of trust is dependent on the desire of fun-loving employees to collaborate and share their optimism, hope, and humergy practice for the purpose of maximizing living. (See Figure 7.1.) The more fear-filled the work environment and the more control that exists, the lower the level of trust.

In Chapter 2, it was mentioned that the basis of human trust is play (Brown, 2009). Play sends signals of acceptance and support from leaders who are willing to share humor and laughter with their employees. Leaders can take this research into consideration when providing instructions at or during meetings. If you are looking for ways to improve fun at your staff meetings, there are several webinars (including mine) at ELN (Education Learning Network) listed in the resources and references.

Don't force humor. Use your humor to make people feel more comfortable.

—Mike Myatt

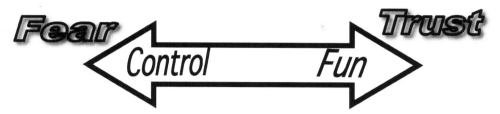

Figure 7.1   Fun: An Indicator of Trust

Creating Commitment

When humor is shared it reinforces a desire to continue relationships and fulfill commitments. Many people initially volunteer for organizations to provide a needed service but find they really just enjoy being with the others in the group. This spirit of networking strengthens the willingness to commit time and energy to the mission of the organization. The next time you are at a meeting of active community volunteers, listen for the laughter. People gravitate towards groups that are fun.

Take a quick look at the fundraising activities that are going on in your community. A review of my local events includes a tennis shoe prom, a golf ball drop, a take-off on "Dancing with the Stars," and mud volleyball. While all of these events require a significant commitment on the part of many people, it is usually an enjoyable activity for the volunteers. The leadership for this type of fundraising requires creative brainstorming so that it will be enticing for the public to attend. Just quietly observe the interaction at your next volunteer meeting. Infuse some fun and watch the reaction!

Community Building

AATH is an organization built on the mission of service "as a community of professionals who study, practice and promote healthy humor and laughter." Humor and laughter are purposefully used to build community within this group of committed volunteers. It is a great example of using humor to build community (AATH website). Think about the organization that you belong to. How does the mission encourage building a community of trust? Both Karyn Buxman and Chip Lutz have provided this type of leadership for AATH. Their ideas are woven throughout this book, but it is important to focus on their insights into leadership and humor here. Chip Lutz has formulated his business, called Covenant Leadership, based on trust.

In today's crazy world, there's never been a better time to learn how to build covenants with the people around you. Covenants built on the foundations of humor, hope and humanity that provide an atmosphere of trust, integrity, and a willingness to collectively move towards achieving a common goal. (Lutz, personal communication)

Karyn Buxman is the immediate past president of AATH, a Lifetime Achievement Award winner, and currently an instructor and advisor for the Humor Academy. She has earned the National Speakers Association's (NSA) Certified Speaking Professional (CSP) designation (held by less than 7 percent of professional speakers), and is one of only 176 experts (32 women) in the world awarded admission into the NSA Speaker Hall of Fame. Her research and experience have shaped her views. She shares her humor journey and practice as part of this book. For the past several years she has been a mentor and partner in the creation of the Humor Academy. Her work is an exemplar of how so many leaders are forging new paths in the field of laughter and humor.

For over twenty years, I have dedicated my entire career to the strategic use of applied and therapeutic humor. I have had the wonderful opportunity to share with people of all ages, from around the world, how humor and laughter can improve their health, their profitability, their relationships, and their happiness. Because of my background in nursing, much of my work is in the healthcare field. I have been able to demonstrate to nurses and other healthcare professionals how they can use humor for themselves to improve their stress levels, their resilience (It's a tough job!), and their effectiveness with their patients. I have also been able to show patients how they can use humor to better cope with and manage their illnesses, and experience a higher quality of life. I've worked with businesses and corporations showing them how to use humor to improve employee morale, creativity, productivity, customer service, and sales. And recently I've had the privilege of working with the military, sharing how humor and laughter can be a powerful tool in their arsenal in dealing with such debilitating issues such as PTSD and suicide among their ranks.

Right now I am most excited about my work with patients and their family members on how to better cope with their chronic conditions such as diabetes, heart disease, and cancer. Our field of psychoneuroimmunology is in the pioneering stage, but already we have seen studies demonstrating benefits of humor and laughter to the cardiovascular system, the immune system, the respiratory system, and much more. This is merely validating what most of us already know: "A merry heart doeth good like a medicine." It is incredibly rewarding to see people grasp the power at their fingertips to make a difference in their own lives and the lives of those they serve. (Karyn Buxman, personal communication)

Nurturing the Spirit

Humor nurtures the spirit and nourishes the soul (Kwan, 2002). If you observe the humor of a leader, you will get a glimpse of the heart and soul of his or her leadership style and insight into his or her personal beliefs.

People usually choose their careers because they want to be engaged in work that matters. Most people want to laugh, have fun, and be involved in creating an energized, productive workplace. There is a longing to work with others who desire a joy-flow collaborative environment. The joy-flow experience identified in Chapter 2 is the purposeful practice of optimism and positive emotionality. It's evident within cultures that strive for shared leadership. It is evident in cultures that continuously strive to maximize productivity and create a climate that is hopeful, engaging, supportive, and fun.

Leaders today face incredible challenges. People in positions of leadership are scrutinized, evaluated, criticized, and under enormous pressure to perform. How is it that some leaders seem to not only survive but also thrive in these circumstances? Observe the humor style of successful leaders and chances are you will find that service is at the heart of their leadership style.

Jackie Kwan, a colleague and friend in AATH, has worked extensively with patients with Alzheimer's and dementia at the Hebrew Home in Rockville, MD. Her experiences include using laughter and humor to encourage connections on a spiritual level. Jackie mirrors the patients' gestures so that she feels "in sync" with them. She often sings along with them so that the patients can see, hear, and feel her on their level and form a connection. She says that while the others may not laugh or giggle, she sees the corners of their eyes begin to crinkle and the corners of their mouths lift. She notices a spark return to their faces. She feels she has impacted both their lives and hers in a profound way (Kwan, 2002).

Fif Fernandes, mentioned several times in this book, cofounded a peace camp for kids brutalized by the twenty-two-year-old civil war in northern Uganda. She uses laughter and humor to assist kids when faced with bullying. She believes that laughter empowers these kids and nurtures their wounded spirits. Leadership includes this kind of initiative that transcends the normal skills and embraces a spiritual commitment to sharing joy and laughter with others.

Good leaders must first become good servants.

—Robert Greenleaf

FRAMEWORK FOR LEADERSHIP: INDICATORS OF HUMOR

This framework (Figure 7.2) depicts the elements commonly identified as a foundation for the leadership process but arranges them into a visual portrayal of how humergy impacts the system. In order to fully explore the role of humergy in an environment, let's look at this framework to visualize the indicators that will maximize the joy-flow experience within a culture.

> *If you think you're too small to be effective you have never been in bed with a mosquito.*
>
> —Bette Reese

Content = What

The inner circle is what I think usually gets the most attention. It answers the question: What needs to be accomplished? Is there a clear focus on the mission, values, and the work that need to be addressed? What is the purpose of your organization? How can humor be used to promote and market your services or your product? What are the written policies of your organization?

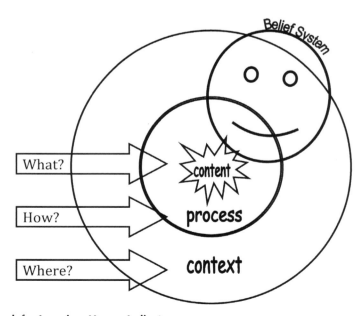

Figure 7.2 Framework for Learning: Humor Indicators

Often the rules and regulations of the workplace bog employees down. Many of these are unwritten rules, but these can drive much of what is done. There may be an unwritten rule that "productive employees" eat lunch at desks while working. What are the unwritten rules in your place of work? Are there unwritten rules about behavior?

> *Only one man in a thousand is a leader of men—the other 999 follow women.*
>
> —Groucho Marx

Process = How

The middle circle depicts the process the individual leader uses to facilitate the work of the organization. It also depicts the process the leader employs to engage the staff in collaborative efforts to address cultural issues. It has a focus on *how* to learn, develop, plan, and implement policy. Imaging technology is providing biological information about how brains work. Humor can be an integral component of the organizational process. An optimal method for the process circle will include the collaborative management of time, space, energy, and resources (Sylwester, 2005). It also is dependent on continual staff development for employees so they have the resources and time for developing their talents.

The importance of movement, the arts, sleep, nutrition, and learning styles are all considerations for the leader who is managing and supporting each and every one of the unique brains floating around in his or her workplace. Each person's brain is different and requires specific conditions for optimal productivity. This type of research is currently being studied and is the subject of numerous books and articles. Check out Dr. Earl Henslin's book, *This Is Your Brain on Joy* (2008). As discussed in Chapter 3, happy brains "look" different from brains that are depressed. Stress reduction is a vital aspect of using humor in leadership. Again, the role of humor is sometimes mentioned as a part of the workplace process, but it has not been specifically identified in many publications on leadership.

Throughout this book, there are various strategies for integrating the processes that would embody the joy-flow concept. How do you use humor to "get the job done"? A review of Chapter 6 provides numerous strategies for adapting the concept of humergy for various groups and organizations. There is a section at the end of each chapter titled "Powerful Practice—Strategies for Leaders." The "Jest for Fun" boxes highlight ideas that have been used by other leaders in various fields.

Want to use humor as a change agent? The "Study Group Focus" and "Café Conversations" included at the end of each chapter are designed to assist leaders as they purposefully implement humor as a change agent in their workplace. There are numerous ways that employees can collaborate on improving their knowledge and skills related to humor practice. They can mentor and coach each other and support each other in their humor practice. Recognizing accomplishments is a great way to encourage humor practice.

Quick Ideas for Recognition

- Use an old trophy as a traveling prize for employee recognition.
- Give deserving staff members a pretty stone with the letter "U" written on it—"U ROCK"!
- Give a deserving employee a can of beets with a note saying, "You can't be beet!"
- Put happy notes or jokes in mailboxes with a congratulation note.

Humor is the vehicle that can help companies return to the place where work is fun. *Happiness, fun, play, mirth, comedy, joy,* and *jokes* are all terms that have been used to define humor. Positive emotionality is a powerful mind–body connection that can create a remarkable feeling of control over one's life. This element of humergy can make a powerful difference in the culture of organizations.

> *I never did a day's work in my life. It was all fun.*
>
> —Thomas Alva Edison

Context = Where

The context circle represents the climate and culture where work occurs. Do the environment and available resources facilitate optimal productivity? This circle encompasses the research on how positive emotionality influences the environment, including the emotional state of both the leader and the employees or members. As mentioned previously, anger, excess fear, and stress can create a tense and stressful environment that will inhibit productivity. In order to maximize the opportunities of humergy, a look at the context (workplace culture) must be addressed first. In other words, addressing the issues of a culture is of utmost importance. Of course, numerous leadership articles and books provide information on how to make this happen, but few address the importance of purposefully using humor for an optimal change to take place.

Let's take a look at humergy as a contextual component of leadership. There are several examples from the world of business that highlight the importance of creating an environment of fun and laughter. Pixar was mentioned earlier in this chapter. There are numerous others.

Google was named the top company to work for by CNN in 2007. It was still ranked at number four in 2011. They provide free food in the cafeteria, a climbing wall, and free laundry. Generous pay increases and bonuses are included in the college-like atmosphere. When you look at the pictures of work life at Google, it looks like a playground for adults. Other companies in the top 100 list offer health benefits including fitness centers, summer camps for kids, beauty salons, and child care. Zappos is part of the Amazon.com family. They are known for their quirky, happy culture with the idea to "create fun and a little weirdness" as one of the company's guiding tenets (CNN, 2011).

In one workplace several employees had babies during a year. The administrator found the space and resources to provide in-house infant care for those employees, many of whom were nursing mothers. This was just one example of his efforts to provide a joy-flow environment. Hope, fun, optimism, and trust were evident in this work environment.

Leslie Yerkes, in her book *Fun Works* (2001), highlights companies that have profited from an infusion of fun in the workplace. The Pike Place Fish Market in Seattle has capitalized on this concept in a huge way. They have actually packaged their marketing program via their FISH video, website, and FISH camps for all who are interested. Their marketing programs are known worldwide for their emphasis on having fun as a means to profit (Yerkes, 2001). Productivity improves as fun and play are integrated into the workplace. The business world is often taking a serious look at the role that fun, play, and humor contribute to an optimal work environment and to increasing productivity.

If the fish vendors can profit from having fun, why can't others benefit from having fun within their own workplace or organization? If fun is thought of as anything that makes learning engaging, exciting, and challenging, it seems that the focus on rules and regulations is counterproductive. Unnecessary regulations and policies decrease or eliminate fun.

> *The more rules, the less fun.*
>
> —Mary Kay Morrison

When there is laughter, there are fewer humordoomers. Laughter begets fun and joy. Leaders can inspire a spirit of humergy.

Stress is frequently emerging as a topic of concern as addressed in several parts of this book. Addressing the stress levels of employees is becoming more of a priority for leaders. The health of employees plays a significant role in productivity and in insurance costs. There is a growing need to find ways to counteract both personal and work-related demands on staff. Many agencies have faced growing budget cuts and decreased staff morale. This is evident in the numerous requests received by those in the humor therapy business:

- "Can you come and give a humor workshop? I need to get my staff in a good mood because we have had serious budget cuts."
- "We are going to spend the day on regulations; can you suggest something to improve the attitudes of the participants?"
- "We have some serious issues here after our downsizing; I want our people to move on."
- "We need to find ways to motivate our employees."
- "Can you do something on humor to help improve our work environment?"
- "Our stress levels have been increasing. Everyone is just so burnt out."

The leaders who make these calls are striving to improve the culture and climate of their organizations. It is possible, in a workshop, to create an awareness of humor and to escalate the energy of a group on a short-term basis. However, in order to address multifaceted climate issues, the components of thoughtful planning, focused staff development, and reflective practice must be a part of a continuous process for improvement. Humor relieves stress, and productivity will increase with a reduction in stress.

A large corporation recently hired several cannibals. "You are all part of our team now," said the Human Resources Department chief during the welcoming briefing. "You get all the usual benefits, and you can go to the cafeteria for something to eat, but please don't eat any of our employees."

The cannibals promised they would not.

Four weeks later, the boss remarked, "You're all working very hard and I'm satisfied with your work. However, one of our secretaries has disappeared. Do any of you know what happened to her?"

The cannibals all shook their heads "No."

After the boss left, the leader of the cannibals said to the others, "Which one of you idiots ate the secretary?" A hand rose hesitantly. "You fool!" the leader said. "For four weeks we have been eating managers and no one noticed anything. But NOOOooo, you had to go and eat the secretary!" (Thanks to my cousin, Jerry Mattingly)

Beliefs and Feelings

The smiley face that overlays all three circles represents the belief system of the leader and those in the organization. Individual beliefs drive behavior. It is important to have the beliefs written to drive the goals of the organization. Does your mission statement include words like *humor*, *fun*, or *joy*?

Regardless of the mission statement of the organization, the beliefs of the administrator, the governing body and its rules and regulations, and employees or members *will* dictate the cultural environment of the group. Some will not agree with the written mission of the organization and can secretly sabotage the efforts of leadership. Changing belief systems is difficult. Humor is the invisible elephant in the center of the room; everyone knows it's there, but no one pays any attention to it unless it disappears or steps on someone. It can also magically appear at times of stress and change. Employees can feel a humor void. They know if they are the brunt of sarcasm or negative humor. Belief systems must be addressed in order to release the potential of positive emotionality within a culture.

Having worked as a gender equity consultant in the 1980s, it has been my observation that many women in management positions feel they need to be "tough" and "demanding" in order to prove that they can be effective. These "glass ceiling" rules are being broken more frequently now, and women are finding the freedom to be participatory leaders rather than feeling they need to be authoritarian in order to be effective. If you are a woman in leadership, do not be afraid to have fun and practice humor.

> *A leader without a sense of humor is like a lawn mower at a cemetery.*
> *A lot of people under him, but no one is paying any attention!*

Review your workplace culture by using the information in Table 7.1, "Worksheet for Analysis of Culture." This instrument is another tool that you can use to assess your work environment. It was created to provide a quick overview of

indicators of either a stress- and fear-based culture or a joyful environment filled with humergy.

Table 7.1 Worksheet for Analysis of Culture

Mark "x" in the center column nearest the description of your workplace culture. Note the pattern and decide where improvement can occur.

Fear and Stress Culture	Measures on Organizational Indicators of Humergy	Joy-flow Culture
Controlled		**Choice**
Production focused		Discovery focused
Content based		Neuroscience based
Bored participants		Engaged participants
Drudgery		Excitement
Low energy levels		Humergy (high energy/humor)
Linear		Chaotic
Low trust/low fun		High trust/lots of fun
Victimization		Empowerment
Hopeless, martyrs		Hope, optimism
Intense stress		Balance and focus
Disrespect: Few belief systems		Respect: Honor all belief systems
Individual efforts		Collaboration, teamwork
Sarcasm, put downs		Laughter, play

Source: Developed by Mary Kay Morrison

THE TOP TEN WAYS YOU CAN IDENTIFY A FUN LEADER OR ADMINISTRATOR

10. Has yo-yos, slinkies, balloons, and other toys in desk drawers. He consistently chooses a positive response pattern in life. The capacity to do this emerges from a focus on creating an affirmative environment (even a mental one) in which to operate.

9. Plans surprises for colleagues. She finds joy in change, incongruity, and uncertainty and has the confidence to think outside of the box and see numerous possibilities. If a situation does not progress as planned, she finds several other options.

8. Teaches the staff to juggle with scarves (balls come later) when budget cuts are announced. He purposefully uses laughter to ease pain, realizing that laughter is a way to relieve stress.

7. Plans frog races (ok—fun activities) for staff meetings. She understands that humor is a coping skill that can be a response to all change (from small annoyances to major crises). She has a lot of enthusiasm and energy!

6. Colors hair orange at Halloween and claims it was the original color. He uses self-deprecating humor as an exaggerated statement of truth, with the knack of laughing at mistakes and difficulties.

5. Puts the staff newsletter on the inside of faculty bathroom doors and titles the newsletter *The Flush*. She has the ability to understand and empathize with other people. She is able to assist others in seeing the humor in difficult situations and elicit laughter in the situation.

4. Evaluations include jellybeans and joking about challenges. Feedback includes listening and making collaborative decisions for improvement. He knows that gentle good-natured teasing is a good way to build collegial relationships.

3. She tries every fun leadership activity that was ever invented and drives the staff crazy doing so. She also has the ability to joke about driving everyone crazy. Highly skilled humergists are able to ease the tension in group meetings by promoting laughter at the situation or at themselves.

2. Has staff meetings in the local pizza place and buys the pizza. He is able to use reframing as a shift in context that allows groups to look at a situation in a more useful way.

1. She offers a $1 bill to any person to whom she forgets to say, "Thank you for working/volunteering here today. What can I do to make your job easier?"

If at first you don't succeed, skydiving isn't for you!

SUMMARY

Several management styles were reviewed, including authoritarian, laissez faire, and collaborative/participatory. Humergy is likely to be most evident by leaders in collaborative cultures. Servant leadership and humor go hand in hand as these folks use humor to effectively motivate, inspire, and communicate with their employees or volunteers.

Trust is an indicator of a joyful atmosphere. In order to address the issues that create a culture of trust, leaders need to examine the context, process, and content of the work environment. The context includes the issue of "where," process addresses "how," and content includes the "what" of organizational structures. Belief systems permeate all three of these areas. Excess stress impacts the ability of leaders to be effective. It negatively impacts the positive emotionality of the environment. An abundance of unnecessary rules and mandates can contribute to this stress.

Effective leaders promote collaborative learning and a positive emotional culture. They are eager to address the issues that contribute to negativity and stress. Building trust through the use of fun, laughter, and humor is embedded in their leadership style.

> *Laughing first (as a leader) sets the tone and paves the way for others to let go and do the same.*
>
> —Chip Lutz, Covenant Leadership

POWERFUL PRACTICE—STRATEGIES FOR LEADERS

- Make sure you have a sunshine committee to offer support to those going through tough times or to celebrate the good times. Be creative in your recognitions. Have each person find a joke to share with that person or select a cartoon without a caption and come up with a few captions that fit the occasion.
- Assist workers by asking them how you can assist them in balancing work and family. Provide a child care resource guide. Have a list of options for exchange of goods and services. One employee might mow in exchange for craft items or another might trade babysitting services for fresh produce.
- Be on the lookout for stress relief and wellness strategies. Maybe provide an in-service day devoted to wellness and stress management. Have a yoga class, offer chair massages, and provide time for workers to collaborate.
- Have staff bring in pictures of their pets and put them all on a bulletin board. Give a prize to the person who has the best guesses for matching the pets with their owners.
- Celebrate with an English tea-and-cookies event or have an ice cream sundae bar.
- Have everyone bring in white elephant gifts for an auction. Donate the money to a favorite charity.
- Many offices do canned food drives over the holidays, but do one over the Fourth of July or Valentine's Day. Research the needs in your community and see how your organization can have fun and raise money at the same time for local agencies. Offer time as well as resources, volunteering for Habitat for Humanity or food pantries.
- Create the position of Humor Resources Manager! Ask the staff to come up with a job description.

STUDY GROUP FOCUS

- Observe the humergy in your workplace. Make a list of the observations. The worksheet for analysis of culture can also be used (see Table 7.1).
- How can humor be used to improve leadership communication?
- Discuss how you have used humor to relieve stress. Strategize ways to reduce stress in your workplace.
- Write your reflections on what you appreciated in this book. Do a pair/share and then discuss with the group.
- Brainstorm ways your group can provide service to others. What leadership skills are needed to make this happen?

CAFÉ CONVERSATIONS

- Discuss the characteristics of a happy work environment or organization. What are the key indicators? How can humor be employed to build trusted relationships and a positive culture?
- What are some successful fundraisers that you are aware of? Why were they a success?
- Share past experiences in situations that were stressful and how these challenges were addressed. What techniques were successful? Why? How does stress impact your workplace? What resources are currently available to workers to alleviate stress? What resources are needed? Review the "Take It and Make It Funny" worksheet in Appendix 8.

APPENDIX 1

HUMOR TERMINOLOGY AND CATEGORIES: COMING TO TERMS WITH HUMOR

HUMOR TERMINOLOGY*

adaptability. Describes how easily a child adjusts to changes and transitions. A sense of humor is closely related to our flexibility for change. The ability to laugh in new situations is apparent even with very young children. Some are at ease right away while others may hide behind a parent in a new situation.

anger. A term for the emotional aspect of aggression as a basic aspect of the stress response in animals in which a perceived aggravating stimulus "provokes" a counterresponse, which is likewise aggravating and threatening of violence.

approach/withdrawal. A child's initial response to novelty: "new places, people, situations or things" (Kristal, 2005). It takes a certain degree of risk taking to experiment with humor. Class clowns, for instance, are pretty comfortable with new places and situations. They approach situations with enthusiasm, zest, and unbridled risk taking.

attachment theory. A theory, or group of theories, about the psychological tendency to seek closeness to another person, to feel secure when that person is present, and to feel anxious when that person is absent.

---

*Thanks to Steve Wilson, WLT, for his contributions to this list.

attention. The brain's focusing system, activated by emotional arousal. Also the cognitive process of selectively concentrating on one thing while ignoring other things.

attitude. A key concept in psychology. Attitudes are positive or negative views of an "attitude object," that is, a person, behavior, or event.

behavior. The actions or reactions of an object or organism, usually in relation to the environment. Behavior can be conscious or unconscious, overt or covert, and voluntary or involuntary.

brain. The control center of the central nervous system.

class clowns. Students who stimulate laughter in a classroom setting. Usually cheerful, positive individuals who relish being the center of fun.

cognitive science. Scientific study either of mind or of intelligence.

content circle. Describes what needs to be learned.

context circle. Describes where learning occurs.

cortisol. Stress hormone secreted by the adrenal glands during stress.

depression. A condition characterized by feelings of pessimism and sadness.

emotion. A neural impulse that moves an organism to action, prompting automatic reactive behavior that evolved as a survival mechanism.

emotion detector. A skill used to understand the emotions of self and others.

emotional intelligence. Also called EI or EQ, a term that describes an ability, capacity, or skill to perceive and assess emotion.

emotional knowledge. The level of perception and assessment that an individual has of his or her emotions at any given moment in time. To manage the emotions of oneself, of others, and of groups.

emotional memory. Memories that are sparked by remembering the feelings about something that happened. Emotional arousal activates the attentional center of the brain and is a powerful trigger for learning and memory.

fear. An unpleasant feeling of perceived risk or danger, whether real or imagined.

flourish. The focus of positive psychology, including the concept of flow. A part of the positive emotions that include peak humor experiences and humergy.

flow. The feeling of complete and energized focus in an activity, with a high level of enjoyment and fulfillment, as originally described by Mihaly Csikszentmihalyi.

frontal lobes. Part of the cerebral cortex of the brain that functions in initiating actions, solving problems, and making decisions.

fun. Anything that makes learning engaging, exciting, and challenging.

games. Usually performed by competing individuals or teams who have the same clearly defined goal. Although many animals play, only humans have games. The existence of rules and criteria that decide the outcome of games implies that games require intelligence of a significant degree of sophistication.

geliophobia. Fear of laughter.

gelos (jee-los). The Greek word for laughter.

gelosis. Denoting the condition of laughing more and more.

gelotherapy. Therapeutic laughter programs.

geloticia. Referring to materials and paraphernalia, props, toys, movies, and so forth to stimulate laughter.

gelotology. Study of the physiology of laughter.

gelotonia/gelotonic. The condition of achieving a healthy balance with laughter.

gelotrophic. The state or condition of being nourished by and or growing due to laughter. An organism exhibiting growth as a result of being stimulated by laughter.

group glee. Wave of laughter emerging from a group of young children.

happiness. Emotional or affective state in which we feel good or pleasure.

hippocampus. Structure in the brain involved with the formation and retrieval of memory.

hope. An emotional belief in a positive outcome related to events and circumstances within one's personal life.

humergist. Person who effectively employs humor to facilitate communication.

humergy. The energy that emerges from the humor, joy, and optimism of our inner spirit, reflects our unique personality, and nourishes a healthy mind–body balance.

humor. The quality that makes something amusing or laughable.

humor paradox. Discrepancy in a society that claims to place a high value on humor, when in reality fears keep us from initiating and sustaining humor practice.

humor physiology. Events that occur in the human body in association with humorous experiences.

humor practice. The art and craft of purposefully applying humor to everyday life.

humor respiration. Laughing, giggling, or chortling that disrupts cyclic breathing, increases ventilation, and accelerates residual air exchange. This results in enhanced intake of oxygenated fresh air.

humordoomer. A person who consistently uses negative humor to control and manipulate others.

humorobics. The physical act of laughing.

humorologist. Person who practices the art and science of healthy humor.

humorology. The art and science of humor.

humorphobia. A fear of fun, laughter, and humor.

hyperacademics. Overly intense focus on academics.

impact versus intent. Comparison between the purpose of the humor as perceived by the conveyor and the feelings evoked by the recipient of the humor.

intensity. The reactive energy of a response, whether happy, sad, or angry, or expressive. The emotional response varies greatly among young children. For instance, some children will smile a little at peek-a-boo games while others laugh loudly.

joke. A short story or short series of words spoken or communicated with the intent of being laughed at or found humorous by the listener or reader.

joy. The emotion of great happiness.

joy-flow. Term used to describe positive emotionality as exhibited by enthusiasm, energy, joy, and hope. The peak experiences most of us identify with experiencing one's sense of humor.

laughter. The biological reaction of humans to moments or occasions of humor, an outward expression of amusement. Human response to a social connection (Provine, 2000).

learning. The process of acquiring knowledge, skills, attitudes, or values, through study, experience, or teaching, that causes a change of behavior that is persistent, measurable, and specified or allows an individual to formulate a new mental construct or revise a prior mental construct (conceptual knowledge such as attitudes or values). It is a process that depends on experience and leads to long-term changes in behavior potential.

long-term memory. Memory that can last as little as thirty seconds or as long as decades.

love. Emotion of primary value associated with an intense attraction to a person, place, or thing.

memory. The ability of the brain to store, retain, and subsequently recall information.

mood. The basic quality of disposition. It may be more positive (a happy or cheerful child) or more negative (a cranky or serious child). Some researchers think that mood is parallel to or overlays our basic temperament.

optimism. The tendency to believe, expect, or hope that things will turn out well. The attitude of somebody who feels positive or confident.

peak experience. Term used to describe an optimal experience of positive emotionality.

peek-a-boo. Term used to describe the first stage of humor development in infants.

perception. The process of acquiring, interpreting, selecting, and organizing sensory information.

pessimism. Describes a belief that things are bad and will become worse.

play. Describes an unrestrained, amusing interaction with people, animals, or things, often in the context of learning.

positive emotionality. A state of being in which the individual is said to flourish. The research is based on the belief that positive emotions extend the capacity of attention, cognition, and action.

process circle. Describes how learning occurs.

pseudogelotic. Referring to false or fake laughter.

psychoneuroimmunology. The study of the interactions between the brain and the immune system that combines psychology, neuroscience, and immunology.

pun fun. Stage of humor development of children ages ten through fourteen.

riddle-de-dee. Stage of humor development of children in grades 3 through 5.

roast. An event in which an individual is subject to publicly hearing insults, praise, outlandish true and untrue stories, and heartwarming tributes about him- or herself. It is seen as a great honor to be roasted, as the individual is surrounded by friends, fans, and well-wishers, who can receive some of the same treatment as well during the course of the evening. The party and presentation itself are called a roast. The host of the event is called the roast master. In short, it is both the opposite of and the same as a "toast."

safe humor. Practice of humor in safe situations.

sarcasm. Sneering, jesting, or mocking a person, situation, or thing. It is strongly associated with irony, with some definitions classifying it as a type of verbal irony.

self-deprecating humor (or self-effacing humor). The ability to laugh at ourselves, to make fun of our human foibles, and maintain a sense of perspective. It is also powerful in defusing confrontations.

sense of humor. The capacity of a human being to respond to life challenges with optimistic enjoyment.

short-term memory. Sometimes referred to as "primary" or "active" memory—the part of memory that stores a limited amount of information for a limited amount of time (roughly fifteen to thirty seconds).

stages of humor development. Sequential process for the development of a sense of humor.

stress. Roughly the opposite of relaxation. A medical term for a wide range of strong external stimuli, both physiological and psychological, which can cause a physiological response called the general adaptation syndrome, first described in 1936 by Hans Selye in the journal *Nature*.

stress management. Techniques intended to equip a person with effective coping mechanisms for dealing with psychological stress.

stressors. Any factor that causes stress is called a stressor. There are two kinds of stressors: processive stressors and systemic stressors. Processive stressors are elements in the environment perceived by the organism as potential dangers. These do not cause damage directly but are processed in the cerebral cortex. The processed information is then sent via the limbic system in the hypothalamus, where it activates the supreme centers of the autonomic nervous system. This results in the fight-or-flight (or sympathetico-adrenal) response. Systemic stressors cause a disturbance in the organism's homeostasis, as well as tissue necrosis, hypotension, or hypoxia. Often both types of stressors occur simultaneously. They are usually accompanied by pain or intense emotions.

survivor humor (group). A specific type of humor response that is an active defense mechanism to help cope with threats and fears instead of surrendering to them (definition provided by Sandfa Ritz, nurse researcher).

teasing. The act of playfully disturbing another person, either with words or with actions. In mild cases, and especially when it is reciprocal, it is essentially a form of playing (friendly teasing). However, teasing can also be used as painful harassment (cruel teasing), if the teasing is one way. In extreme cases it may escalate to real violence and may even result in abuse (in the case of a child, child abuse).

temperament. The general nature of an individual's personality, such as introversion or extroversion.

therapy. A treatment that is the attempted remediation of a health problem, usually following a diagnosis.

trust. Having confidence in and reliance on good qualities, especially fairness, truth, honor, or ability. The ability to take the responsibility for taking good care of somebody or something.

working memory. The collection of structures and processes used for temporarily storing and manipulating information.

CATEGORIES OF HUMOR**

absurd. That which obviously lacks reason, which is foolish or ridiculous in its lack of good sense; includes nonsense, the nonsensical use of logic and language; the preposterous, arising from the incongruity of reality and fantasy; and whimsy, a fanciful or fantastic device, object, or creation, especially in writing, art, or decoration.

defiance. Primarily the release of hostility or aggression through rebellion; includes the violation of conventions, the perpetration of situations socially unacceptable to adults, the expression of forbidden ideas, and the violation of adult authority.

**Adapted from Kappas (1967).

exaggeration. Using an obvious over- or understatement, including such things as physical characteristics, data, feelings, or experiences.

human predicaments. Situations in which a character appears foolish or bested. Includes the humor of superiority and degradation, which is based on self-aggrandizement or the release of hostility through the discomfiture, failure, or misfortune of others; and comic predicaments, which is based on an attitude of sympathetic acceptance of the human predicament and can be seen in situations in which either oneself or someone else appears foolish or bested by life for the moment. In this case, however, no hostile feelings are intended to be aroused or expressed.

incongruity. Connecting two generally accepted opposites, the lack of a rational relation of objects, people, or ideas to each other or to the environment.

ridicule. Primarily the teasing and mockery of others or oneself; can be seen expressed, for example, in the mockery of adults, their world, and its customs, institutions and so forth. Negative ridicule finds its source in feelings of self-aggrandizement or the release of hostility through the mockery of others. Playful ridicule, on the other hand, is based on the sympathetic acceptance of human foibles. Satire is primarily a sophisticated artistic form of humor arising from both types of ridicule.

slapstick. The form of humor that depends for its effect on fast, boisterous, and zany physical activity and horseplay, often accompanied by broad, obvious, rowdy verbal humor.

surprise. Exploiting the occurrence of the unexpected—whether fact, thought, feeling, or event; in its more sophisticated form it becomes irony.

verbal humor. The manipulation of language through word play, puns, jokes, sarcasm, wit, name-calling, and the like; may contain either a positive or negative emotional content, but differs from the other forms in being a verbal rather than a situational form of humor.

APPENDIX 2

HUMOR STYLES INVENTORY

Self-awareness is a critical component in the journey of discovering your humor strength. This instrument is designed as an awareness aid for your own experience with a sense of humor. If you are serious about humor, you may want to begin to journal data on what tickles your funny bone. Jot down what makes you smile and when you laugh out loud. Review the categories in the humor list and the humor terminology list to assist you in identifying the type of humor that appeals to you. Colleagues can generate observations and suggestions for your humor practice.

1. What makes you laugh?
2. Identify your favorite:
    Comedians
    Movies
    Television shows
3. What form of humor do you practice? (Refer to the Appendix 1 categories list and glossary.)
4. When are you comfortable using humor?
5. How do you play?
6. What is your first choice when you want to have fun?
7. The ability to laugh at yourself is called self-deprecating humor. (Examples are physical characteristics, the aging process, mistakes made, etc.) When do you use this kind of humor?
8. Reflect on the type of humor your parents exposed you to. What kind of humor did you experience when you were growing up?
9. What kind of humor being do you want to practice?
10. Estimate how many times a day you laugh and when it most often happens.

APPENDIX 3

IDENTIFYING YOUR SENSE OF HUMOR

1. During an average day, I laugh out loud (keep a log for a few days to be sure):
    a. Once or not at all
    b. Two or three times
    c. At least once an hour
    d. Constantly—I may need professional help.
2. When I am alone and read, see, or hear something funny, I:
    a. Smile to myself
    b. Laugh out loud but look around to see if anyone saw me
    c. Laugh out loud and find someone with whom to share it
    d. Let whoever made me laugh know I appreciate it, even if it's 3:00 a.m.
3. In the past year, I can remember:
    a. At least one time I spent at least a whole minute laughing
    b. At least two to five times I spent at least a whole minute laughing
    c. More than five times I spent at least a whole minute laughing
    d. Being escorted out of a restaurant for disrupting the other patrons with my annoying laughter
4. I choose friends who:
    a. Are more serious than I am
    b. Are as serious as I am

---

    c. Laugh a little more than I do

    d. Are probably in need of medication, but they're fun to be around

5. When faced with everyday frustrations (voicemail, missed deadlines, rush hour traffic, etc.), I respond with a laugh:

    a. Never

    b. Sometimes

    c. Often

    d. Always; it's my only emotion

6. I intentionally do things to make myself laugh

    a. Never

    b. Sometimes

    c. Often

    d. There's another way to live?

7. The people I spend most of my time with:

    a. Leave me feeling drained and depressed

    b. Don't really affect my attitude

    c. Make me laugh a lot

    d. Are a bunch of clowns—literally

8. I would rate my family (the people with whom I live) as:

    a. Extremely serious

    b. Mostly serious

    c. Pretty light-hearted

    d. A laugh riot

9. My inner voices often say:

    a. "That's not funny and people will look at me strangely if I laugh."

    b. "It's kind of funny, but I'd better not embarrass myself."

    c. "Go ahead and laugh; no one's looking."

    d. "Why isn't everyone else already laughing?"

10. I have friends who can always make me laugh.

    a. 0

    b. 1–2

    c. 3–5

    d. Thousands, if you count Facebook

11. I laugh at myself:

    a. Only when I'm not in the room

    b. Sometimes

    c. Often

    d. Always; if you laugh at yourself you'll always be amused

12. When I hear people laughing at work, the first thing I think is:

    a. "I wish I could get paid to goof off."

    b. "I wish I knew what the joke is."

    c. "How wonderful that they're having a good time; I think I'll join them."

    d. "It's Saturday and I shouldn't be at work."

13. When in a large group of people, I generally laugh:
    a. Far less than most of them
    b. A little less
    c. About as often as they do
    d. So often they usually assume I know something they don't

14. If I'm the only one in a group who laughs at something, I usually:
    a. Get embarrassed and walk away
    b. Pretend I misunderstood
    c. Ask, "Hey, didn't you think that was funny?"
    d. Don't notice; I'm too busy laughing

15. On average, when something embarrassing happens to me, this is how long it takes until I find it funny:
    a. A long, long time; continents would drift first.
    b. Probably longer than it should
    c. A few days; I know I should let things go sooner though.
    d. I try to find the funny right away; after all, everyone else is laughing at me anyway.

16. Check off the things on the list below that I would NEVER find funny under any circumstances.
    a. Death
    b. Break-up of a relationship
    c. Chronic disease
    d. Financial ruin
    e. Someone else getting hurt, either physically or emotionally
    f. Animal abuse or neglect
    g. Racist jokes
    h. Ageist jokes
    i. Sexist jokes
    j. Homophobic jokes
    k. Other (specify)

17. How much does my sense of humor depend on who I'm with, where I am, and how I feel?
    a. A lot
    b. Quite a big amount
    c. Not much
    d. Not at all; I laugh when I want to.

18. People often tell me my sense of humor is:
    a. Nonexistent

  b. Great when I use it

  c. What they like best

  d. Intoxicating

19. The types of humor I find funniest from the following list are:

  a. Sarcasm

  b. Political humor

  c. Word play

  d. Intellectual humor

  e. Playful humor

  f. Pranks and practical jokes

  g. Animals and children

  h. Hanging with my friends

20. The types of humor I find least funny from the following list are:

  a. Sarcasm

  b. Political humor

  c. Word play

  d. Intellectual humor

  e. Playful humor

  f. Pranks and practical jokes

  g. Animals and children

  h. Hanging with my friends

How to score: for all questions except 16, 19, and 20, a = 0, b = 1, c = 2, d = 3.

<17 You are suffering from humor malnutrition. Even your funny bone is sad. Your case is so serious that you may actually need a humor transplant if you don't do something immediately.

17–33 You occasionally have a good laugh, but laughter is like exercise—you have to do it regularly to get the full benefit. Use it or lose it.

34–50 You are humorously fit. Not only do you approach life with the right amount of humor and benefit from it, you also probably make other people's lives more enjoyable.

50+ You're downright silly, aren't you? Don't stifle that childish instinct. Sure, they told you in school that the class clown would never go anywhere in life. But they were wrong. Look at Robin Williams, Jim Carrey, Seth Rogan, Wanda Sykes, and Tina Fey!

Questions 16, 19, and 20 are to help you get a better sense about your sense of humor. Your goal should be to know where your boundaries are and to state them but not to have so many that you miss out on the stress-reducing laughter altogether.

APPENDIX 4
COMEDIAN LIST

Abbott and Costello
Tim Allen
Woody Allen
Jeff Altman
Lucille Ball
Gina Barrecca
Mel Brooks
Kathy Buckley
Carol Burnett
Drew Carey
George Carlin
Jim Carrey
Judy Carter
Bill Cosby
Rodney Dangerfield
Ellen Degeneres
W. C. Fields
Jeff Foxworthy
Bob Hope
Andy Kaufman
Buster Keaton

Alan King
Loretta LaRouche
Laurel and Hardy
Jay Leno
David Letterman
Jerry Lewis
Steve Martin
Eddie Murphy
Rosie O'Donnell
Paula Poundstone
Don Rickles
Joan Rivers
Adam Sandler
Jerry Seinfeld
Sinbad
Smothers Brothers
The Three Stooges
Carrot Top
Dick Van Dyke
Robin Williams

APPENDIX 5

HUMOR REFLECTIONS

Analysis of past emotional experiences:

- What are my strongest emotional memories?
- What do I fear?
- What makes me laugh?

Awareness of current emotional state or feelings:

- What is my current comfort zone in expressing my emotions?
- What self-talk do I engage in during the day?
- How can my ongoing awareness of my feelings assist with creating an environment for optimal learning?

Ability to let go of what cannot be controlled, (Look for the absurdity of human behavior, beginning with yourself. Risk-taking confidence comes from an assurance of purpose that is constant amid the change and chaos of humor practice.):

- What fears inhibit my learning?
- Do I blame others (the students, the parents, the teachers, the administrators, the school board) for the inability to control many factors of my teaching and learning environment?
- Do I accept the decisions of others even though I might not agree? Can I trust others to make the right decisions?

Skill of reading the emotions of others (emotional literacy):

- Do I really listen to what the other person is saying?
- Can I read body language that mirrors the emotions of others?
- Do I notice when I tweak their sense of humor?
- How can I make a conscious effort to elicit humergy in others?

Focus on hope and optimism to maintain the joy of humergy:

- Am I willing to take the time for humor? Do I frequently choose play and fun?
- What new form of play am I willing to try?
- Am I willing to take the risks necessary to experiment with humor?

What does a peak experience feel like for me?

APPENDIX 6

HUMOR BELIEF INVENTORY

Please answer by selecting the most appropriate score: 1 = seldom/never or disagree and 5 = often/all of the time or agree.

ASSESSMENT	1	2	3	4	5
1. Humor is a skill that I use with intent and purpose.	1	2	3	4	5
2. I have a good sense of humor.	1	2	3	4	5
3. I intentionally use humor to optimize learning.	1	2	3	4	5
4. I intentionally use humor to build a relationship with students, educators, and parents.	1	2	3	4	5
5. I know and understand my humor style.	1	2	3	4	5
6. I believe humor is inherited.	1	2	3	4	5
7. If a classroom of students is laughing and joking, an observer will assume the class is not learning.	1	2	3	4	5
8. Humor can be an effective tool for students with serious behavior challenges.	1	2	3	4	5
9. Humor relieves stress.	1	2	3	4	5
10. Humor promotes healing.	1	2	3	4	5
11. Humor increases productivity.	1	2	3	4	5
12. Humor requires a culture of trust.	1	2	3	4	5
13. The ability to laugh at yourself can be used to gain the trust of others.	1	2	3	4	5
14. The "class clown" is usually perceived in our work environment as being a disruption to learning.	1	2	3	4	5
15. Humor is the number one characteristic students desire in a teacher.	1	2	3	4	5

16. Playing and having fun in the classroom is a
    waste of precious learning time.   1 2 3 4 5

17. Humor is not a measurable characteristic and
    therefore has a questionable role in education.   1 2 3 4 5

18. If there is a perception that I am a fun seeker,
    I will not be considered professional.   1 2 3 4 5

19. While humor is important, learning requires
    a serious work environment with little time for
    fun, humor, and play.   1 2 3 4 5

20. I am not comfortable initiating fun, play, and
    humor in my current work culture.   1 2 3 4 5

APPENDIX 7

TOY LIST

I have had great luck finding toys and games at garage sales. Some games can be made or created by the students. This is just a brief list to get you started. The possibilities are endless.

Balloons*
Bean bags
Bubbles
Clapping hands*
Hula hoops
Jacks
Kazoos*
Paddle balls
Pick-up sticks
Puppets
Makeup and dress-up costumes
Mood rings
Mr. Potato Head
Play money
Rubik's Cube
Slide puzzles
Slinkies
Squish balls
Spinning tops
Tic Tac Toe

* recommended for group use

APPENDIX 8

TAKE IT AND MAKE IT FUNNY

This activity is designed to purposefully take the difficulties in your life or work and look at these challenges in a humorous way. Think of a problem or issue facing you right now and play with ways to turn it into fun. Here are some ideas to get you started:

- Take two incongruent items and see how you can make them relate. Here are some examples:

  Complying with audits is like a microwave because . . .

  Our staff is like the Beatles because . . .

  Our budget is like blueberries because . . .

- Create a top ten list of why this particular challenge is a good thing. For example, a group had just had major budget cuts, and there were no more light bulbs to be purchased for the year. They had a top ten list of why it was great to be in the dark, including:

  Can't see the dust bunnies

  Can't observe any behavior problems

  Don't need sunglasses

- Do a "survivor" show. Make a list of all of the worst things that have ever happened to staff members. Staff members write these on papers (anonymously), and a list is compiled. Teams are created to brainstorm survivor strategies.

- Exaggerate the problem. Be creative.
- Brainstorm how cheese can be used as a strategy to market your business. Have a wine and cheese party, and bring the book *Who Moved My Cheese?* (Johnson, 1998). Wear a cheese head (Wisconsin Packers fans will assist you here). Ideas generate lots of additional ideas, and fun happens!

CONTRIBUTORS AND RECOMMENDED RESOURCES

Balmer, Chris
    Counselor, professor, researcher, administrator
    http://www.laughwell.com
    cbalmer@shaw.ca

Barreca, Gina
    Professor, author, speaker
    http://www.ginabarreca.com/index.html
    regina.barreca@uconn.edu

Berk, Lee
    Professor, researcher, speaker
    lberk@llu.edu

Berk, Ron
    Professor, speaker, author
    http://www.ronberk.com/
    rberk@son.jhmi.edu

Boyd, Hamish
    Playwright, actor
    http://www.laughingpeace.com
    Hamishboyd@shaw.ca

Buxman, Karyn
    Speaker, nurse, author
    http://www.KarynBuxman.com
    karyn@karynbuxman.com

Carter, Judy
>Author of *The Comedy Bible*, motivational humorist, comedy coach
>http://www.judycarter.com
>judy@judycarter.com

Caskey, Kay
>Professor, Western Michigan University
>http://www.laughways.com/
>info@laughways.com

Conklin, Pat
>Certified Laughter Yoga leader and teacher
>http://www.laughteryogaorlando.com/
>LaughilyEverAfter@gmail.com

Cortino, Becky
>Therapeutic clown, speaker, media consultant, author
>http://www.aheart4clowning.com/about/
>aheart4clowning@gmail.com

Covey, Dwayna
>Counselor, educator, life coach
>http://www.newseasoncoaching.com
>dwayna@newseasoncoaching.com

Edmondson, Adrienne, MA, CLL, CCP
>President and CEO, Edmondson & Associates, Inc.
>http://edmondsonandassoc.com/Bio-Affiliations.html
>solutionshr@sbcglobal.net

Epperson, Kelly
>Author, speaker, happiness coach
>http://kellyepperson.com
>kelly@kellyepperson.com

Fernandes, Fif
>Therapeutic clown, Alberta Children's Hospital; speaker and certified Laughter Yoga teacher/leader; Laughing Peace
>http://www.laughingpeace.com
>fif@laughingpeace.com

Gauldin, Deb
>Nurse, speaker, musician
>http://www.debgauldin.com/
>deb@debgauldin.com

Gold, Roberta, RTC
>Recreation therapist and humor therapist
>http://www.laf4u.com
>laf4u@sbcglobal.net

Granirer, David
  Author, speaker, CEO of Stand Up for Mental Health
  http://www.standupformentalhealth.com/
  david@standupformentalhealth.com
Hart, Debra Joy, RN, BFA, CLL
  Nurse, humor educator, therapeutic clown
  http://www.debrajoyhart.com
  debrajoyhart@gmail.com
Harty, Kris
  Author, speaker, thought leader on perseverance with Strong Spirit Unlimited
  http://www.StrongSpiritUnlimited.com
  Info@StrongSpiritUnlimited.com
Hoesl, Nick
  Pharmacist, author, speaker
  http://laughterdoc.com/
  nhoesl@yahoo.com
Jacobson, David
  Social work administrator, speaker, author
  http://www.davidmjacobson.com/bio.html
  david.jacobson2@va.gov
Jasheway, Leigh Anne
  Speaker, accidental comic, author
  http://www.accidentalcomic.com
  lajfun@accidentalcomic.com
Keaton, Kathy
  Keynote speaker, hospital humor therapist, therapeutic clown
  http://www.piccolotheclown.com
  kpiccolo28@juno.com
Klein, Allen
  Speaker, author
  http://www.allenklein.com/
  humor@allenklein.com
Kwan, Jackie
  Social worker, author, speaker, caring clown, certified Eden Energy
    Medicine practitioner
  http://www.hahalogy.com/
  jacki@hahalogy.com
Laurenhue, Kathy
  CEO of Wiser Now, trainer, author
  http://www.wisernow.com/
  Kathy@WiserNow.com.

Lutz, Chip
    President of Covenant Leadership, speaker, author, retired navy officer
    http://www.covenantleadership.com/
    cwlutz@gmail.com
McElravy, Lois
    Founder of "Lessons from Lois," speaker, author
    http://www.lessonsfromlois.com/
    lois@lessonsfromlois.com
McGhee, Paul
    President of Laughter Remedy, researcher, author, educator
    http://www.laughterremedy.com/
    paulmcghee@verizon.net
Nilsen, Don L. F., and Nilsen, Alleen
    Professors, researchers, authors
    http://www.hnu.edu/ishs/ISHS%20Documents/Nilsen25Article.pdf
    don.nilsen@asu.edu
Oberg, Cheryl
    Speaker, therapeutic clown, laughter leader
    cheryloberg@shaw.ca
Olds, Sharon
    Elementary school principal, assistant superintendent of curriculum,
        researcher, author
    http://www.nbcusd.org/poplargrove.shtml
    oldssharon@nbcusd.org
Osterlund, Hob
    Clinical nurse specialist, researcher, author, Chuckle Channel creator,
        actress
    http://www.youtube.com/watch?v=AdbjidOuJYU
    chucklechannel@hawaii.rr.com
    hob@hawaii.rr.com
Passanisi, Kathleen
    Speaker, medical professional, author
    http://www.kathleenpassanisi.com/index.php
    kathleen@kathleenpassanisi.com
Puckett, Katherine
    National director of mind/body medicine, Cancer Treatment Centers
        of America
    http://www.cancercenter.com/
    katherine.puckett@ctca-hope.com

Robbins, Amy
Anesthesiologist, internal medicine, critical care medicine (ICU);
Domestic Abuse advocate/activist
amy88rmd@aol.com

Roberts, Bronwyn
Australia Corporate Health Programs; Laughter Yoga leader
http://www.letslaugh.com.au/
bronwyn@letslaugh.com.au

Schwartz, Enid
Nurse, educator, author, researcher
enidschwartz@mac.com

Schwartz, Joel
Emeritus chair of staff, Department of Psychiatry, Abington Memorial
Hospital; speaker, author
http://stresslessshrink.com/
joel@stresslessshrink.com

Singer, Ed
Researcher
esinger@alliant.edu

Sparks, Susan
Minister, author, lawyer, comedian
Revssparks@gmail.com
http://susansparks.com

Sukenick, Ron
Speaker, trainer, author
http://www.ronsukenick.com/
rs@ronsukenick.com

Trunfio, Tony
Speaker, professor
http://laughfirstproject.com/about/
laughfirstproject@yahoo.com

Wandell, Heather
Speaker, author, laughter leader
http://www.anotherwaytoseeit.com/
haw@anotherwaytoseeit.com

Wilson, Steve
Psychologist, humor/laughter therapy, CEO of World Laughter Tour
http://www.worldlaughtertour.com/sections/about/history.asp
steve@stevewilson.com

Yerkes, Leslie
 Speaker, author, management consultant, entrepreneur
 http://www.changeisfun.com/about/leslie.html
 fun@catalystconsulting.net
Young, Laurie
 Professor at Western Michigan University
 http://www.laughways.com/
 info@laughways.com

REFERENCES AND RESOURCES

BOOKS AND ARTICLES

American Physiological Society. (2009, April 17). Laughter remains good medicine. *Science Daily*. Retrieved August 26, 2011, from http://www.sciencedaily.com/releases/2009/04/090417084115.htm.

Armstrong, T. (2006). *The best schools: How human development research should inform educational practice.* Alexandria, VA: Association for Supervision and Curriculum Development.

Bacall, A. (2002). *The lighter side of educational leadership.* Thousand Oaks, CA: Corwin.

Bany-Winters, L. (2002). *Funny bones.* Chicago: Chicago Review Press.

Barth, R. S. (2001). *Learning by heart.* San Fransisco: Jossey-Bass.

Battat, S., & Saltman, J. (2010). *Thin thread: Teachers and mentors.* Woodbridge, CT: Kiwi Publishing.

Baum, B. R. (2002). Infusing humor in the education of students with emotional and behavioral disorders. *Perceptions*, 35(2), 2–6.

Bennett, E. L., Diamond, M. C., Krech, D., & Rosenzweig, M. R. (1964). Chemical and anatomical plasticity of brain. *Science*, 164, 610–19.

Berk, L. (2009). Laughter remains good medicine. *Science News*. http://www.science-daily.com/releases/2009/04/090417084115.htm.

Berk, L. S., et al. (1989). Neuroendocrine and stress hormone changes during mirthful laughter. *American Journal of the Medical Sciences*, 298, 390–96.

Berk, L. S., Felten, D. L., Tan, S. A., Bittman, B. B., Westengard, J. (2001, March). Modulation of neuroimmune parameters during the eustress of humor-associated mirthful laughter. *Alternative Therapies in Health and Medicine*, 7(2), 62–76.

Berk, L., & Tan, S. (1997, April 17). The laughter–immune connection. Available from http://www.touchstarpro.com/laughbb3.html.

Berk, L., & Tan, S. (2009). Mirthful laughter, as adjunct therapy in diabetic care, increases HDL cholesterol and attenuates inflammatory cytokines and hs-CRP and possible CVD risk. Paper presented at 122nd Annual Meeting of the American Physiological Society, Experimental Biology conference, New Orleans, April 18–22.

Berk, R. A. (1996). Student ratings of 10 strategies for using humor in college teaching. *Journal on Excellence in College Teaching, 7*(3), 71–92.

Berk, R. A. (2000). Does humor in course tests reduce anxiety and improve performance? *College Teaching,* 48, 151–58.

Berk, R. A. (2001). The active ingredients in humor: Psychophysiological benefits/risks for older adults. *Educational Gerontology,* 27, 323–39.

Berk, R. A. (2004, July/August). Coping with the daily stressors of an academic career: Try mirthium®. *Academic Physician and Scientist,* 2–3.

Bernstein, A. J. (2001). *Emotional vampires: Dealing with people who drain you dry.* New York: McGraw-Hill.

Brown, S. (2009). *Play.* New York: Penguin Group NY.

Bryk, A. S., & Schneider, B. L. (2002). *Trust in schools: A core resource for improvement.* New York: Russell Sage Foundation.

Buckley, K. (2003). *If you could hear what I see.* New York: Penguin Group.

Burgess, R. (2000). *Laughing lessons: 149 2/3 ways to make teaching and learning fun.* Minneapolis, MN: Free Spirit.

Buxman, K. (2008). *Amazed and amused.* CA: Karyn Buxman Publications.

Caine, G., & Caine, R. (1997). *Education on the edge of possibility.* Alexandria, VA: Association for Supervision and Curriculum Development.

Carrica, J. L. (2008). Humor styles and leadership styles: Community college presidents. Dissertation, Wichita State University. http://www.grin.com/en/doc/235387/humor-styles-and-leadership-styles-community-college-presidents.

Carter, J. (2001). *The comedy bible.* New York: Fireside.

Carter, R. (2009). *The human brain book.* New York: DK Publishing.

Charnetski, C. J., & Brennan, F. X. (2001). *Feeling good is good for you: How pleasure can boost your immune system and lengthen your life.* Emmaus, PA: Rodale.

Conant, D., & Norgaard, M. (2011). *Touch points.* San Francisco: Jossey-Bass.

Connors, N. A. (2000). *If you don't feed the teachers they eat the students!* Nashville, TN: Incentive Publications.

Cousins, N. (1979). *Anatomy of an illness as perceived by the patient: Reflections on healing and regeneration.* New York: W. W. Norton.

Cousins, N. (1989). Proving the power of laughter. *Psychology Today,* 23, 22–25.

Cousins, N. (1990). *Head first: The biology of hope and the healing power of the human spirit.* New York: Penguin.

Covey, S. R. (1995), *Principle centered leadership.* New York: Simon and Schuster.

Crawford, C. B. (1994). Strategic humor in leadership: practical suggestions for appropriate use. Paper presented to the 1994 Kansas Leadership Forum, Salina.

Cronin, R. (1997). *Humor in the workplace.* Rosemont, IL: Hodge-Cronin and Associates.

Csikszentmihalyi, M. (1990). *Flow: The psychology of optimal experience.* New York: Harper & Row.

Csikszentmihalyi, M. (1997). *Finding flow: The psychology of engagement with everyday life.* New York: Basic Books.

Curtis, D. B., & Hansen, T. L. (1990, April). *Humor in the workplace: A communication tool. An annotated bibliography.* Annandale, VA: Speech Communication Association. (ERIC Document Reproduction Service No. ED 319 085).

Damasio, A. (1999). *The feeling of what happens: Body and emotion in the making of consciousness.* San Diego, CA: Harcourt.

Davidson, R. (Ed.). (2000). *Anxiety, depression and emotion.* Oxford, UK: Oxford University Press.

Davidson, R. J., Scherer, K., & Goldsmith, H. H. (Eds.). (2003). *Handbook of affective sciences.* Oxford, UK: Oxford University Press.

Deal, T. E., & Peterson, K. D. (1991). *Shaping school culture: The heart of leadership.* San Francisco: Jossey-Bass.

Derks, P. (1997). Laughter and electorencephalagraphic activity. *Humor,* 10, 285–300.

Diamond, M., & Hopson, J. (1998). *Magic trees of the mind: How to nurture your child's intelligence, creativity, and healthy emotions from birth through adolescence.* New York: Penguin Putnam.

Dickmann, M. H., & Standford-Blair, N. (2002). *Connecting leadership to the brain.* Thousand Oaks, CA: Corwin Press.

Diener, E., & Chan, M. (2010). *Happy people live longer: Subjective well-being contributes to health and longevity.* University of Illinois and The Gallup Organization University of Texas at Dallas.

Dugatkin, L. A. (2002). Turtles with toys: It's more than just (animal) play. *Cerebrum* 4(3), 41–52.

Duman, R. S., Malberg, J., & Thome, J. (1999). Neural plasticity to stress and antidepressant treatment. *Biological Psychiatry,* 46(9), 1181–91.

Duncan, W. J., & Feisal, J. P. (1989). No laughing matter: Patterns of humor in the workplace. *Organizational Dynamics,* 17, 18-30.

Dunn, J. R. (1999). What is a sense of humor? An interview with James A. Thorson. *Humor & Health Journal,* 8(2).

Edwards, K. R., & Martin, R. (2011). Humor creation ability and mental health: Are funny people more psychologically healthy? *Europe's Journal of Psychology,* 6(3), 196–212.

Endres, S. (2005). *Teaching is too important to be taken seriously.* Chicago: Spectrum Press.

Estroff, M. H. (1999, March/April). Depression: Beyond serotonin. *Psychology Today Magazine.*

Farah, M. J., Noble, K. G., & Hurt, H. (2005). Poverty, privilege and brain development: Empirical findings and ethical implications. In J. Illes (Ed.), *Neuroethics in the 21st century.* New York: Oxford University Press.

Farris, P. J., Fuhler, C. J., & Walther, M. P. (1999). That's a good one! Humor in the primary classroom. *Delta Kappa Gamma Bulletin,* 65(3), 5–8.

Fell, C. (2011). *Sunny side up: Health and happiness by the dozen.* AZ: Wheatmark.

Forsyth, A. G., Altermatt, E. R., & Forsyth, P. D. (1997, August 16). *Humor, emotional empathy, creativity and cognitive dissonance.* Paper presented at the annual meeting of the American Psychological Association.

Franzini, L. R. (2002). *Kids who laugh: How to develop your child's sense of humor*. New York: Garden City Publishers.

Fredrickson, B. (2003). The value of positive emotions. *American Scientist*, 91, 330–35.

Fry, W. F. (1992). The physiologic effects of humor, mirth, and laughter. *Journal of the American Medical Association*, 267(13), 1857–58.

Fry, W. F. (1994). The biology of humor. *HUMOR: International Journal of Humor Research*, 7(2), 111–26.

Fry, W. F. (2002). Humor and the brain: A selective review. *HUMOR: International Journal of Humor Research*. 15(3), 305–333. DOI: 10.1515/humr.2002.017.

Fry, W. F., & Salameh, W. A. (Eds.). (1993). *Advances in humor and psychotherapy*. Sarasota, FL: Professional Resource Press.

Fry, W. (2010). *Sweet madness* (2nd rev. ed.). Edison, NJ: Transaction Publishers.

Führ, M. (2002). Coping humor in early adolescence. *HUMOR: International Journal of Humor Research* 15(3), 283–304.

Führ, M., Proyer, R. T., & Rulch, W. (2009). Assessing the fear of being laughed at (gelotophobia): First evaluation of the Danish GELOPH<15>. *Nordic Psychology* 61, 62–73.

Garland, R. (1991). *Making work fun*. San Diego, CA: Shamrock Press.

Glatthorn, A. A. (2002). *Publish or perish: The educator's imperative*. Thousand Oaks, CA: Corwin.

Goleman, D. (1995). *Emotional intelligence: Why it can matter more than I.Q.* New York: Bantam.

Goleman, D. (1998). *Working with emotional intelligence*. New York: Bantam.

Goleman, D., Boyatzis, R., & McKee, A. (2002). *Primal leadership: Realizing the power of emotional intelligence*. Boston: Harvard Business School.

Goodman, J. (1988a). Anatomy of Norman Cousins. *Laughing Matters*, 2(3).

Goodman, J. (1988b). The Family Circus. *Laughing Matters*, 3(4).

Goor, M. (1989, September). *Humor in the classroom: Options for enhancing learning*. Paper presented at the National Conference of the Council for Exceptional Children/ Council for Children with Behavior Disorders, Charlotte, NC.

Granier, D. (2006). *The happy neurotic*. Warwick Publishing.

Green, L. (1994). *Making sense of humor: How to add joy to your life*. Manchester, CT: KIT.

Greenleaf, R. K. (1991). *The servant as leader* (rev. ed.). Indianapolis, IN: Robert K. Greenleaf Center.

Greenleaf, R. K. (2002). *Servant-leadership: A journey into the nature of legitimate power and greatness (25th anniversary edition)*. (L. C. Spears, Ed.). New York: Paulist Press.

Grothe, M. (2008). *I never metaphor I didn't like*. New York: Harper Collins Books.

Hansen, P. G. (1985). *The joy of stress*. New York: Andrews and McMeel.

Harty, K. (2011). *A shot in the arm and a strong spirit: How health care givers help patients persevere . . . no matter what!* CO: Strong Spirit Unlimited.

Harvey, L. C. (1998). *Humor for healing: A therapeutic approach*. San Antonio, TX: Therapy Skill Builders.

Hernsath, D., & Yerkes, L. (2001). *301 ways to have more fun at work*. San Francisco: Barrett-Koehler.

Henslin, Earl. (2008). *This is your brain on joy.* Nashville, TN: Thomas Nelson.

Hoesl, Nick. (2010). *Laughter: The drug of choice.* Eau Claire, WI: EC Printing.

Holmes, J., & Marra, M. (2006). Humor and leadership style. *HUMOR: International Journal of Humor Research,* 19(2), 119–38. DOI: 10.1515/HUMOR.2006.006.

Hubel, D. H., & Wiesel, T. N. (1962). Receptive fields, binocular interaction and functional architecture in the cat's visual cortex. *Journal of Physiology,* 160, 106–54.

Hurley, M. M., & Dennett, D. C., & Adams, R. B. (2011) *Inside jokes: Using humor to reverse-engineer the mind.* Cambridge, MA: MIT Press.

Hurren, L. (2006). The effects of principals' humor on teachers' job satisfaction. *Educational Studies,* 32(4), 373–85.

Jasheway, L. A. (1996). *Don't get mad, get funny!* Duluth, MN: Pfeifer-Hamilton.

Jensen, E. (1994). *Brain-based learning.* Del Mar, CA: Turning Point.

Jensen, E. (1994). *The learning brain.* Del Mar, CA: Turning Point.

Jensen, E. (1998). *Teaching with the brain in mind.* Del Mar, CA: Turning Point.

Johnson, S. (1998). *Who moved my cheese? An amazing way to deal with change in your work and in your life.* New York: Putnam.

Jonas, P. (2004). *Secrets of connecting leadership and learning with humor.* Lanham, MD: Rowman and Littlefield.

Jones, S. (2003). *Blueprint for student success.* Thousand Oaks, CA: Corwin Press.

Kappas, K. H. (1967). A developmental analysis of children's responses to humor. *Library Quarterly,* 37, 68–69.

Kataria, M. (2002). *Laugh for no reason* (2nd ed.). Mumbai, India: Madhuri International.

Kessler, R. (2000). *The soul of education: Helping students find connection, compassion, and character at school.* Alexandria, VA: Association for Supervision and Curriculum Development.

Kilcup, K. (2001). Studies in American humor. *The Journal of the American Humor Studies Association,* 3(8).

Klein, A. (1989). *The healing power of humor.* New York: Tarcher/Putnam.

Klein, A. (1998). *The courage to laugh.* New York: Tarcher/Putnam.

Klein, A. (2011). *Learning to laugh when you feel like crying.* New York: Goodman Beck.

Köhler, G., & Ruch, W. (1996). Sources of variance in current sense of humor inventories: How much substance, how much method variance? *HUMOR: International Journal of Humor Research,* 9, 363–97.

Kolberg, K. J., & Loomans, D. (1993). *The laughing classroom: Everyone's guide to teaching with humor and play.* Tiburon, CA: H. J. Kramer.

Kotulak, R. (1996). *Inside the brain: Revolutionary discoveries of how the mind works.* Kansas City, KS: Andrews and McMeely.

Kristal, J. (2005). *The temperament perspective: Working with children's behavioral styles.* New York: Paul H. Brookes.

Kwan, J. (2002). *Almost home: Embracing the magical connection between positive humor & spirituality.* PA: Cameo Publications.

LeDoux, J. (1996). *The emotional brain: The mysterious underpinnings of emotional life.* New York: Simon and Schuster.

LeDoux, J. (2002). *Synaptic self: How our brains become who we are.* New York: Viking.

Linksman, R. (2007). Setting up an effective pre-school reading program. *Illinois ASCD Newsletter*, 52(4).

Logan, M. *Ask Mike the Counselor* (blog). http://www.healinglovenotes.com/ask-mike-the-counselor-aka-mike-logan.html.

Lundkin, S. C. (2000) *FISH*. New York: Hyperion.

Lutz, C. (2010). *Chipper the skipper's lavatory leader*. Sevierville, TN: Insight Publishing.

Mallan, K. (1993). *Laugh lines: Exploring humor in children's literature*. Newtown, New South Wales, Australia: Primary English Teaching Association.

Marijuan, P. C., & Navarro, J. (2010) *The bonds of laughter: A multidisciplinary inquiry into the information processes of human laughter*. Spain: Bioinformation and Systems Biology Group, Instituto Aragones de Ciencias de la Salud.

Martin, R. A. (1996). The situational humor response questionnaire (SHRQ) and coping humor scale (CHS): A decade of research findings. *HUMOR: International Journal of Humor Research*, 9(3–4), 251–72.

Martin, R. A. (2000). Is laughter the best medicine? Humor, laughter, and physical health. *Current Directions in Psychological Science*, 11, 216–20.

Martin R. A. (2001). Humor, laughter, and physical health: Methodological issues and research findings. *Psychological Bulletin*, 127, 504–519.

Martin, R. A. (2007). *The psychology of humor: An integrative approach*. Amsterdam: Elsevier.

Maslow, A. (1968). *Toward a psychology of being* (2nd ed.). New York: D. Van Nostrand.

McElherne, L. N. (1999). *Jump starters: Quick classroom activities that develop self-esteem, creativity, and cooperation*. Minneapolis, MN: Free Spirit.

McGhee, P. E. (1999). *Health, healing and the amuse system*. Dubuque, IA: Kendall/Hunt.

McGhee, P. E. (2002a). *Stumble bees and pelephones: How to develop a powerful verbal sense of humor*. Dubuque, IA: Kendall/Hunt.

McGhee, P. E. (2002b). *Understanding and promoting the development of children's humor: A guide for parents*. Dubuque, IA: Kendall/Hunt.

McGhee, P. E. (2010). *Humor: The lighter path to resilience and health*. Bloomington, IN: AuthorHouse.

Medina, J. (2008). *Brain rules*. Seattle, WA: Pear Press.

Mellin, L. (2010). *Wired for joy*. Carlsbad, CA: Hay House.

Mendler, A. N. (2001). *Connecting with students*. Alexandria, VA: Association for Supervision and Curriculum Development.

Millard, E. N. (1999). Humor can be a serious strategy. *Delta Kappa Gamma Bulletin*, 65(3), 9–14.

Morreall, J. (1991). Humor and Work. *Humor: International Journal of Humor Research*, 4(3–4), 359–74. DOI: 10.1515/humr.1991.4.3-4.359.

Morreall, J. (1997). *Humor works*. Amherst, MA: HRD Press.

Morrison, M. K. (2000). *Humor is a funny thing*. Madeira Beach, FL: Florida Association for Supervision and Curriculum Development.

Morrison, M. K. (2005). *Humor is a funny thing*. Retrieved from http://www.susanjjones.com/growbrain2.html.

Morrison, M. K. (2008). *Using humor to maximize learning: The links between positive emotions and education.* Lanham, MD: Rowman and Littlefield.

Mroczek, D. K., & Spiro, A., III. (2005). Change in life satisfaction over 20 during adulthood: Findings from the VA Normative Aging Study. *Journal of Personality and Social Psychology,* 88, 189–202.

Nilsen, A. P., & Nilsen, D. L. F. (2000). *Encyclopedia of 20th-century American humor.* Phoenix, AZ: Oryx.

Northhouse, P. G. (2007). *Leadership: Theory and practice* (4th ed.) Thousand Oaks, CA: Sage.

Nunley, K. F. (2001). *Layered curriculum: The practical solution for teachers with more than one student in their classroom.* Kearney, NE: Morris Publishing.

Olds, S. D. (2011). *A qualitative study of the strategic use of humor by women in district leadership and the superintendency.* Unpublished doctoral dissertation, Aurora University.

Olliff, V. J. (1999). Lighten up! *Delta Kappa Gamma Bulletin,* 65(3). Special issue: Impact of humor on education and learning.

Osterlund, H. (2011). *Impact of humor on outpatients receiving chemotherapy: The comic study.* Honolulu, HI: Pain and Palliative Care Department, Queen's Medical Center.

Panksepp, J. (2003). Review of emotions and the brain. *Discover,* 24(4).

Panksepp, J., & Burgdorf, J. (2003). "Laughing" rats and the evolutionary antecedents of human joy? *Physiology and Behavior* 19, 533–47.

Panksepp, J., Dong, Y., Wayman, G., & Guerra, D. (2009). *Hope for depression flourishing.* Washington State University. file:///Users/marykaymorrison/Desktop/book/research/ Hope%20for%20 depression%20 research%20WSU.webarchive.

Papousek, I., Ruch, W., Freudenthaler, H. H., Kogler, E., Lang, B., & Schulter, G. (2009). Gelotophobia, emotion-related skills and responses to the affective states of others. *Personality and Individual Differences,* 47, 58–63.

Park, N. C. P., & Ruch, W. (2009). Orientations to happiness and life satisfaction: National comparisons. *Journal of Positive Psychology* 4, 273–79. (Special issue: What makes for a good life? International and interdisciplinary perspectives.)

Passanisi, K., & Passanisi, A. (2009). *Spark magazine.* FL: New Perspectives/Movere.

Paulson, T. L. (1989). *Making humor work.* Mississauga, Ontario, Canada: Crisp Learning.

Pellis, S., & Pellis, V. (2009). *The playful brain: Venturing to the limits of neuroscience.* Oxford, England: Oneworld Publications.

Pert, C. (1997). *Molecules of emotion: Why you feel the way you feel.* New York: Scribner.

Peterson, C., & Seligman, M. (2004). *Character Strengths and Virtues.* New York: Oxford University Press.

Phillips, B. (2009, April 14). Hope for depression research flourishing. *Washington State University News.* http://wsunews.wsu.edu/pages/publications.asp?Action=Detail &PublicationID=14348.

Pink, D. H. (2006). *A whole new mind.* New York: Riverhead Books.

Platt, T., & Ruch, W. (2009). Gelogophobia and bullying: The assessment of the fear of being laughed at and its application among bullying victims. *Psychology Science Quarterly,* 135–47.

Posner, M. I., & Rothbart, M. K. (2007). *Educating the human brain.* Washington, DC: American Psychological Association.

Prerost, F. J. (1993). A strategy to enhance humor production among elderly persons: Assisting in the management of stress. *Activities, Adaptation and Aging,* 17(4), 17–24.

Priest, R., & Swain, J. E. (2006). Humor and its implications for leadership effectiveness. *HUMOR: International Journal of Humor Research,* 15(2), 169–89. DOI: 10.1515/humr.2002.010, 12/06/2002.

Provine, R. R. (2000). *Laughter: A scientific investigation.* New York: Viking Penguin.

Purkey, W. W. (2006). *Teaching class clowns (and what they can teach us).* Thousand Oaks, CA: Corwin.

Ranpura, A. (1997). *Weightlifting for the mind: Enriched environments and cortical plasticity.* Retrieved from http://www.brainconnection.com/topics/printindex.php3?main=fa/cortical-plasticity.

Ratey, J., with Hagerman, E. (2008). *Spark: The revolutionary new science of exercise and the brain.* New York: Little, Brown and Company, Western Schools.

Rath, T. & Harter, J. (2010). *Wellbeing: The Five Essential Elements.* New York: Gallup Press.

Rayl, A. J. S. (2002). Humor: A mind-body connection. *The Scientist,* 14(19), 1.

Reeves, D. B. (2006). *The learning leader.* Alexandria, VA: Assoc. for Supervision and Curriculum Development.

Roberts, B. (2011, July). *Happiness hotline newsletter.* Australia.

Roe, B., Alfred, S., & Smith, S. (1998). *Teaching through stories: Yours, mine and theirs.* Norwood, MA: Christopher-Gordon.

Rowe, M. R. (2001). *Puntoons! Jest for the health of it!* Bloomington, IN: Authorhouse.

Ruch, W. (1992). Assessment of appreciation of humor: studies with the 3WD humor test. In *Advances in Personality Assessment, Vol. 9,* eds. C. D. Spielberger & J. N. Butcher (27–75). Hillsdale, NJ: Lawrence Erlbaum Associates.

Ruch, W. (2002). Computers with a personality? Lessons to be learned from studies of the psychology of humor. School of Psychology. Queens University, Belfast Ireland. 57–70.

Ruch, W. (1993). Exhilaration and humor. In *The Handbook of Emotions,* eds. M. Lewis & J. M. Haviland (605–616). New York: Guilford Publications.

Ruch, W. (2009a). Amusement. In *The Oxford Companion to the Affective Sciences,* eds. D. Sander & K. Scherer (27–28). Oxford, England: Oxford University Press.

Ruch, W. (2009b). Fearing humor? Gelotophobia: The fear of being laughed at: Introduction and overview. *HUMOR: International Journal of Humor Research* 22(1–2), 1–25.

Ruch, W., & Proyer, R. T. (2008) The fear of being laughed at: Individual and group differences in gelotophobia. *HUMOR: International Journal of Humor Research* 21(1), 47–67.

Ruch, W., Proyer, R. T., & Weber, M. (2010). Humor as character strength among the elderly: Theoretical considerations. *Zeitschrift für Gerontologie und Geriatrie,* 43, 8-18.

Salameh, W. A., & Fry, W. F., Jr. (2001). *Humor and wellness in clinical intervention.* Westport, CT: Praeger.

Sapolsky, R. J. (1998). *Why zebras don't get ulcers: An updated guide to stress, stress-related diseases, and coping.* New York: W. H. Freeman.

Sapolsky, R. J. (1999, March). Stress and your shrinking brain. *Discover,* 116–22.

Schwartz, E A. (1999). Humor development in children from infancy to eighth grade. *Research for Nursing Practice,* 1(2), 1–6.

Schwartz, E. (2010) *Humor in health care* (2nd ed.). MA: Western Schools.

Seligman, M., & Csikszentmihalyi, M. (2000). Positive psychology: An introduction. *American Psychologist,* 55(1), 5–14.

Seligman, M. (2011). *Flourish: A Visionary New Understanding of Happiness and Wellbeing.* New York: Free Press.

Senge, P. M., Kleiner, A., Roberts, C., Ross, R., & Smith, B. J. (1994). *The fifth discipline: Strategies and tools for building a learning organization.* New York: Currency and Doubleday.

Sergiovanni, T. J. (1983). *Supervision: Human perspectives.* New York: McGraw-Hill.

Shade, R. A. (1996). *License to laugh: Humor in the classroom.* Englewood, CO: Teachers Ideas.

Shammi, P. (1999). Humour appreciation: A role of the right frontal lobe. *Brain,* 122(4), 657–66.

Shammi, P., & Stuss, D. T. (2003). The effects of normal aging on humor appreciation. *Journal of the International Neuropsychological Society,* 9, 855–63.

Siegel, D. J. (1999). *The developing mind: Toward a neurobiology of interpersonal experience.* New York: Guilford.

Sims, P. (2011). *In on the joke.* Fast Company Expert (blog). http://www.fastcompany.com/1749246/little-bets-peter-sim-pixar.

Singer, E. (2010). *Individual humor style characteristics and the "Big Five" personality traits.* PowerPoint presentation at the 2010 AATH conference in Orlando Florida.

Sousa, D. A. (2001). *How the brain learns.* Thousand Oaks, CA: Corwin.

Sparks, S. (2010). *Laugh your way to grace.* Woodstock, VT: Skylight Paths Publishing.

Sprenger, M. (1999). *Learning and memory: The brain in action.* Alexandria, VA: Association for Supervision and Curriculum Development.

Sprenger, M. (2002). *Becoming a wiz at brain-based teaching: How to make every year your best year.* Thousand Oaks, CA: Corwin.

Stephenson, S., & Thibault, P. (2006). *Laughing matters: Strategies for building a joyful learning community.* Bloomington, IN: Solution Tree.

Sternberg, E. M. (2000). *The balance within: The science connecting health and emotions.* New York: W. H. Freeman.

Stewart, D. W., & Furse, D. H. (1986). *Effective television advertising: A study of 1000 commercials.* Lexington, MA: Lexington Books.

Stopsky, F. (1992). *Humor in the classroom: A new approach to critical thinking.* Lowell, MA: Discovery Enterprises.

Stronge, J. H. (2004). *Qualities of effective teachers.* Alexandria, VA: Association for Supervision and Curriculum Development.

Sultanoff, S. M. (1994). Therapeutic uses of humor. *California Psychologist,* 25.

Sultanoff, S. M. (2002). Integrating humor into psychotherapy. In *Play therapy with adults*, ed. C. Shaefer. New York: Wiley and Sons.

Sylwester, R. (1995). *A celebration of neurons: An educator's guide to the human brain.* Alexandria, VA: Association for Supervision and Curriculum Development.

Sylwester, R. (2003). *A biological brain in a cultural classroom.* Thousand Oaks, CA: Corwin.

Sylwester, R. (2005). *How to explain a brain.* Thousand Oaks, CA: Corwin.

Sylwester, R. (2006). *Mirror neuron update.* Retrieved from http://www.brainconnection .com/content/226_1.

Tan, S., & Berk, L. (2008). Therapeutic benefits of laughter. *Humor and Health Journal.* http://agedcareact.wordpress.com/2008/02/14/what-is-humor-therapy/.

Teicher, S. (2005, July 12). Practice scenes for the tough choices of adolescence. *Christian Science Monitor.*

USA Weekend. (2011, September 2). Where the playgrounds are: America's most playful cities. http://www.usaweekend.com/article/20110902/HOME02/110902001/Where -playgrounds-are

Volkmar, F. R., & Greenough, W. T. (1972). Rearing complexity affects branching of dendrites in the visual cortex of the rat. *Science,* 176, 1445–47.

Weber, M. (2003). Coping with malcontents: You can deal with negative staff and prevent yourself from becoming negative. *School Administrator,* 60(2), 6–11.

Weinstein, M. (1997). *Managing to have fun.* New York: Simon and Schuster.

Wheatley, M. J. (2002). *Turning to one another: Simple conversations to restore hope to the future.* San Francisco: Berrett-Koehler.

Wolfe, P. (2001). *Brain matters: Translating research into classroom practice.* Alexandria, VA: Association for Supervision and Curriculum Development.

Wolk, S. (2001). The benefits of exploratory time. *Journal of Educational Leadership,* 59(2), 56–59.

Wood, C. (1997). *Yardsticks: Children in the classroom ages 4–14.* Turner Falls, MA: Northeast Foundation for Children.

Wood, R. S. (1995). *Have more fun: Play your way to success.* Novato, CA: Condor Books Publisher Services.

Wooten, P. (1996). *Compassionate laughter: Jest for your health.* Salt Lake City, UT: Commune-a-key.

Wright, W. E. (2002). The effects of high stakes testing in an inner-city elementary school: The curriculum, the teachers, and the English language learners. *Current Issues in Education,* 5(5).

Wurtman, J. (1998). *Neurotransmitters and food: Managing your mind and mood through food.* New York: Harper and Row.

Yerkes, L. (2001). *Fun works: Creating places where people love to work.* San Francisco: Berrett-Koehler.

Ziv, A. (1984). *Personality and a sense of humor.* New York: Springer.

Ziv, A., & Ziv, N. (2002). *Humor and creativity in education.* Paris: Creatrix Editions.

INFORMATIONAL WEBSITES

For quick access to links go to Humor Quest, http://www.questforhumor.com/.

Follow Mary Kay Morrison on LinkedIn and Twitter, and check out Humor Quest blog at http://humor-quest.blogspot.com!

AATH (Association for Applied and Therapeutic Humor): http://www.aath.org/

Alliance for Childhood: http://www.allianceforchildhood.net/projects/play/play_fact_sheet.htm

Alliance for Servant Leadership, Indiana State University: http://www.indstate.edu/asl/

American Humor Studies Association: http://www.slu.edu/academic/ahsa/journal home.htm

American Medical Association journals: http://www.ama-assn.org/med_link/peer.htm

Ask Mike the Counselor, Michael Logan's blog: http://www.askmikethecounselor2.com/index.html

Association for the Study of Play: http://www.csuchico.edu/kine/tasp/index.html

Brain Lab: http://www.newhorizons.org/blab.html

Brain Net: http://www.brainnet.org/

Comedy Cures (Saranne Rothbeg): http://www.comedycures.org/saranne.html

Changing Minds on Servant Leadership: http://changingminds.org/disciplines/leadership/styles/servant_leadership.htm

CNN 2011 Top 100 Companies to Work For: http://money.cnn.com/magazines/fortune/bestcompanies/2011/full_list/

Covenant Leadership: http://www.covenantleadership.com/

Dana Foundation: *Brain Work, the Neuroscience Newsletter*: http://www.dana.org

Dave, Lenny: http://www.creativity123.com/

Education Learning Network, ELN Webinars by Morrison: http://www.edleadersnetwork.org/Home/

Fun Squad with Charles Lutz: http://www.funsquadinc.com/

How Rats Laugh (Panksepp 2007): http://www.youtube.com/watch?v=ieP3lpyOHtU&feature=related

Humor for Teachers: http://www.learninglaffs.com/

Humor for Your Health: http://www.humorforyourhealth.com/humor_articles.html

Humor Project: http://www.humorproject.com/

Humor Quest, Mary Kay Morrison's website: http://www.questforhumor.com/index.html

Humor X with Karyn Buxman: http://www.humorx.com/KB_humorx_home.html

IEA-Pedia: http://iae-pedia.org/Main_Page

IAE-Pedia—Using Humor to Maximize Learning: http://iae-pedia.org/Using_Humor_to_Maximize_Learning

Institute for the Emotionally Intelligent: http://www.teacheq.com/

International Society for Humor Studies: http://www.hnu.edu/ishs/

Jest for the Health of It: http://www.jesthealth.com/frame-articles.html

Journal of Nursing Jocularity: http://www.journalofnursingjocularity.com/

Jollytologist Allen Klein: http://www.allenklein.com/recommend.htm

Lab for Effective Neuroscience: http://psyphz.psych.wisc.edu/web/index.html

Laugh Doctor: http://www.natural-humor-medicine.com/the-laugh-doctor.html

Laughter Arts and Sciences Foundation with Steve Wilson: http://www.laughter foundation.org/

Layered Curriculum, by Kathie Nunley: http://help4teachers.com

Leigh Anne Jasheway, Don't Get Mad, Get Funny: http://www.accidentalcomic.com/books/dont_get_mad.php

Let's Laugh Bronwin Roberts: http://www.letslaugh.com.au/the-latest-happiness-hotline-newsletter-0

Lighthouse Professional Alliance, by Susan J. Jones: http://www.susanjjones.com

Live the Joy Newsletter: http://kellyepperson.com/category/live-the-joy/

McGhee, Paul: http://www.laughterremedy.com/

Museum of Humor: http://www.museumofhumor.com/

National Institutes of Health: http://www.nih.gov

Nurse Talk: Interview with Mary Kay Morrison: Paper Wad Ideas, by Scott Endres: http://www.paperwadideas.com/

"Play," by Stuart Brown (2009 TED video): http://www.ted.com/talks/stuart_brown_says_play_is_more_than_fun_it_s_vital.html

Play Therapy: http://www.a4pt.org/ps.playtherapy.cfm

Wavelength, Communication through Comedy: http://www.wavelengthinc.com/

Whole Brain Atlas (anatomy of the brain, CATs, MRIs, etc.): http://www.med.harvard.edu/AANLIB/

World Laughter Tour: http://www.worldlaughtertour.com/index.asp

"Your Voice": How Humor Affects Learning (television interview with Cheryl Jackson and Mary Kay Morrison):

MEDIA

Dr. Fred Goodwin, director of the Center on Neuroscience Medical Progress in Society, George Washington University, and host of *The Infinite Mind* on National Public Radio.

Schoolhouse Rock song "Three Is a Magic Number," by Bob Dorough. http://www.schoolhouserock.tv/Three.html

Stress: Portrait of a Killer. (2008). National Geographic Society. DVD.

INDEX

Brooks, Mel, 2
Brown, S., 32
Buckley, Kathy, 111
bully humor, 102–3, 109; and control, 91;
    victims of, 92–93; violence, potential
    for, 91. *See also* aggressive humor;
    bullying; dark humor; hostile humor;
    negative humor
bullying: and humor, 187; and
    humordoomers, 92–93, 102, 109;
    in workplace, 90–91. *See also* bully
    humor
Burnett, Carol, 101
Bush, George W., 125
Buxman, Karyn, 26, 91, 135, 175, 185–86

Calgary Children's Hospital, 152
Canada, 47, 172
Cancer Treatment Centers of America
    (CTCA), 144
caregivers: and humor, 5, 155
Carson, Johnny, 23
Carter, Judy, 144–45
Carter, Rita, 59
Caskey, Kay, 77
Catalyst Consulting, 141
censorship, 98–99
Center for Spiritual Living, 171
Certified Laughter Leaders (CLLs), 158
Chaplin, Charlie, 20, 170
Character Strengths and Virtues (Peterson
    and Seligman), 60
chemotherapy: and humor, 72–73,
    162–63
Children's Miracle Network, 170
China, 47, 172
Chuckle Channel, 163
Clarke, Mark, 120
clowns: in classes, 30, 44–45; and clown
    noses, 157; in hospitals, 102, 170–71;
    in offices, 174
Clown on Down program, 170
cognitive research, 53; and fear, 57

comedy, 20
Comedy Cures, 24
Comedy Workshop Productions, 144
COMIC (comedy in chemotherapy)
    Study, 163
computer mouse, 53
Conklin, Pat, 159
Cortino, Becky, 170
Cosby, Bill, 22
Cousins, Norman, 21, 27, 57, 73
Covenant Leadership, 185
Covey, Dwayna, 128, 140–41
Covey, Steven, 179
creativity: and humor, 1, 4, 9–11, 15; and
    play, 49
Csikszentmihalyi, Mihaly, 45, 75
Cuppy, Will, 110

Damasio, Antonio R., 57
Dangerfield, Rodney, 100
dark humor, 70, 86, 90, 98–99; and
    anger, 115. *See also* aggressive humor;
    bully humor; hostile humor; negative
    humor
Davidson, Richard, 18
Davis, William, 19
DeGeneres, Ellen, 105
Department of Defense, 136
Derks, Peter, 68
depression, 31, 60; brain circuitry,
    malfunctions in, 62; and humor, 64,
    76; as neurodegenerative disorder,
    64; and play, 32, 49, 63; serotonin,
    shortage of, 62; symptoms of, 63
Diller, Phyllis, 110
Don't Get Mad, Get Funny (Jasheway),
    128
Donuts, Danny, 170
Drucker, Peter F., 177
Dugatkin, Lee Alan, 33
Duncan-Eller, Beth, 118

Eban, Abba, 110

ABOUT THE AUTHOR

Mary Kay Morrison is a teacher who has taught at virtually every level of the educational spectrum while facilitating keynote presentations and workshop sessions for the past thirty years. Her work includes integrating what we know about cognitive research on the emotions (particularity humor) and movement to classroom application.

In addition to humor and stress management, Mary Kay frequently conducts seminars on brain research, leadership, ADHD, group facilitation, parenting, and mentoring. Mary Kay is founder and director of Humor Quest. She currently serves on the board of directors for the Association of Applied and Therapeutic Humor (AATH) and was the 2010 conference chair.

In 2009, she founded and directed the international AATH Humor Academy graduate study and certificate program. As a member of the Illinois NCLB implementation team, she conducted "Train the Trainer" sessions for the State Board of Education on school improvement and mentoring. The YMCA Northeast Branch of Rockford named her 2009 Volunteer of the Year. Mary Kay served on the Tedx committee for the Rockford Area Economic Development Council. She is in the Seedlings Garden Club and is on the board of directors for Rockford Network of Women.

BOOK

Her publication *Using Humor to Maximize Learning: Exploring Links between Positive Emotions and Education* is the text for humor studies courses at several universities and is the text for the groundbreaking international graduate Humor Academy offered by AATH.

ARTICLES WRITTEN

Creating an Appropriate 21st Century Education: The Top Ten Reasons Why Humor is FUNdamental to Education. IAE Newsletter. Issue 83. February 2012. http://i-a-e .org/newsletters/IAE-Newsletter-2012-83.html.

Using humor to maximize learning (n.d.). IAE-Pedia. http://iae-pedia.org/Using_ Humor_to_Maximize_Learning

Using Humor to Maximize Learning. Illinois Association for Supervision and Curriculum Development newsletter. Hot topic number 67. Winter 2011. http://www.illinoisascd .org/pdfs/Hot%20Topic%20PDF/HotTopic67.pdf.

INTERVIEWS

Go with your strengths. (2010, May). *Journal of Nursing Jocularity* http://www.journal ofnursingjocularity.com/index.php?s=mary+kay+morrison.

How humor affects learning. (2009). Canada TVO Station live broadcast http://www .youtube.com/watch?v=XaG678AzVs4.

Seriously funny. (2010, July). *CMA Today.*

BOOK REVIEWS BY OTHERS

American Association of School Administrators (AASA). (2009, November). *The School Administrator.*

Sylwester, R. Our elusive sense of humor. *The Brain Connection.* April 2008. http:// brainconnection.positscience.com/content/268_1

WEB RESOURCES

Humor Quest website	http://www.questforhumor.com/
Humor Quest blog	http://www.humor-quest.blogspot.com/

Webinars (AATH Humor Academy)
  March 2010

AATH featured interview by Becky Cortino,
  October 2010

ELN (three webinars available on Education Learning Network) http://www.edleadersnetwork.org/home/

Facebook: Mary Kay Morrison http://www.facebook.com/marykaymorrison

Twitter http://twitter.com/

YouTube http://www.youtube.com/user/MaryKayMorrison

LinkedIn: Mary Kay Morrison http://www.linkedin.com/home

PDK Online http://pdkconnect.leveragesoftware.com/login.aspx

KEYNOTE ADDRESSES

- YMCA, 2012, Rockford, IL
- AATH International Conference, 2011, Orlando, Florida
- Humor in Education Conference, 2010, Izmir, Turkey
- AATH International Humor Academy, 2010, Disneyland, California
- IASCD Kindergarten Conference, 2010, Schaumberg, IL
- Bradley University Student Leadership Conference, 2010, Peoria, IL
- Art Council Workshop, 2010, Rockford, IL
- ISHS International Society for Humor Studies, 2009, Long Beach, CA
- Chicago Principal Association, 2009, Chicago, IL
- Kishwaukee College Fall Orientation, 2009, Malta, IL
- Barnes and Noble Education Week Seminar, 2009, DeKalb, IL
- Strategic Planning Harrison School District, 2009, Wonder Lake, IL
- Using Humor School Seminar, 2009, Phoenix, AZ
- YMCA Leadership Workshop, 2009, Rockford, IL
- Rock Valley College Tutor Conference, 2009, Rockford, IL
- 4-H Leaders Conference, 2009, Winnebago County, IL
- Commencement Address, 2008, College of Education National Louis University, Lake Geneva, WI
- Parent Academy, 2008, Wonder Lake, IL
- Early Childhood Spring Conference, Highland College, 2008, Freeport, IL

WORKSHOP OFFERINGS

- *Using Humor to Maximize Living.* This workshop provides an overview of the benefits of humor with a focus on what we have learned from brain research. The relationship between learning, stress, and memory are explored. Humor-doomer behavior and humorphobia are discussed. The goal is that participants will be able to identify their humor style and focus on strategies that they can use to improve their humor practice.

- *Humor: The Educator's Toolbox (1–3 hours)*. Fish for humor strategies that have been indicated in current research to improve communication and increase long-term memory. Jump on board with this action-packed session, and you will fall "hook, line, and sinker" for this approach to maximize learning! You will navigate the cognitive research that identifies the benefits of using humor in the classroom. Opening the "educator tackle box," you will explore purposeful ways to use humor to strengthen relationships and increase memory retention. Leave with a "catch" of powerful ways to (1) capture attention with humor (hook); (2) learn how to manipulate information in the working memory using humor (line); and (3) use humor in assessment and feedback to increase memory retention (sinker). Leave this session with joy in your heart and humor strategies for your classroom.

- *Staff Meetings with Pizzazz*. One-third of the population hates meetings. Make sure your staff meetings are both focused and FUN! Find out how humor and laughter can increase productivity, increase communication, and build trust.

- *Stress and Learning: The Bucket Strategy (1 hour)*. If you suspect that excess stress negatively impacts student learning—you are right on! Stress impacts all of us, including teachers, administrators, and students. Explore the research on how excess stress can lead to depression and how a sense of humor can reduce anxiety. You will leave with a bucketfull of strategies to help you enhance your learning environment.

- *What Is Your Humor Style? (1 hour)*. Take a humor styles inventory in this interactive session designed to help you explore your sense of humor. You will leave knowing the benefits of humor and how you can improve your humor practice.

- *It's All about ME! (Movement and Emotions) (1–2 hours)*. Movement and the emotions are emerging from cognitive research as the power-charged tools that optimize student learning. Find out how to create an environment that creates positive emotional change. This is an action-packed session with an abundance of FUN activities.

- *Humor Is a Funny Thing (1 hour)*. Include some fun in your day! This session will encourage participants in the practice of humor, not only as a personal tool to optimize a healthy lifestyle but to maximize the benefits of humor for healthy living. If you love laughter, this session is for you!

- *Research Causes Cancer in Rats (2 hours)*. What is humor, exactly? How do you get a sense of humor? Once you find yours, how do you use it to maximize learning? If it is so important, why is it rarely mentioned in teacher preparation without some clues for finding and using it? Participants will complete a humor styles inventory and practice increasing their individual sense of humor.

- *Got Stress? Survival Strategies (2 hours)*. Stress seems to creep up on many of us—creating unexpected problems when we least expect it. Participants will examine their current lifestyle and identify their own key stress indicators. Resources for reducing stress will be shared. Participants will focus on achieving maximum mind–body balance.

TESTIMONIALS

"I have had the privilege of experiencing Mary Kay Morrison's talents through presentations, workshops, webinars, teleconferences, and the facilitation of a board meeting. I don't know of anyone who can match her enthusiasm, expertise, and passion. She has presented around the country and internationally—the results are the same regardless of the language—she blows people away! Anyone wanting to chat with me personally about her abilities may contact directly. Be prepared—I can go on about her for hours." —Karyn Buxman, RN, MSN, CSP, CPAE, president

"When we decided to hold a conference about the power of humor in education in our school, I did some research about experts in the field and found Mary Kay Morrison. I emailed her to give information about our conference and ask her if she would be willing to come to Turkey to lecture Turkish teachers. I did not know that I was going to gain a wonderful friend. For months, we corresponded about the content of the conference to meet the needs of Turkish teachers and about cultural differences in humor. It turned out that Mary Kay's humor is universal! Except for a few jokes that are based on language differences, we could use everything she suggested.

Our conference was for 250 Turkish teachers and academicians from all over Turkey. One of the teachers wrote on her feedback form: 'I had great fun in learning today, and I am going to carry everything I learned today to my classroom!'

When all the teachers who attended the conference start to use more humor in their classrooms, Mary Kay will have touched the lives of at least 5000 Turkish children!" —Handan Oktar, administrator, Isikkent School, Izmir, Turkey

"Mary Kay is an inspirational force in today's 'not so inspirational' world. Mary Kay and I have worked alongside each other for the past year on the Board of Directors for the Association of Applied and Therapeutic Humor and I have always found her to be insightful, dedicated, and never afraid to roll up her sleeves and get dirty to get the job done. Due to her coaching, I was able to see varying perspectives that, previously, I had not considered. She is never dull, always positive, and the footprint she is leaving in this lifetime is enormous!" —Chip Lutz, CLO of Covenant Leadership; president-elect of AATH

WORKSHOP COMMENTS

From the International Humor Academy graduate class:

"I have definitely been influenced by all the research! I absolutely love it!! At times I wish that the world would just believe what they feel, rather than having to have it proved, yet I know that research gives it the reality, the science behind the thoughts. I have a stack of books, from Mary Kay's to Kathy Buckley (both of which I have taken much from). I use the book as a resource on a regular basis."

From school bus drivers:

"I learned ways to control my stress and handle my stress."
"Needs to come back to our welcome meeting."

From administrators in a six-hour session:

"Excellent presentation. Liked incorporation of current brain research."
"Absolutely wonderful!"

From community college retired attendees:

"I loved every minute of this class. Mary Kay was terrific."
"Very interesting. Thought provoking research."